DULCE WARRIORS

Aliens Battle for Earth's Domination

DULCE WARRIORS

Aliens Battle for Earth's Domination

DULCE WARRIORS - Aliens Battle for Earth's Domination

By Timothy Green Beckley, Sean Casteel, Tim R. Swartz

Addition Material by: Tom Adams, Otto Binder, Maria D'Andrea, Ben Eno, Paul Eno, Charla Gene, Dr. Jean-François G. Gille, Adam Gorightly, Allen Greenfield, William Hamilton III, Ben Hanson, Norio Hayakawa, Hercules Invictus, C. Lois Jessop, Jorge Martin Miranda, Paul Dale Roberts, Albert Rosales, Diane Tessman, Christa Tilton, Joshua P Warren, Don Worley

Copyright © 2021 by Timothy Green Beckley dba Inner Light/Global Communications

All rights reserved. No part of these manuscripts may be copied or reproduced by any mechanical or digital methods and no excerpts or quotes may be used in any other book or manuscript without permission in writing by the Publisher, Inner Light/Global Communications, except by a reviewer who may quote brief passages in a review.

Published in the United States of America by

Inner Light/Global Communications

PO Box 753

New Brunswick, NJ 08903

ISBN-13: 978-1-60611-962-4

Staff Members: Timothy G. Beckley, Publisher

Carol Ann Rodriguez, Assistant to the Publisher

Sean Casteel, General Associate Editor

Tim R. Swartz, Formatting, Graphics and Editorial Consultant

William Kern, Editorial and Art Consultant

www.ConspiracyJournal.com

CONTENTS

DEDICATED TO THE MEMORY OF TIMOTHY GREEN BECKLEY 9

SECTION ONE - Seven Levels of Hell 36

1. A TERRIFYING INTRODUCTION - WHAT HAPPENED ON OUR WAY TO DULCE.............37

2. THE STRANGE SAGA OF PAUL BENNEWITZ AND THE UNDERGROUND "ALIEN" BASE AT DULCE 47

3. EXPOSING THE EXISTENCE OF THE DULCE BASE - SEVEN LEVELS OF HELL..............54

4. FRENCH SCIENTIST'S DIARY 70

5. GABE VALDEZ CATTLE MUTILATIONS 78

6. MEANWHILE, BACK AT THE (ABANDONED) RANCH.................................86

7. THE DULCE CHATTER - PUBLIC SCUTTLEBUTT ON A TOP SECRET MYSTERY...............92

8. DULCE MAY EVENTUALLY COME TO A BIG CINEMA SCREEN NEAR YOU..................112

SECTION TWO - The Faces Behind Dulce 120

9. ENIGMATIC PERSONALITIES BEHIND THE INITIAL DULCE BASE RUMORS 121

10. JOHN LEAR'S INCREDIBLE DULCE THEORIES—AND BEYOND — WAY BEYOND!........134

11. UFOLOGISTS' LIVES MATTER - BILL COOPER SPEAKS FROM THE GRAVE...................154

12. THE MYSTERIOUS JASON BISHOP III 164

13. THE FASCINATING LIFE OF CHERRY HINKLE - HER STORY OF DULCE........................168

14. PHILIP SCHNEIDER - MYSTERIOUS DEATH OF A DULCE WHISTLE-BLOWER.............174

15. BIRTH OF AN ALIEN HYBRID - THE CHRISTA TILTON STORY PART ONE 186

16. LED BY THE HAND THROUGH A DEEP AND DARK LAND A Q AND A WITH CHRISTA TILTON 203

SECTION THREE - Underground Bases 214

17. THE DEADLY TRUTH ABOUT UNDERGROUND BASES 215

18. DULCE AND OTHER UNDERGROUND BASES AND TUNNELS 230

19. MALTA - ENTRANCE TO THE CAVERN WORLD 254

20. ADDITIONAL BASES SCATTERED AROUND THE GLOBE 266

21. BROWN MOUNTAIN, N.C. - SECRET MILITARY BASE UNDERGROUND? 284

22. RALPH LAEL AND THE LIGHTS FROM VENUS 294

23. MYSTERY OF ALIEN INFESTATIONS: ARE STRIP MINES AND NOISY UNDERGROUND CONSTRUCTION PARTS OF THE ALIEN PHENOMENA? 298

24. OPERATION TANGO - UNDERGROUND BASE IN KOREA 306

25. ADAM GORIGHTLY - THE SPOOKS AND KOOKS OF DULCE 310

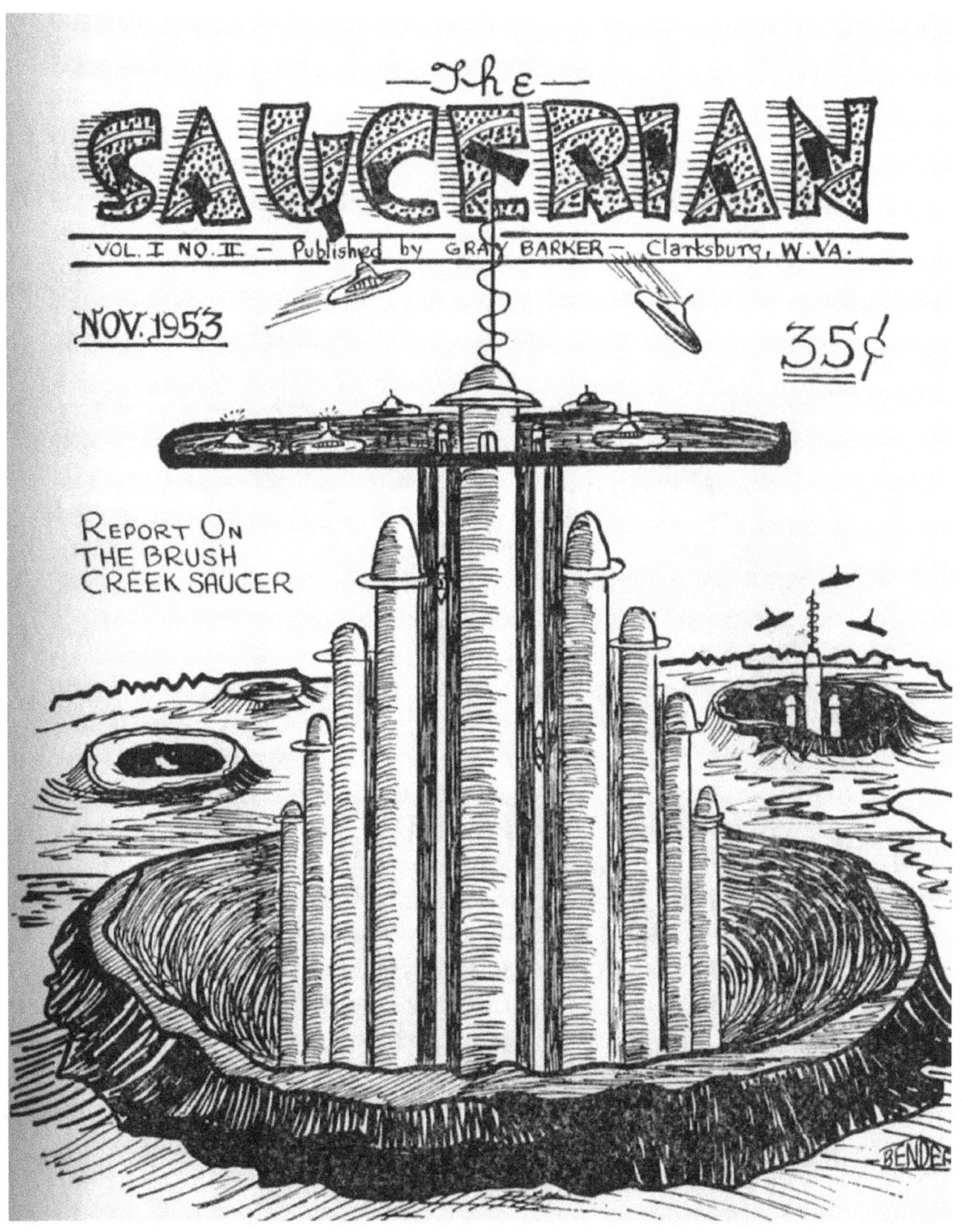

Underground alien bases have been a part of UFO mythology right from the start. A secret base on the moon is illustrated here in Gray Barker's 1952 "UFO-Zine" "The Saucerian."

Timothy Green Beckley - "Mr. UFO" - hitching a ride with a friend to the mothership.

DEDICATED TO THE MEMORY OF TIMOTHY GREEN BECKLEY

July 13, 1947 – May 31, 2021

When Timothy Green Beckley passed away on May 31, 2021, he left behind a body of work that has few equals in the realms of Ufology and the paranormal.

Tim steadfastly pursued the truth underlying the great mysteries of human existence, beginning as a child, hiding underneath his bed covers to read *"FATE Magazine"* by flashlight or listening to all-night paranormal radio host Long John Nebel, whose call-in show on a major New York station became the template for shows that came later, like Art Bell's Coast to Coast. In the early 1960s, Tim began his publishing efforts as a teenager, grinding out UFO magazines on an old-fashioned mimeograph machine and building a goodly-sized mailing list of subscribers.

Working as a freelance stringer for *"The National Enquirer,"* he covered a great many stories of UFO landings and alien abductions. Tim thus earned a kind of "street cred" as a journalist of off-the-beaten-path type subjects. For a time he published a newsstand magazine called *"UFO Universe"* that ran for several years, as well as the newsletter "The Conspiracy Journal," which got its title long before Q-Anon gave conspiracy theory a bad name.

Tim was even better known for the books he published through his Global Communications and Inner Light Books publishing houses. Most of them are still available from Amazon.com. Do a search there and you may be pleasantly surprised at the wealth of what is on offer.

For the sake of paying homage to "Mr. UFO," we have assembled memories and testimonials from some of Tim's most prolific and – and grateful – authors and friends.

A dapper Timothy Green Beckley.

Timothy Beckley – Always A Free Spirit

By Maria D'Andrea   MsD, D.D.,DRH

Maria D'Andrea is a fulltime psychic who wrote several books that Tim published; books she always adamantly declared were written to be used only in the most positive of ways. She wrote several "How-To" books that teach the reader to awaken the psychic powers within and put them to benevolent use for a myriad of reasons. One of Maria's titles is "*Supernatural Words of Power*," part of her "Yes, You Can!" series in which she helps the reader achieve a kind of "self-empowerment." She also contributed chapters to many books Tim assembled as group efforts in which several writers would offer their insight into a given paranormal topic.

Maria D' Andrea

DULCE WARRIORS

Tim affected so many lives while he was on this planet that we can't even count all of them. With his passing, we are also finding out about things he did to help others that he never spoke about. He just helped everyone he cared about without looking for a "thank you" or acknowledgements. He never mentioned when he was buying food for someone, paying someone's rent, contributing to helping someone's career or any of the other selfless things he did. He truly came from his heart and will be deeply missed.

I met Tim in 1985, when I was working at a psychic event doing Readings. He was already accomplished doing eight million things in his life, and was there promoting his books as a publisher. We started chatting and realized we had much in common and were in sync on a friendship level. Because of our levels of knowledge in the spiritual, psychic, paranormal and UFO fields, he asked me to write a book for him. I explained that I'd never written one. He countered by explaining that I COULD and gave me a subject he needed a book on at the time. So I gave him the first chapter. After he stopped laughing, he said, "I told you so. And we're going to do a lot more."

Now I laugh because Tim started me on this path with support and friendship. I have somewhere around 60 books out, including several that I co-authored with talented people. I was a guest on Tim's radio show with his co-host Tim Swartz, (Tim was also gracious enough to be on my TV and radio show). I was also able to do numerous types of media work, as well as teaching and speaking in my fields and so on...and it ALL stemmed from him having a gigantic heart and introducing me to many different fields years ago.

He was my confidant, close friend, family, travel partner, publisher and partner in crime. Free spirits tend to be this way, right? Tim was always funny. He would come up with hilarious thoughts in an instant and then forget about them. I wish I remembered all of them because they would have made a great book.

He would go to some of the same places to eat in his neighborhood in Manhattan and got to know the people who were working there. At times, some of us would get together and go. He would already know what to recommend off the menu that was good and he knew each of us enough to recommend food that fit our individual tastes. Tim loved to get us experimenting with different foods. He was very aware and thoughtful that way.

DULCE WARRIORS

He knew at an early age what his Path of Life was. He started a magazine while young and expanded his horizons as he went along life's pathways.

I remember when we would go ghost hunting in various states. Even though it was for work, we always had fun. I would find the spirit, if there was one (if a sighting wasn't real, he would never make something up) check it out, deal with whatever came up and Tim would write about the experience as a prolific author and speak about it in the media. He loved to enlighten the public on the odd things in our universe.

His sense of humor was always there. We would send pictures back and forth as friends and then we would have separate work pictures. He would call me and come up with a title and just say for me to write a book about the subject. Teamwork is always a good thing. So on one occasion, his title for me was *Traveling The Waves Of Time* and he put a "friend" picture on the back cover. First I was a little upset, because it was a picture of me on my motorcycle, and here I am being professional. When I called him, Tim said he thought it worked because the book was on travel and that's what I was doing. He thought it fit and was fun. What can I say? That was Tim.

Another time we spoke about our various UFO experiences He had a few and he also had experiences channeling. He traveled to numerous places on a global level. Tim said one of his favorite places was Bora Bora. I remember him telling me about his visit to Hawaii and the book that came from traveling there. After his book came out about Kahuna Power, for a while we were calling him Daddy Kahuna. He always found out the most interesting, obscure information and then wrote about what he discovered. He was a phenomenal researcher and author. Tim was interested in everything from science to the mystical and the other realms beyond.

He was a filmmaker and also acted in some films, plus he was in a book where he looked very "dapper."

Once during our travels, we were reminiscing, and he told me how, many years ago, he went to a party thrown by the Beatles with sitar music and rock stars among the guests. I was asking more about the party and he looked at me and said it was just one more great party he went to. He loved parties. It just goes to show you how much he got around. Tim was an experienced promoter and had his own band for a while. That is only one example of the interesting contacts he had and many turned into lifelong friends. Tim was really great at anything he set his mind to.

He loved to travel and when we would go on a trip I would love to listen to his stories and adventures. He was a larger-than-life person without any ego and a soft heart.

We would go to UFO conventions and people would know him and ask his opinion on various matters. He would take the time to give them a real answer from his point of view and not just give a meaningless quick one, even when he was tired.

The title "Mr. UFO," as Tim was known in many circles, came about due to his articles, lectures, books and magazines being on the supernatural, the odd, the offbeat and the unexplained.

There's no doubt that I loved Tim very much and that he was there for me when it came to my work and my personal life. But if I were to sit here and write about all of his adventures I would be afraid that the police would have to dig him up and arrest him.

I am sure there are beings in various realms mourning Tim and wondering what he is up to where he is. After all, being inspirit doesn't mean it is an ending, just a different vibrational shift.

He was so diverse that it's impossible to mention all that he was and all that he did. Anyone knowing Tim was going to enter into unknown territory in a wonderful way. I feel blessed to have been his friend and considered part of his family.

First Contact! – With Timothy Green Beckley

By Diane Tessman

Diane Tessman is another fulltime psychic, in her case in partnership with an alien named "Tibus" that Diane has been familiar with since childhood. She wrote for Tim extensively and he published her first book in 1983, as well as serving as a constant source of guidance and encouragement for her as a writer. When you read what Diane says below here, you will likely agree that Tim was truly a great romantic at heart. He frequently referred to Diane as a "Time Traveling Star Goddess," among other worshipful monikers.

Diane with her dog Hannah.

In 1979, I was teaching school in St. Petersburg, Florida, and, in my spare time, I was chasing UFOs and their secrets, as always. I enjoyed UFO Review, published out of New York City by Timothy Green Beckley. I decided to submit an article to it. However, nothing happened, no response, and I thought, "Oh, well."

Then one evening at home in St. Pete, I heard a knock on my door, and there was Timothy Green Beckley! I was shocked and delighted; I asked if he always flew around the country to see someone who had sent him an article.

Tim responded, "Well, you sent your picture too."

Yes, Tim and the ladies were a match made in heaven.

He took me to dinner at the fanciest place I could find in St. Pete (that was his request), and we did have a good talk regarding those elusive UFOs and their occupants. The next day, Tim took my daughter Gianna and me to the beach. Then he flew back to New York.

We kept phone contact but not a whole lot of it, and in 1982, my daughter, our animals, and I, moved to San Diego. I had intended to get into teaching out there but could not. A hiring freeze was in effect due to a recession, plus I didn't have my master's degree.

I was soon in real financial trouble out there. However, there was a knock on my door in San Diego, and there was Timothy Green Beckley, again!

This time he stayed a while, and he suggested to me that I do psychic readings door to door. I had never heard of such a thing, but he put an ad in the local Reader, and I nervously began a psychic career. It turned out really well; Tim had gotten me out of my financial bad straits.

Soon I was writing my own publication, The Star Network Heartline, and Tim promoted my work, suggesting I write my first book, "The Transformation." I did, he published it, and it sold thousands of copies. My life's career had begun, and I've never looked back. Thanks, Tim!

Also, my lifelong friendship with Tim Beckley had begun. We were business friends, we were personal friends. I treasure the Christmas I spent with him and Brad and Sherry Steiger. Tim had come to Iowa to spend Christmas with us and we had a wonderful time.

www.youtube.com/watch?v=-8vAxXRbgy8

I miss you, Tim.

The Honor of Working For Timothy Beckley

By Hercules Invictus

Hercules Invictus is a fairly recent addition to Tim's stable of writers, though he took inspiration from Tim for many decades. Hercules takes his name from the hero of Greek mythology and believes the gods of Olympus live on in our modern world, albeit filtered through a technological haze that we call UFOs and aliens. Over the past few years, Hercules has contributed chapters to books like "*Incredible Alien Encounters*," for which he wrote "A Confrontation With Greys," as well as numerous others.

Hercules Invictus

DULCE WARRIORS

I first became aware of Tim Beckley and Inner Light/Global Communications back in the 1970s. Having had paranormal experiences throughout my (then) young life, I eagerly sought some answers, and Tim's publishing companies provided not only reprints of obscure and hard to find texts but collections of ongoing phenomena on our planet and in the heavens above.

Comforted by learning that I was not alone, I fervently hoped that someday my own accounts would be added to these chronicles. I started writing down some of my own experiences.

In the latter half of the decade (though still technically a teen) I was the Deep Trance Medium for a small Theosophical-Spiritualist group in New York City and had started speaking publicly on matters metaphysical.

Invited to visit relatives in New Brunswick, New Jersey, I leapt at the chance. Though I truly loved these relatives and sincerely wished to see and spend time with them, I also had an ulterior motive: New Brunswick was the point of origin of my cherished tomes from Inner Light/ Global Communications. Questing for the writers and their offices did not prove fruitful on that occasion – but I tried, given the time I had.

During the 1980s I attempted to live a "normal" life. Tim Beckley (aka Mr. UFO) and his intrepid band of explorers and chroniclers of the unknown provided me with a much-needed connection to the unusual life (I thought) I'd left behind through their many publications.

Tim and his late friend the highly controversial John Keel, author of "*Mothman Prophecies*" and other pop items.

The 1990s dawned with my re-embracing my totality and diving back into the fringes of reality. I finally met Tim Beckley and some of my other heroes at the Fortean Society's formal meetings and informal gatherings in the Big Apple.

In the early 2000s I reconnected with Tim (aka Mr. Creepo) and got to know him. He was, during this period, cheerfully engaged in publishing, making movies and having other exciting adventures. I reviewed some of these books, CDs and films and interviewed some of the folks involved on my podcasts – including Tim Beckley.

This continued on and off for over a decade. I got to meet many interesting people through Tim and have gotten close with some of them. The end of the 2010s saw me as a contributor to Tim's paranormal anthologies and by the start of the 2020s my writings had appeared in sixteen of these books.

Tim, alas, passed on May 31st, 2021. Though we were not buddies, we were friendly and had communicated for a long span of years. I greatly enjoyed working (and interacting) with Tim. He was one of my role models growing up and I was greatly honored to be part of his band of otherworldly chroniclers. Looking back, my only regret is my decision to wait until he felt better before I called to say "Hi! How are you?" and explore what projects were looming on the horizon.

Thank you, Tim Beckley, for enriching over half a century of my life with your unique self-expression, generosity and unbridled creativity! And thanks to all who have kept and who will continue to keep Tim Beckley's legacy alive!

Onwards!

Hercules Invictus

Timothy Green Beckley: The Teacher Who Opened My Eyes

By Sean Casteel

By the time Sean Casteel began writing for Timothy Green Beckley, he had already spent years toiling in the world of mainstream journalism, writing about government programs that worked to help the poor and disabled and other attempts to cure America's social ills in general. When Casteel discovered the world of UFOs and alien abductions, an entirely new career opened up for him and he never looked back. Casteel contributed articles to "*UFO Universe*" and "*The Conspiracy Journal*" for many years before Tim began publishing Casteel's books. Tim not only let Casteel write books on his own favorite topics, like UFOs and religion, he brought Casteel into new worlds the freelancer had never even dreamed of. Casteel's first book was called "*UFOs, Prophecy and the End of Time*," and is still available on Amazon.com.

Tim Beckley with Sean Casteel.

In spite of knowing that Tim had been in failing health for the last several years, his sudden death by heart attack still came as quite a shock, a shock that lingers now and a loss that will be felt forever.

I first began to work for Tim in earnest in the winter of 1995, after he had published my Q and A with pioneering abduction researcher Budd Hopkins and subsequently my Q and A with film director Robert Wise, who had helmed the UFO classic "The Day the Earth Stood Still." Thus began the 26 years of our relationship, which would involve magazine articles, books and appearances on Tim's podcast, "Exploring the Bizarre," co-hosted with Tim R. Swartz.

Tim Beckley once told me that there were two basic kinds of UFO enthusiasts. There are the dilettantes, who are at first totally absorbed by the topic, but then, when their personal pet theory doesn't work out or they must confront the fact that absolute answers to the various mysteries remain elusive, abandon the subject in frustration.

Then Tim said that the other kind of UFO enthusiast is a "lifer," someone whose devotion to finding out the truth is at times obsessive but never flags or weakens as the years go by. Tim was certainly such a lifer himself, and he died in the midst of laboring over yet another book, in this case an examination of the alleged joint human/alien underground facility said to be located in Dulce, New Mexico. He left no stone unturned as he chipped away at the boulder that is the unknown and the paranormal.

Like many of his generation, Tim started out as a "nuts-and-bolts" believer, at first convinced that UFOs were a higher physical technology piloted by flesh-and-blood aliens. As the years passed, he more and more embraced the nonphysical, paranormal approach, believing that the visitors were from another dimension and capable of many phenomena we call "supernatural." Or at least an advanced technology that seems supernatural to we humans.

Tim ultimately espoused the theory that UFOs, ghosts, NDEs, spiritualism, etc., were all part of one continuum and that mankind was subject to a large spectrum of phenomena that sprang from a single source. When you studied one facet of the paranormal, it always included ties to another facet.

In his later years as a publisher, Tim struggled mightily with the dark side of the subject. Titles like *"Screwed by the Aliens"* and *"UFO Hostilities and the Evil*

Alien Agenda" mince no words about his sometimes negative take on the UFO occupants.

But he will likely be remembered for his lighter take as well. The last book Tim and his team of writers completed before his death was "*Alien Lives Matter, It's OK To Be Grey.*" Even though some of us on Tim's team thought the title might be seen as "trivializing" the Black Lives Matter Civil Rights movement, Tim countered by saying that the concept had been appropriated already by Hawaiians (Hawaiian Lives Matter) and Jewish people (Jewish Lives Matter) and there was even a section on Amazon where a totally separate business was selling "Alien Lives Matter" t-shirts.

The book turned out to be a struggle for Tim and our entire team, but it also turned out to be a relative bestseller for us. Whenever I spoke the title to someone, it never failed to get a chuckle and a word of encouragement about how it would be a popular title, and it was. Tim made sure to include several chapters on Black UFO experiencers and believers as well, people whose contacts were for the most part very positive.

I can never thank Tim enough for exposing me to so many aspects of the paranormal that I had never taken an interest in prior to working for him. I was called upon to research subjects like ghosts and hauntings, mediums and séances, even the clairaudience of Joan of Arc and the spiritualist beliefs of Sir Arthur Conan Doyle. Tim had a way of leading me down paths I'd never trod before and expanding my horizons considerably.

Toward the end of his life, he did combat with his own understanding of the determinism of "the Matrix," and gathered his team together to do a book on it with the wordy title "*The Matrix Control System of Philip K. Dick and the Paranormal Synchronicities of Timothy Green Beckley.*" It was a subject he sometimes saw the malevolent side of as he wondered whether "synchronistic" experiences, or "nonrandom coincidences," somehow undermined human free will. If our lives are not under our own control, then who IS controlling everything? Like Jacob wrestling with the angel in the Book of Genesis, Tim made a determined combat to maintain his sense of personal autonomy.

Tim Beckley will always be an inspiration to me and a person I am glad to have shared my life with.

Tribute to Tim Beckley

By Paul & Ben Eno

Paul & Ben Eno are a world-famous team of father-son paranormal adventurers, broadcasters, authors and lecturers who have combined experience of over 65 years in the field of the unexplained. Between the two of them, they have investigated hundreds of cases all over the world, and they have lectured all over America and in Europe. Their Sunday destination radio show "Behind the Paranormal with Paul & Ben Eno" airs on 1240 AM and 99.5 FM in the Boston-Providence market at noon Eastern, 9AM Pacific and 5PM GMT.

Ben Eno, Tim Beckley, Paul Eno

In the 1960s, the name of Timothy Green Beckley moved in and out of my early UFO studies like an intriguing shadow. He was only five years my senior, but I wouldn't meet him in the flesh until the following millennium. Tim was a lover of synchronicities, and our connection began in just that way some 50 years before we actually rendezvoused at the Amtrak Station in Lovecraft-haunted Providence, Rhode Island, on August 18, 2014.

That connection came in the form of another 1960s UFO great, Joseph L. Ferrierre, described by Tim as one of his first correspondents in the flying saucer field.

It happened thus: Joe Ferrierre was one of the early UFO "contactees" ("experiencers" we might call them today), having bizarre UFO and alien encounters around southern New England since the mid-1940s. By the late 1950s, Joe was publishing amateur magazines like "*Controversial Phenomena*" and "*Probe.*" By the early 1960s, Joe added radio to his repertoire, hosting the big, and decidedly non-paranormal, daily talk show on a mom-and-pop AM radio station in northern Rhode Island - WWON 1240 in Woonsocket.

Tim, still a kid, was already doing similar things, so contact of the postal kind was inevitable. In 1964, I'm not sure just when, Joe invited Tim to Rhode Island to be on his radio show. They had a great time talking flying saucers, a new subject for most of Joe's audience. Tim and Joe were friends for many years.

Fast forward to 2009. Joe Ferrierre was still hosting the afternoon talk fest on what was now WOON 1240, and just after him in the Monday lineup was a new show: "Behind the Paranormal with Paul & Ben Eno." The former was me and the latter my second-born. In one of our between-show conversations, Joe, Ben and I started talking about Tim, who was to become a frequent guest on "Behind the Paranormal" in the ensuing years.

Joe passed in 2012 at the age of 73, the same age as Tim when he passed in 2021. More synchronicities?

Tim was scheduled to do our show on August 18, 2014, with the subject being just that: synchronicities. But this time we wouldn't do a phone interview. To mark 50 years since his first in-person appearance on 1240 AM, Tim hopped on a train in the Big Apple early that day and headed for Little Rhody. I met him at the Providence Station in my white Ford F-150 pickup truck, and we were brothers from the start.

"Almost all interviews today are done over the phone," Tim declared as we left the station. "It will be great to be at a real radio station for a change and to remember our friend Joe!"

My truck was parked across the street, in front of the Rhode Island State House (state capitol). We got in and, in an appropriately weird scene; a bizarre man in an old coat (probably a member of the legislature) stepped up to the truck, looked at the parking meter, then stared at us through the window. Tim and I just stared back.

Tim could be pretty spooky (Mr. Creepo and all that), and our spectator suddenly stumbled back and ran away.

We drove to Woonsocket, met Ben at the radio station, reminisced about good old Joe Ferrierre, and then had a great show of our own. We had dinner at a local eatery afterward, and then hung out as long as we could before Tim had to catch the train back to New York.

Tim later became a special guest co-host of "Behind the Paranormal," and we enjoyed many guest spots on the great show he did with another good friend, Tim Swartz, "Exploring the Bizarre."

Truly, it can be said of Timothy Green Beckley what has been said of other greats: His like will not be seen again.

Joe Ferrierre always ended his show with "Keep watching the skies!" Tim would enthusiastically agree. Godspeed, my friend. Your memory will be eternal!

Tim Beckley Kept on Trucking Forever

By Charla Gene

Charla Gene says that she was an artist at the age of four when, not knowing that she couldn't, she drew her pet bird. Her parents enrolled her in John McCrady Art School at the age of ten. She remembers that when she was a teeny bopper, she was reading Timothy Beckley's magazines off the newsstand at the neighborhood QuickStop. "So, I already kind of felt I grew up relating to Timothy Green Beckley and his UFO Universe!"

Charla first met Tim at her friend Allen Benz's mini conference at Rancho Vistoso, Oro Valley, AZ. It became apparent right away that Tim was a kindrid spirit. It began in 2010, and Tim wanted to make a jaunt to Northern Arizona to visit and interview more of his UFO buddies. It turned out for the next three years he would come back and give talks to his Tucson friends and head up north again.

"It was great for me to be his chauffeur and I had fun taking photos of all the beautiful spots in AZ," Charla said. "The energy was extraordinary when Tim did interviews and I took photos. Tim and the researchers shared interesting stories which were later included in his many books and YouTube videos. It was so special to share these warm hearted times with Tim."

Charla Gene' with Tim Beckley

Tim's life was full of synchronicities! In 2012 (the end of the Mayan Calendar), here in Sedona, we were expecting a parallel universe experience! Upon entering we're greeted by the iconic Bell Rock Vortex. It's the most magical place and Tim made many trips back to Sedona.

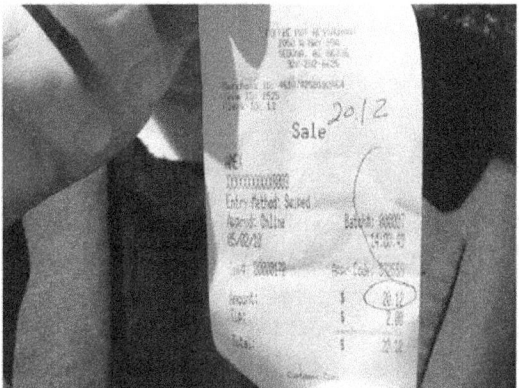

Tim Beckley's favorite place for breakfast was the Coffee Pot Restaurant. After enjoying breakfast the receipt came to $20.12! When we returned to get in my car, the car parked next to us had a plate with APRO on it which was a UFO organization once based in Tucson.

While in Tucson, Tim was express mailed a "ghost detector" to use for hauntings in Jerome. He gave a lecture consisting of tales of his youth living in a haunted house. By now, his paranormal experiences were all natural to him and he considered no one weird. We had a good-old weird time in Jerome. We met up with other ghost busters and Tim was interviewed on a radio show about the spooky tales of the local area.

DULCE WARRIORS

After a fantastic interview with Tom Dongo, we all decided to venture up to one of the most magical places in the world. Good thing I have a 4-wheel drive because the road had not been maintained and driving it was treacherous! The beautiful scenery was worth it.

Charla Gene and Tim Beckley - Schnebly Hill, Sedona AZ

The "Teen UFOlogy Movement"

By Allen Greenfield

I first met Tim Beckley through the "Saucer Club News" free ad section of Ray Palmer's Flying Saucers Magazine, the source of the entire 'teen UFOlogy Movement' -- Gene Steinberg, Rick Hilberg, Tim, myself, Dave Halperin et al. This was in 1961-62, and we had a relationship ongoing right up to my last appearance on his podcast, which was Christmas Eve 2020. In between, we were both fixtures at the National UFO Conference, and we attended the reunion in Cleveland (where the NUFOC began in 1964), and recorded another radio program. We were both guests together on the three hour WOR-Radio Show with Jim Randi hosting (Long John had moved over to WNBC) during the run-up to Jim Moseley's GIANT SAUCER SHOW during the Summer of Love, 1967. Tim later told me that the program was a frequent rebroadcast.

We did an investigation of the Brown Mountain Lights including a visit with contactee Ralph Lael, other local witnesses, and a scary Christmas Eve skywatch on the peak of a mountain overlooking Brown Mountain, with Jim Moseley, his daughter Betty, Tim and myself. The next day I had a really mysterious visitor in my motel room, a true man in black. Tim and I had good relations throughout that 50 plus years.

Tim was my friend from the early 1960s on. He is missed already; the stuffed shirt stick up the arse UFOlogists may be glad he is gone...but, as with Barker, Moseley and other "trickster UFOlogists" he as shockingly close to the truth.

DONATIONS ALWAYS WELCOME via paypal to bishop171@gmail.com

THE ENIGMA SOLVER - http://thesecretcipher.com/

Or...

https://lexicon.thesecretcipher.com/

PRIME SITE https://mewe.com/p/allengreenfielsmostlysageobservations

TRADITIONAL MODERNIZED PAGE- http://tallengreenfield.com/index.html

MY FAMILY - https://wordpress.com/view/greenfieldsimowitz.wordpress.com

THE GRAIL WITHIN - True Quest for the Holy Grail by Allen H. Greenfield with Olav Phillips

www.amazon.com/Grail-Within-Western-Magick-Tradition/dp/B08TSLL8BP

The Complete SECRET CIPHER Of the UfOnauts Paperback New Combined Edition!

By Allen H. Greenfield (Author), Olav Phillips (Introduction)

The Complete SECRET CIPHER Of the UfOnauts Paperback New Combined Edition!

By Allen H. Greenfield (Author), Olav Phillips (Introduction)

www.paranoiamagazine.com/2016/07/complete-secret-cipher-ufonauts/

Decryption key for the secret cipher - http://thesecretcipher.com/

CAUSES PAGE - www.causes.com/campaigns/929080-encourage-people-to-affiliate-with-free-illuminism

At center (l-r) are Timothy Green Beckley, Author of UFO Silencers and CEO of Inner Light Publications and T Allen Greenfield, author of Secret Cipher of the UFOnauts and Secret Rituals of the UFOnauts. 32nd National UFO Conference.

My Friend, Timothy Green Beckley

By Tim R. Swartz

One of the first books about UFOs that Tim R. Swartz bought from Gray Barker's Saucerian Press turned out to be the first book that Timothy Green Beckley wrote… *"The Shaver Mystery and the Inner Earth."* **Even though they didn't realize it at the time, Tim R. Swartz and Tim Beckley's paths would cross several times before they actually met. Starting when he was a teenager, Tim R. Swartz investigated and wrote about UFOs and the paranormal for various UFO-related magazines, but his career in television often sidelined his interest and research in the world of the weird. Thanks to Timothy Green Beckley, Tim was able to renew his love for the unexplained and reach a worldwide audience who was eager to learn just how wonderfully strange our universe actually is.**

Timothy Green Beckley was such a unique and charismatic character that I wish the way we first got to know each other were as spectacular as the way he lived his life.

Our first introduction, however, came about thanks to the United States Air Force.

In 1983, when I was working for a television station in Dayton, Ohio, I was able to secure an interview with UFO investigator J. Allen Hynek. Hynek was in town to give a talk about Project Blue Book at the National Museum of the U.S. Air Force at Wright-Patterson Air Force Base.

After my story ran on the local news, it was picked up by the CBS satellite feed, which allowed CBS stations all across the country to run the story as well. Timothy Green Beckley saw my story on WCBS in New York and managed to track me down to ask for a VHS copy and a transcript, which I was happy to provide for him.

From that point on, barely a week went by where I didn't hear from Tim one way or another. He would either call me, or send me a letter (this was pre-internet), to talk about UFOs, movies, or any of the other things that we were mutually interested in.

When he started publishing "*UFO Universe*," he asked me if I would be interested in providing him with some articles, do research and help punch up articles from other writers. Of course I was excited to help out with his new UFO magazines…I had written articles for magazines like "*Saga's UFO Report*" when I was in college, but it had been years since I had written anything for publication.

From magazines to books, to direct to video movies, Timothy Green Beckley was always coming out with new and interesting things for us to attempt. I often thought his ideas were insane, and I would tell him so…but, for the most part, I was always game to go along with his crazy ideas simply because they sounded like fun.

If you listen to any archived episode of our radio show "Exploring the Bizarre," which aired on the KCOR Digital Radio Network, you can hear how much fun we were having, and Tim was always a treasure trove of UFO knowledge. In fact, the rare times that at the last minute, one of our guests couldn't do the show, Tim and I could easily do the entire two-hours just talking about all of the weird things in this world that forever intrigued us.

DULCE WARRIORS

It is difficult to write about all the great times that Timothy Green Beckley and I had because I never thought they would end. I keep expecting him to call me up with another of his wild adventures...in fact, I wouldn't be the least bit surprised if he did manage to do so from wherever he has gone after leaving this mortal coil.

So when my days on this planet draw to a close, I hope that Mr. UFO swings by on his mothership to pick me up so we can continue on with our adventures. This time, however, there will be no limits; we will have the entire universe to explore. I am looking forward to that.

Photo by Charla Gene

DULCE WARRIORS

SECTION ONE

Seven Levels of Hell

1.

A TERRIFYING INTRODUCTION

WHAT HAPPENED ON OUR WAY TO DULCE
By Timothy Green Beckley

We have every right – as you shall see – to use the engaging title "*Dulce Warriors – Aliens Battle For Earth's Domination*," for the work you are about to read.

It may turn out to be a frightful, but I guarantee an engaging study.

For when we speak of Dulce we speak of:

- Monster Factories.

- Alien Cloning.

- Underground Tunnel Systems.

- MK Ultra Soldiers – Disguised As Greys.

- Aliens torturing Humans.

- Children Disappearing.

- Government germ warfare weapons.

- Human and animal mutilations.

- Breakthrough on the suicide or murder of numerous researchers associated with Dulce.

But we are concerning ourselves not just with one supposed underground base occupied by aliens and humans (at the same time). But in a treaty between our government and "theirs," as well as an endless string of underground and cavern stories admittedly meant to titillate and shock.

"Even before the reign of Philip of Mascedonia," the ancient Roman philosopher Seneca wrote in his *"Questions of Nature,"* – "Men forced their way into caverns, where it is impossible to tell the day from the night and penetrated to the deepest hiding places. They saw great rushing rivers and vast still lakes, sights that made them tremble with horror.

"They descended to a world where the whole of nature is reversed. The land hung above their heads while winds whistled hollowly in the shadows. In the depths, frightful rivers lead nowhere into a perpetual and alien night. After accomplishing so much, these men now lived in fear, having tempted the fires of hell."

Caverns have always exacted a magnetic hold on the human spirit. Speleologists say no other experience comes close to crawling in tube-like tunnels to the guts of the Earth. Even the casual visitor to a tourist cave is enthralled by cathedral-sized subterranean domes and chambers.

Going back more than a decade and I half, when our research was far from complete on Dulce, this is the first report I officially printed in Issue 13 of "The Conspiracy Journal." My remarks were based upon a limited knowledge of the scope and complexity of the enormous situation confronting us from our perch back east, when all the activity was taking place in the state of New Mexico, and in an isolated part of that state in addition.

This is what the front page article in our humble newsletter reported – and it was to begin our journey.

As you shall see, we will be engaging the assistance – willingly or otherwise – of a host of unusual characters. It's kind of like being on the UFOlogical set of "Hello Shorty."

But here we go!

* * * * * * * * *

"It is an absolutely incredible story," says Timothy Beckley, the publisher of "Bizarre Bazaar" and "Conspiracy Journal."

"Since the mid-to late-1970s there have been all sorts of claims made about an underground laboratory beneath the town of Dulce, New Mexico, which was taken over by the greys after a fierce battle with government troops. "The UFO Hunters" show on the History Channel featured an entire episode on this strange event that is taking place on Native American soil, and a few days later George Noory and Coast to Coast plunged headfirst into trying to make sense out of the various accounts that have – pardon the expression – surfaced."

ENTER PAUL BENNEWITZ

Beckley admits that it is difficult to pinpoint exactly when this macabre saga started to develop.

"Probably an engineer by the name of Paul Bennewitz can be given the credit. Bennewitz had been 'called' to the area when aliens started to communicate with him over a radio receiver. He had been 'directed' to this area after observing UFOs over Kirtland Air Force Albuquerque nuclear storage facility.

"Standing near some of the tall cliffs outside Dulce, Bennewitz took a series of photographs showing unidentified craft diving into the mountain through what he claimed were entrance ways that could be opened and closed. The ships passed by so fast they could not be seen with the unaided eye. Somehow, he knew where to aim his camera. He also managed to get a shot of a strange Bigfoot-like creature standing in a nearby clump of trees. The area around these mountains seemed to be alive with all sorts of paranormal activity."

Beckley says that at one of the UFO/Conspiracy conferences he organized in the Southwest he had the opportunity to meet a lady who had dug deeply into the Paul Bennewitz case as well as numerous animal mutilations in the vicinity.

"There were dozens of them and the ranchers were freaking out. Many of the mutilations were associated with strange balls of light and UFO-type phenomenon that would be seen on the nights when the animals were apparently being butchered.

"I offered to purchase a self-published, rather thick report that Christa had put together on the Bennewitz affair. I put it out but never really promoted it and the cover was less than professional, so it didn't get the readership it deserved."

There were other rumors about underground UFO activity in Dulce states Tim Beckley, adding that, "A claim was made of a last man standing war in which the aliens took over the lower levels and set up containers where they could breed humans, turning them into hybrids. One military personnel said he managed to escape, but later 'disappeared,' while another individual, Phil Schneider, 'mysteriously' committed suicide after he began speaking in public about the ongoing events in Dulce."

He offered as evidence of his being caught in an interplanetary confrontation the fact that he had lost three fingers.

"And even if one discounts some of the more speculative episodes, there have been – and this is a matter of public record – any number of unexplainable sightings of 'saucers' in and around the town. Some of them made by the local Native Americans, others by no less a credible authority than the Chief of Police."

Beckley says apparently the local citizenry have known about the UFO presence for some time. The Native Americans might well have equated it with the re-appearance of their gods, but these appearances seemed a bit more negative . . . but not all of them! Paul Villa (whose book of seemingly authentic UFO photographs we published) spoke of meeting advanced humanoid beings probably within a stone's throw of Dulce. His pictures are quite spectacular as the objects are shown landing on tripod extensions. In March of 2009, veteran researcher Norio Hayakawa decided he wanted to get to the bottom of the mysterious happenings at Dulce. Was there really an alien base inside the mountain, were locals actually seeing UFOs, or was something perhaps a bit more sinister taking place? Norio decided to call a town hall meeting in Dulce itself. Feeling strongly that the city's board and the local Native American tribe would not be anxious for him to proceed with any plans for a mini-conference, he decided to go ahead and organize such an event anyway.

As it turned out, not only did he receive no objections from the city council, but some members helped with promotion and offered to provide their own testimony on what they had seen or been involved in. The event was such a success that at the last minute, Norio had to move the conference from a hotel meeting room to a larger auditorium. A lot of new information was forthcoming and the day after the presentations were made, Norio filed the following report.

DULCE BASE CONFERENCE ENDS: A FULL REPORT

By Norio Hayakawa

March 30, 2009 – "Dulce Base Conference Ends With More Questions Than Answers."

DULCE, NEW MEXICO – Close to 120 people showed up for the first "underground base" conference ever to be held in Dulce, New Mexico, on Sunday, March 29. The event made a rather tumultuous start at the Best Western Jicarilla Inn at 10 a.m. By that time the entire bar lounge area began to be filled beyond capacity. And by the time the first speaker (former Dulce ranch owner, Edmund Gomez) began his presentation, many people had to stand and wait in the adjacent restaurant area. It was then that the Fire Department said that the conference must immediately be moved elsewhere. Halfway through the speaker's fascinating presentation, the Fire Department issued a stern second warning saying that the number of people inside the conference room far exceeded its capacity. Panic then began to be felt by the event's organizer, Norio Hayakawa of Rio Rancho. Hotel employees frantically made phone calls to find out if there were any other locations available for the conference to go on.

It was then that Hoyt Velarde, former Dulce police officer and head of the Public Safety Department, suggested to Hayakawa that the conference be moved to a civic hall inside a small shopping center across the street from the hotel. With Velarde's swift assistance in making the arrangements, and after a short intermission, the entire "Dulce Base: Fact or Fiction?" conference and public forum finally resumed and continued the rest of the day at the new location.

As an interesting side note, on Sunday morning, when it was still dark outside, many guests at the Best Western Jicarilla Inn were awakened shortly before 6 a.m. by a thunderous roar of blades of helicopters above. Local residents nearby reported that there was a rare low flight of two military helicopters above Dulce.

In the afternoon session of the conference, two local residents also testified that they witnessed the military helicopters circling above Dulce and that they passed slowly above the hotel. They told Hayakawa that there are occasional appearances of military helicopters over the town but the flights were never as low as what they saw early Sunday morning.

As organizer and moderator of this conference, Hayakawa several times alluded to an allegation that the government, beginning in the early 1970s and lasting till the early 1980s, may have conducted clandestine operations in the area involving experiments with bovine diseases, anthrax and other substances as part of biological warfare research. He also alluded to another allegation that there may also have been some illegal dumping or storage of toxic chemicals and other biohazardous materials in the nearby areas.

Hayakawa stated that he tends to support a theory that the government may have purposefully created some "convenient" cover stories (underground alien base concept) to conceal those clandestine activities and may even have staged a series of fake "UFO-type" incidents in the area, utilizing high tech equipment such as holographic projection devices. However he also stated that he cannot deny any possibility that there may indeed be some unknown interdimensional phenomenon in the area which happens to be filled with fascinating cultural and spiritual beliefs of the Jicarilla Apache nation.

WHAT THE SPEAKERS HAD TO SAY

The speakers at the conference and their main points expressed were as follows:

Edmund Gomez, spokesman for the entire Gomez family, who owned a large ranch in Dulce, said that their ranch lost more than 17 cows during the height of cattle mutilations incidents and experienced substantial financial loss over the years. Gomez stated that gas masks were found near the mutilation sites and that specific cows were each tracked with phosphorescent markings a few days before the mutilations actually took place. He is convinced that this was done by the government and that no aliens were involved. He asserted that the government was conducting some type of germ warfare experiments. He concluded by stating that there is definitely a governmental underground facility there.

Hoyt Velarde, former Dulce police officer and head of the Public Safety Department, asserted that he has not located the base yet but it is an undeniable fact that there have been (and still are) many UFO sightings in the area. Velarde even suggested that he is willing to organize an escorted group expedition soon for the public to the top of the Archuleta Mesa if such a request is made in earnest. He surprised the attendees also by saying that another conference on this topic could even be held next time in the conference hall of the Police Department there.

Hayakawa said that he may consider this offer. Gabe Valdez, former New Mexico state patrol officer in charge of the Dulce area, stated that he investigated numerous cattle mutilation cases around Dulce from the mid-1970s to the early 1980s. He declared that this has nothing to do with aliens but that there is something there that is too sensitive for discussion and refused to further divulge what that was.

Christopher O' Brien, researcher of paranormal activities in the San Luis Valley of Southern Colorado, asserted that Dulce may be a diversion from what is more importantly taking place in the San Luis Valley just north of northern New Mexico.

Dr. Michael E. Salla, the initiator of "exo-politics" and author of a book entitled "Exposing U.S. Government Policies On Extraterrestrials" expressed his belief that there is a joint US/alien underground bio-lab beneath the Archuleta Mesa and that this must be addressed as a serious human rights abuse issue.

Greg Bishop, author of "Project Beta," a book in which he describes in detail his investigations of the claims of an Albuquerque scientist by the name of Paul Bennewitz, said that Bennewitz was the initial source behind the rumors of the underground base in Dulce. Bishop asserted that Bennewitz was side tracked by an unofficial disinformation campaign to get him to look away from evidence of sensitive military projects going on in 1979 inside Kirtland Air Force Base in Albuquerque. However, Bishop surprised everyone when he said at the end that he is now beginning to rethink his initial doubts about Dulce and concluded that there could indeed be something there.

Gabe Julian, former Dulce police officer who worked under the late Raleigh Tafoya, former Dulce Police Chief, described his encounters with three metallic, oval-shaped objects hovering at a tree-top level at a ranch in Dulce. He described how he was dispatched to the ranch house of a woman who claimed that small people with strange boxes emitting light were harassing her. Initially skeptical of what his radio dispatcher told him, he drove over to the area and was shaken up when he witnessed those hovering objects there.

Dennis Balthaser, a well-known UFO researcher from Roswell, New Mexico, expressed his conviction, like Salla, that there is a US/alien joint biological laboratory and base under the Archuleta Mesa.

DULCE WARRIORS

Keith Ealy, a researcher with a fascinating interpretation of Dulce as being a space/time portal for inter-dimensionals amazed the audience with his close-up satellite imagery of the Dulce Elementary School building. He told the audience that the contours of the parking lot resemble an ancient stone sculpture in Bolivia. He concluded that the Dulce area is filled with inter-dimensional phenomenon, a belief similarly shared by world famous researchers, Dr. Jacques Vallee and John Keel.

Norio Hayakawa was the organizer and moderator of the 2009 Dulce Conference. Held at the Best Western Jicarilla Inn, the event featured such speakers as former Dulce ranch owner, Edmund Gomez; Greg Bishop, author of the book *"Project Beta"*; researcher Chris O' Brien; former Dulce police officer Hoyt Velarde; and Dr. Michael E. Salla - author of the book *"Exposing U.S. Government Policies On Extraterrestrials."*

PAUL BENNEWITZ - UFO PHOTOS OVER KIRTLAND AFB

Noted "UFO Nukes" researcher Robert Hastings, has this to say about Paul Bennewitz and his UFO photos at Kirtland.

"After Bennewitz approached USAF commanders at Kirtland with his films, and subsequently began giving interviews about his sightings at Manzano to UFOlogists and the press, OSI agent Richard Doty was secretly ordered to neutralize his testimony and evidence through the use of dirty tricks, including providing Bennewitz with forged documents and other bogus information about U.S. government-sanctioned alien operations near Kirtland, and other bizarre subjects - which he was encouraged to publicize - in an effort to undercut his credibility with the media and the public.

Bennewitz was also told that aliens were monitoring his own activities and, as a result, he began wearing a sidearm at home. The ensuing psychological assaults on the hapless Bennewitz resulted in his being temporarily hospitalized for paranoid psychosis and, ultimately, his complete, permanent mental collapse.

In short, Bennewitz became a casualty of the Air Force's determined efforts to direct attention away from the real story – repeated UFO incursions at the Manzano nukes storage site - evidence of which he had captured on film.

Wyoming Gate at Kirtland Air Force Base.

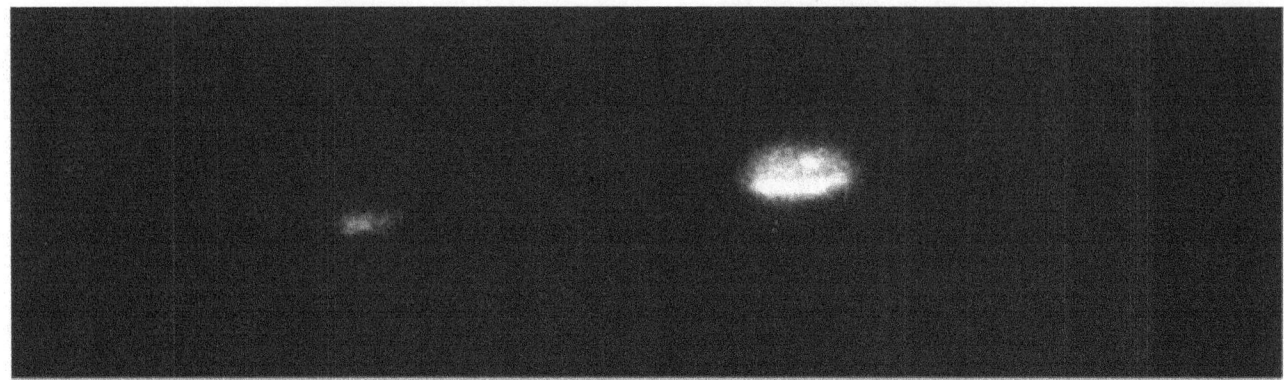
A unique view of the largest vehicle with a smaller one faintly visible in the distance.

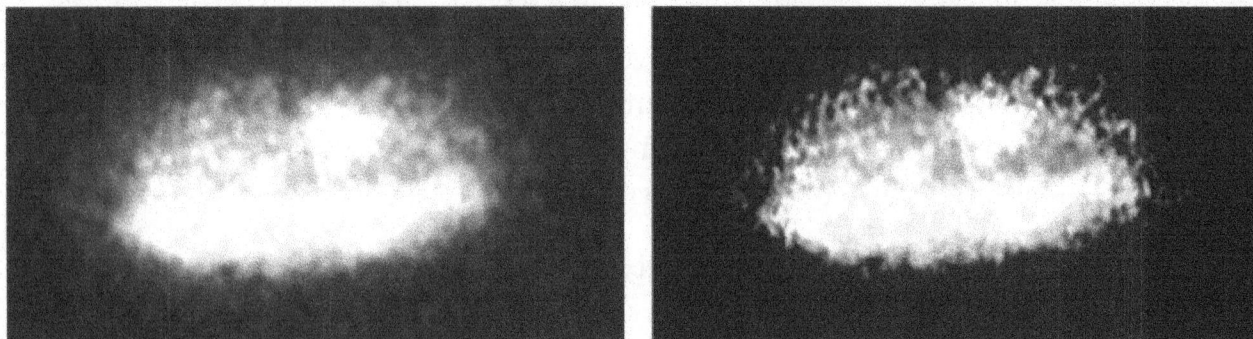
Enhancement shows unusual patterns in the upper energy field, possibly converging at the glowing node.

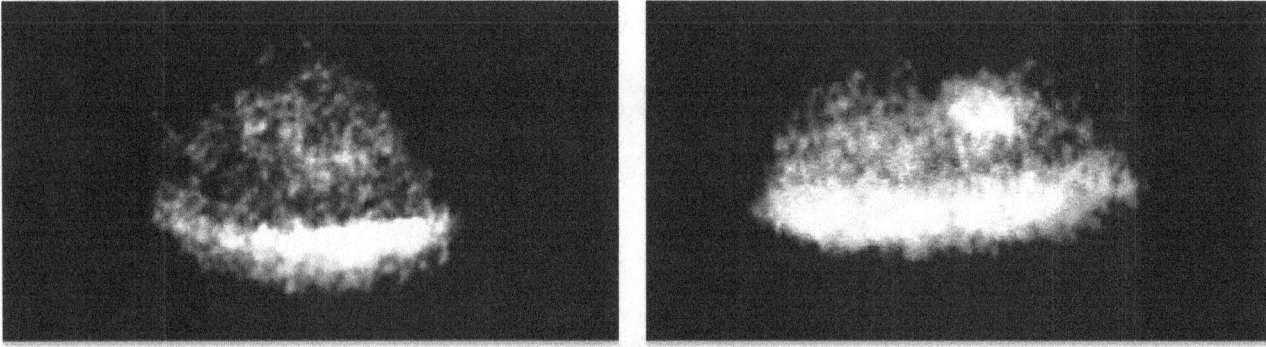
Above left is the vehicle in an apparent low-power state. Above right is a color-enhanced view of the vehicle in flight, the upper surface now engulfed in yellow-orange and the vehicle appears an intense white. The same iridescent blue-green glow stands out along the lower edge.

Copyright © 2012 Christian P. Lambright

2.

THE STRANGE SAGA OF PAUL BENNEWITZ AND THE UNDERGROUND "ALIEN" BASE AT DULCE
By Sean Casteel

Paul Bennewitz owned Thunder Scientific Labs, an electronics firm subcontracted by Kirtland AFB.

The story of Paul Bennewitz is one of the sadder ones in all of Ufology. He seems to have been a victim from the very beginning, though he was not victimized by the aliens he came to believe in but rather the shadowy finagling of a government to whom he mistakenly gave his trust.

Bennewitz's experience, as related in a book on his struggle called "*Underground Alien Bio Lab at Dulce: The Bennewitz UFO Papers*," by Timothy Green Beckley and Christa Tilton, started in 1979. The twisted trail that is the story of Bennewitz took many bizarre turns on its path to UFO and conspiracy theory legend. One of the more mysterious places it led to is the tiny New Mexico town of Dulce, located not far from the Four Corners region of the American Southwest. For my own contribution to the abovementioned book, I spoke to some researchers about the strange rumors continually floating around Dulce, which together form one of the most interesting enigmas of the present age.

Perhaps the most vocal and visible expert on the Dulce mysteries is Norio Hayakawa, who has written many articles on the subject and appeared numerous times on radio and television programs dealing with the town.

"Dulce, New Mexico," Hayakawa said, "is a location filled with mysteries that are still ongoing. I believe it is far more interesting than Roswell. Yes, Roswell was significant in that it is the alleged location of the crash of extraterrestrial vehicles in 1947, but, you know, that was it. But Dulce is something different. It is an ongoing thing that is taking place.

"Not only that," Hayakawa continued, "but Dulce has the highest percentage per population of UFO sightings. This is a fact. Almost the entire town of Dulce, which has a population of about 2,600 now, almost the entire population has experienced a sighting of strange objects in the past 30 years. This is the highest percentage of any community in the United States."

But back to Bennewitz. The story goes that Bennewitz was a scientist living near Kirtland Air Force Base in Albuquerque, New Mexico. In 1979, he began to observe the flights of mysterious objects from his home, which was also adjacent to the Monzano Storage Area, the country's largest underground nuclear storage facility, as well as the Coyote Canyon Test Range.

"Albuquerque is very significant," Hayakawa said, "because it is where German scientists were first transferred in 1945, immediately after World War II, through the Operation Paperclip Program in which the U.S. brought into the country not only scientists from Germany but also many skilled intelligence officers."

Bennewitz began to film and attempt to report on the strange aerial activity he was witnessing, which immediately drew the interest of the government. One theory is that the bewildered scientist was seeing test flights of what are called "UAVs," or Unmanned Aerial Vehicles, pilot-less aircraft that are remotely controlled either on the ground or programmed by onboard computer systems. Whatever the secret flights involved, the government did not want Bennewitz to know the truth.

Apparently, so the story goes, the government brainwashed Bennewitz into believing that he was witnessing a flight of alien discs over Kirtland Air Force Base. Bennewitz received a message somehow, either by radio or over his computer, saying that there is a secret base 150 miles north of Albuquerque in the mountains.

Bennewitz was provided with the exact coordinates of this alien base, which of course turned out to be Dulce.

Bennewitz was never able to prove either the existence of aliens over Kirtland or the government's manipulations of his attempt to document the mysterious overflights. He sank deeper and deeper into an increasingly paranoid frame of mind, unable to cope with the bizarre scenario in which he had been ensnared.

In the years before his death in 2003, he corresponded with a woman named Christa Tilton, an alien abductee who was conducting research into UFOs in an attempt to understand her own experiences with what she felt may have been government agents posing as extraterrestrials. A reprint of her manuscript about her dealings with Bennewitz is included herein, as well as photocopies of newspaper articles that dealt with Bennewitz and other witnesses to the strange craft. The book also reproduces letters exchanged with local law enforcement officials, who totally pooh-poohed any inquiries into the alien rumors around Dulce.

It all coalesces into a very complicated story that leaves one with more questions than answers, but Tilton and the other writers do their utmost to bring some order to the general chaos. For instance, the book offers a lengthy interview with Thomas Costello, who claims to have been employed as a security guard at an underground facility in Dulce. Costello talks at length about interacting with aliens far below the surface and some of the protocols the humans and aliens were required to observe. Costello would sometimes be forced to intervene if a human wandered out of the zones where earthlings were permitted and had to try to smooth things over when an alien felt a human had crossed some kind of agreed upon line.

The interview with Costello, conducted by a writer named Bruce Walton (who also appears under the pseudonym Branton), is fraught with the kind of detailed information about day-to-day human and alien interaction that would seem to be very difficult to conjure out of nothing. Costello died about a year after the interview was conducted, a questionable case of suicide.

In addition, the book includes a report by Dr. Michael Salla in which he attempts to understand the Bennewitz/Dulce story based on primary sources as opposed to secondhand information and hearsay.

"Was Bennewitz just an overzealous UFO researcher," Salla asks, "that accidentally tapped into highly classified Air Force research and development projects? Or was he an electronics genius who single-handedly uncovered the existence of a joint U.S. government/ET underground base where ETs conducted gross human rights violations on abducted civilians? Seeking clear answers to these questions has spurred a number of books, articles and internet websites. A more scholarly effort of analyzing the primary source material available on Dulce is needed to help answer key questions about the alleged base at Dulce."

And just what would that primary source material be? Salla said he started by reviewing whistleblower testimonies that would seem to support Bennewitz as well as analyzing current government whistleblower protection laws. The long and tangled path was not made much clearer, but at least a sensible effort to solve the mystery in real world terms was underway.

There is no easy way to answer the question of "Who can we believe?" Two different government disinformation agents, Richard Doty and William Moore, have both publicly confessed on more than one occasion to feeding disinformation to Bennewitz designed to throw him off the scent of what he had uncovered and documented about Kirtland Air Force Base and Dulce. As stated previously, Bennewitz began to grow increasingly paranoid as a result of their efforts at brainwashing him.

Writer Leslie Gunter contributes a report on Bennewitz to the book in which she firmly declares, "Still, Paul Bennewitz was not a complete nut. The signals he was receiving were real signals and Doty says the National Security Agency, who had their own offices at the base, were doing the sending and receiving. Doty was eventually replaced by NSA agents who wanted to make sure Bennewitz discredited himself by spreading wild stories about UFOs. They also wanted to keep an eye on him to make sure that he wasn't sharing his method of intercepting these signals with Soviet spies posing as UFO enthusiasts."

The pattern of deception extended to the cattle mutilations around Dulce, which the NSA wanted Bennewitz to continue to blame on the alien presence in the area. They also installed some fake air shafts in Dulce that Bennewitz was intended to believe served the underground base below. Sorting through the lies and manipulation, as Dr. Salla seeks to do, would seem a daunting task to say the least.

"In 1988," Gunter writes, "after eight years of constant stress and lack of sleep, Paul Bennewitz had to be taken to a mental hospital. His paranoia had reached an all-time high and he had pretty much barricaded himself in his home. He was hardly eating or sleeping and was sure aliens were coming into his home late at night and injecting him with strange chemicals."

Gunter credits Bennewitz with being the first to state that the alien abductors were inserting implants into their abductees, though Bennewitz felt the implants were some method of mind control as opposed to the more popular theory that they serve as a kind of tracking device that keeps the whereabouts of abductees easy to locate. Bennewitz did show others the needle marks left behind after the alleged alien injections, but it was never certain whether the marks were self-inflicted or were in fact made in the way he claimed.

But leaving aside the story of Bennewitz's personal struggles, his revelations about the underground base at Dulce were nothing short of spectacular. The rumors that have circulated since then are full of nightmare scenarios like huge vats of human and animal body parts used in genetic experiments, perhaps in further efforts to create an alien-human hybrid species or an even stranger chimera that is part human and part animal. One expert says the government and the aliens may be working to create a "perfect soldier," one that is capable of fearlessness and obedience beyond that of the normal GI grunt. There is the case of a female abductee who claimed that she was in one of the lower sections of Dulce when an alien walked right through the wall and raped her. That kind of forced copulation may also be a component of the genetics experimentation said to take place in Dulce, the goal being to impregnate the human female with an alien seed and see what is produced, a scenario already familiar from other stories of alien abduction.

For my part of the book, I also spoke to Bill Birnes, the former publisher of the now-defunct "*UFO Magazine*" and the team leader on the also defunct History Channel program "UFO Hunters." Birnes said that one possibility about what's happening at Dulce may be experiments with various virulent diseases and certain kinds of bacteria. Most of the land there is owned by the government, specifically the Bureau of Land Management, and the base may also lease some of the land from the nearby Indian reservation.

The government could be researching mad cow disease and its penetration into the American beef supply, which may account for some of the cattle mutilations in the area. The secrecy could have something to do with keeping the mad cow problem from panicking an already jittery public. They may also be using cattle to determine how much the ground was penetrated by nuclear fallout following the atomic testing in the last century.

When asked about the "alien stuff," Birnes replied, "Quite frankly, I can understand the alien hypothesis. I really do believe that there are areas where aliens and humans are working together, such as Area 51 and S-4. But whether Dulce is indeed that kind of base or not, everything we've seen – when you talk to Norio Hayakawa, when you talk to Gabe Valdez, a New Mexico state trooper, they really discount the alien connection and talk more about the New World Order. But I mean, the base is top secret, and there are serious things happening at the base. But whether it's because of aliens or because the aliens are a very convenient cover for even more dastardly things going on there – that, I can't tell you."

While Birnes obviously has his doubts about an alien presence in Dulce, he did relate an interesting story about what has come to be called the "Firefight at Dulce."

"The story goes that all the way back in the 1980s," he said, "the extraterrestrials were giving a lecture to some scientists. In that demonstration, a lot of the scientists were getting sick because of what the aliens were doing. So some of our military guards, who were prohibited from entering the area and prohibited from carrying any kind of weapons into that area, suddenly burst in to protect the scientists.

"And the aliens reacted," Birnes continued, "by basically turning their weapons on the security guards, killing them. Some aliens were killed and some scientists were killed. And supposedly we all worked very hard to try to patch it together so there wouldn't be any more incidents like that."

Which brings us back to Paul Bennewitz. Was he just another casualty in a war zone of alien and government conflict? Did he cross some line of knowing that upset the powers that be, again powers that are both human and alien? While these questions cannot presently be answered, and may in fact never be answered, reading *"Underground Alien Bio Lab At Dulce: The Bennewitz UFO Papers"* will at least bring the curious reader up to speed on the ongoing discussion and the seemingly unending tug of war about the truth. Whether we're dealing with human beings and/or an alien contingent, they all seem to be playing this game for keeps.

Underground Alien Bio Lab At Dulce - The Bennewitz UFO Papers.
Published by Inner Light-Global Communications.

3.

EXPOSING THE EXISTENCE OF THE DULCE BASE - SEVEN LEVELS OF HELL

PUBLISHER'S NOTE: I couldn't quite believe what I was seeing. I was streaming the show "UFO Witness" on "Discovery Plus" (Episode 7) and here was respected journalist Ben Hansen off on a trip to investigate the "Aliens Underground" in "the small town of Dulce, New Mexico, which may harbor one of America's darkest secrets." Hansen said he will try to figure out if the rumors are true and in the process uncovers multiple reports of UFO sightings, alien abductions and stories of an underground base below the mesa located on Indian Territory.

In order to proceed with his investigation, Ben has to establish a working relationship with the Native Americans in the area. He knows it will not be an easy task, but it is something he has to do. The local population has been skeptical of all outside visitors and they seem hesitant to share their knowledge with those unsympathetic to the plight of the people.

AND JUST WHO IS BEN HANSEN?

Ben Hansen is a former federal special agent and paranormal investigator. He currently stars in the new Discovery+ series "UFO Witness," where he reopens case files of some of the most astounding UFO encounters in history, files that have been hidden from the public for decades.

Hansen's paranormal inspiration stems from the series, "The X-Files." He grew up obsessed with the series, which gave him an insatiable desire to explore mysteries of the unknown. To transform this passion into a career, Hansen studied at the University of Utah, where he graduated with a degree in sociology and criminology. He worked for several private and public agencies investigating a wide range of crimes, eventually becoming a special agent for the U.S. government. While Hansen has an impressive track record investigating cases at the state and federal level, he is still anchored in his passion for the unknown and pursues paranormal cases.

Hansen's knowledge of both criminal and paranormal investigations has caught the attention of several media outlets. His expertise has been called upon for numerous documentaries and series on networks such as Smithsonian, Destination America, CW and several appearances on Travel Channel. Hansen was the lead paranormal investigator in the Travel Channel series "Ghosts of Morgan City" and was founding host of the SyFy hit television show "Fact or Faked: Paranormal Files." Breaking down captured media of alleged Bigfoot, UFO and ghost events, Hansen provides his expert opinion on some of the most current viral stories in the media. He has presented his research and findings at dozens of conferences across the globe.

Hansen also works as a commercial drone pilot and teaches advanced firearms, active shooter response and CPR courses. He owns a night vision and thermal camera retail business called Night Vision Ops as well as a company that sells bulletproof backpacks and other safety equipment. In his free time, he attempts to surf, enjoys basketball, rock climbing, scuba diving and flying small planes. He also believes firmly in the importance of volunteerism, especially when it comes to disaster preparedness. He serves on his community's FEMA-sponsored community emergency response team and was formerly active with a disaster action team for the American Red Cross. Hansen is also the chief of media and entertainment for PrepperCon, the largest disaster preparedness/survival consumer expo in the country.

Hansen resides in Huntington Beach, California, with his wife and son.

* * * * * * * * *

As it turns out, events go beyond expectation, and, once Hansen is seated in the offices of the Alameda tribe, they go to a locked file drawer and pull out a heavy folder containing a copy of the *"Dulce Case Book"* (also known as *"The Dulce Papers"* and *"The Dulce Base"*), which pretty much looks identical to the initial report issued by Jason Bishop III which initially was only to be passed around to a handful of researchers, but ended up getting wider distribution than anticipated.

The following is Jason's report, the same one that Ben Hansen is privileged to open in full view of the Discovery cameras for his stunned audience.

DULCE WARRIORS

Dissident Grays fought lower level Grays alongside U.S. military personnel at Dulce at one point. The dissidents are 600 years old mostly, and have a different doctrine than the lower level Grays. The lower level Grays are thousands of years old.

The Austra Albus can breed with humans. They are, in fact, 99.99% human. The Honorable Lady Barbara Judge, chairman of Hyperion, is one of them. Hyperion is working out of Dulce and Judge is in charge of the program that intends to sell miniature nuclear reactors as individual-use power devices across the planet. "Pine Gap uses them, Mount Weather, all these underground facilities use them."

The 4-corners area of New Mexico has the highest levels of missing people in the country; women of child-bearing age, and young men from 10 to 15, the prime age for super soldier programs. These military abductions are an outgrowth of things the Grays have been teaching us since the 1940s. "The Dulce facility -- it's horrific what they are doing to these people.".

China has been selected by the new world order to invade the rest of the world after a false flag, mass landing event causes pandemonium. China has built "the mother of underground bases," and is developing stealth technology at an alarming rate. "It's alien technology." A massive human depopulation program is going to be implemented thereafter. What China doesn't know is that "the Chinese are being manipulated by human-alien hybrids who have controlled this planet since the very beginning." The human depopulation program is to begin with them.

Project Leonid is a low Earth orbit defense system successfully launched by the U.S. Using satellites of various sizes, it will combat a space war with the Chinese and ETs. It uses artificial intelligence, however, and has a 30% chance of following its own plans.

The Dulce Base

```
       *********************
ÄÄÄÄÄÄÄÄÄÄ *                   * ÄÄÄÄÄÄÄÄÄÄ
           *  LITERARY FREEWARE  *
           *                     *
           *       FOUNDATION    *
ÄÄÄÄÄÄÄÄÄÄ *                   * ÄÄÄÄÄÄÄÄÄÄ
       *********************

         -=ð P R O U D L Y  ¡  P R E S E N T S ð=-
```

THE FOLLOWING MATERIAL COMES FROM PEOPLE WHO KNOW THE DULCE (UNDERGROUND) BASE EXISTS. THEY ARE PEOPLE WHO WORKED IN THE LABS; ABDUCTEES TAKEN TO THE BASE; PEOPLE WHO ASSISTED IN THE CONSTRUCTION; INTELLIGENCE PERSONAL (NSA,CIA,FBI ECT.) AND UFO / INNER-EARTH RESEARCHERS.
THIS INFORMATION IS MEANT FOR THOSE WHO ARE SERIOUSLY INTERESTED IN THE DULCE BASE. FOR YOUR OWN PROTECTION BE ADVISED TO "USE CAUTION" WHILE INVESTIGATING THIS COMPLEX.

An ongoing investigation:

"THE DULCE BASE"
   by Jason Bishop III

This facility is a "GENETICS LAB" and is connected to Los Alamos, via a "Tube-Shuttle." Part of their research is related to the General Effects of Radiation (Mutations and Human Genetics). Its research also includes other "Intelligent Species" (Alien Biological Life Form "Entities").
In the revised September 1950 edition of "THE EFFECTS OF ATOMIC WEAPONS" prepared for and in cooperation with the U.S. Department of Defense and the U.S. Atomic Energy Commission, under the direction of the Los Alamos Scientific Laboratory, we read about how "complete Underground placement of Bases is desirable". On page #381: "There are apparently no fundamental difficulties in construction and operating Underground various types of important Facilities. Such facilities may be placed in a suitable existing mine or a site may be excavated for the purpose".

CAUGHT IN THE GAME
Centuries ago, Surface People (some say the Illuminati) entered into a pact with an "Alien Nation" (hidden within the Earth). The U.S. Government, in 1933, agreed to trade Animals and Humans in exchange for High Tech Knowledge, and allow them to use (undisturbed) UNDERGROUND BASES, in the Western USA. A Special Group was formed to deal with the Alien Beings. In the 1940's, "Alien Life Forms (ALF)" began shifting their focus of operations, from Central and South America, to the USA.
The Continental Divide is vital to these "Entities". Part of this has to do with Magnetics (Substrata Rock) and High Energy States (Plasma). [See: BEYOND THE FOUR DIMENSIONS (Reconciling Physics, Parapsychology and UFOs by Karl Brunstein. Also: NUCLEAR EVOLUTION (Discovery of the Rainbow Body) by Christopher Hills.]
This area has a very high concentration of Lightning Activity, Underground Waterways and Cavern Systems, Fields of Atmospheric Ions, ect, ect.

"The Dulce Base" by Jason Bishop III (AKA - Tal Levesque.)

THE FOLLOWING MATERIAL COMES FROM PEOPLE WHO KNOW THE DULCE (UNDERGROUND) BASE EXISTS. THEY ARE PEOPLE WHO WORKED IN THE LABS; ABDUCTEES TAKEN TO THE BASE; PEOPLE WHO ASSISTED IN THE CONSTRUCTION; INTELLIGENCE PERSONNEL (NSA, CIA, FBI, ETC.); AND UFO/INNER-EARTH RESEARCHERS.

THIS INFORMATION IS MEANT FOR THOSE WHO ARE SERIOUSLY INTERESTED IN THE DULCE BASE. FOR YOUR OWN PROTECTION BE ADVISED TO "USE CAUTION" WHILE INVESTIGATING THIS COMPLEX.

An ongoing investigation:

DULCE WARRIORS

"THE DULCE BASE"

By Jason Bishop III

This facility is a "GENETICS LAB" and is connected to Los Alamos, via a "Tube-Shuttle." Part of their research is related to the General Effects of Radiation (Mutations and Human Genetics). Its research also includes other "Intelligent Species" (Alien Biological Life Form "Entities").

In the revised September 1950 edition of *"THE EFFECTS OF ATOMIC WEAPONS"* prepared for and in cooperation with the U.S. Department of Defense and the U.S. Atomic Energy Commission, under the direction of the Los Alamos Scientific Laboratory, we read about how "complete Underground placement of Bases is desirable." On page #381: "There are apparently no fundamental difficulties in construction and operating underground various types of important Facilities. Such facilities may be placed in a suitable existing mine or a site may be excavated for the purpose."

CAUGHT IN THE GAME

Centuries ago, Surface People (some say the Illuminati) entered into a pact with an "Alien Nation" (hidden within the Earth). The U.S. Government, in 1933, agreed to trade Animals and Humans in exchange for High Tech Knowledge, and allow them to use (undisturbed) UNDERGROUND BASES, in the Western USA. A Special Group was formed to deal with the Alien Beings. In the 1940's, "Alien Life Forms (ALF)" began shifting their focus of operations, from Central and South America, to the USA.

The Continental Divide is vital to these "Entities." Part of this has to do with Magnetics (Substrata Rock) and High Energy States (Plasma). [See: "BEYOND THE FOUR DIMENSIONS" (Reconciling Physics, Parapsychology and UFOs by Karl Brunstein. Also: *"NUCLEAR EVOLUTION (Discovery of the Rainbow Body")* by Christopher Hills.]

This area has a very high concentration of Lightning Activity, Underground Waterways and Cavern Systems, Fields of Atmospheric Ions, etc., etc.

DULCE WARRIORS

WHOSE PLANET IS THIS?

These Aliens consider themselves "Native Terrans." They are an Ancient Race (descendent from a Reptilian Humanoid Species which cross-bred with Sapient Humans). They are untrustworthy, manipulative Mercenary Agents for another Extraterrestrial Culture (The DRACO) who are returning to Earth (their ancient "Outpost") to use it as a staging area.

But, these Alien Cultures are in conflict over Whose Agenda will be followed for this Planet. All the while Mental Control is being used to keep Humans "in place," especially since the Forties.

The DULCE Complex is a Joint US Government/Alien Base. It was the first built with The Aliens (others are in Colorado, Nevada, and Arizona.)

THE SECRET "ACTIVITY"

Paul Bennewitz reports about his study into the Dulce area: "Troops went in and out of there every summer, starting in '47. The natives do recall that. They also built a road right in front of the people of Dulce and trucks went in and out for a long period. That road was later blocked and destroyed. The signs on the trucks were 'Smith' Corp, out of Paragosa Springs, Colorado. No such corporation exists now – no record exists... I believe the Base - at least the first one was being built then under the cover of a lumbering project...problem - they NEVER hauled logs. Only BIG Equipment."

R&D AND THE MILITARY INDUSTRIAL COMPLEX

THE RAND CORP. became involved and did a study for the Base. Most of the lakes near Dulce were manmade, via Government grants 'for' the Indians.

NAVAJO DAM is the main source for conventional electrical power, with a second source in EL VADO (also, an entrance). Note: If RAND is the mother of "THINK TANKS," then the "FORD FOUNDATION" must be considered the father.

Rand secrecy is not confined to "Reports," but on occasion extends to Conferences and Meetings. On page #645 of The PROJECT RAND, proceedings of the DEEP UNDERGROUND CONSTRUCTION SYMPOSIUM (March 1959) we read: "Just as airplanes, ships and automobiles have given man mastery of the surface of the Earth, Tunnel-Boring Machines... will give him access to the Subterranean World." Note: The Sept. 1983 issue of "*OMNI*" (pg#80) has a color drawing of "THE SUBTERRENE," the Los Alamos nuclear-powered tunnel machine that burrows through the rock, deep underground, by heating whatever stone it encounters into molten rock (magma), which cools after the SUBTERRENE has moved on. These underground tubes are used by electro-magnetically powered "Subshuttle Vehicles," which can travel at great speeds. They connect the "Hidden Empire" Sub-City Complexes. Also, the top-secret project code-named: "NOAH's ARK" uses "TUBE-SHUTTLES" in connection with a system of over 100 "Bunkers" and "Bolt Holes" which have been established at various places on Earth, with other Bases inside the Moon and Mars. Many of these underground Cities are complete with streets, sidewalks, lakes, small electric cars, apartments, offices and shopping malls.

There were over 650 attendees to the 1959 RAND Symposium. Most were representatives of the Corporate-Industrial State, like: THE GENERAL ELECTRIC COMPANY, AT&T, HUGHES AIRCRAFT, NORTHROP CORP., SANDIA CORP., STANFORD RESEARCH INSTITUTE, WALSH CONSTRUCTION COMPANY, THE BECHTEL CORP, COLORADO SCHOOL OF MINES, ETC., ETC.

BECHTEL (pronounced BECK-tul) is a super-secret international corporate octopus, founded in 1898. Some say the firm is really a "SHADOW GOVERNMENT" - a working arm of the CIA. It is the largest construction and engineering outfit in the USA and the WORLD (and some say BEYOND).

The most important posts in the US Government are held by former BECHTEL Officers. They are part of "The WEB" (an interconnected control system) which links the Tri-Lateralist plans, the C.F.R. the Orders of "Illuminism" (Cult of the All-Seeing Eye) and other interlocking groups.

SURVIVING THE FUTURE

The DULCE FACILITY consists of a Central "HUB," the Security Section, (also some photo labs). The deeper you go, the stronger the Security. This is a multi-leveled Complex. There are over 3000 cameras at various High-Security locations (exits and Labs).

There are over 100 Secret Exits near and around Dulce. Many around Archuleta Mesa, others to the south around Dulce Lake and even as far east as Lindrith.

The Dulce Base is said to be located deep beneath the The Archuleta Mesa.

Deep sections of the Complex connect into natural Cavern Systems. A person who worked at the Base, who had an "ULTRA 7" Clearance, reports: "There may be more than seven levels, but I only know of seven. Most of the Aliens are on 5-6-7 Levels. Alien housing is Level Five."

21st CENTURY POWER: "BIO-TECH"

We are leaving the Era of expendable resources, like Oil based products. The Power of the Future is Renewable resources... "Biologically" Engineered. The Dulce Genetic Research was originally funded under the cloak of "BLACK BUDGET" Secrecy. (Billions $$$$)

They were interested in intelligent "Disposable Biology" (Humanoids), to do the dangerous Atomic (Plutonium) Rocket and Saucer experiments.

We cloned "our" own little Humanoids. Via a process perfected in the Bio-Genetic Research Center of the World, Los Alamos! Now we have our own disposable slave-race. Like the Alien "Greys" (EBES), the US Government clandestinely impregnated females, then removed the hybrid fetus, (after three months) and then accelerated their growth in the Lab.

Biogenetic (DNA Manipulation) programming is then instilled - they are "Implanted" and controlled at a distance through RF (Radio Frequency) transmissions.

Many Humans are also being "Implanted" with Brain Transceivers. These act as telepathic "Channels" and telemetric brain manipulation devices. The network-net was set-up by DARPA (Advanced Research Project Agency). Two of the procedures were RHIC (Radio-Hypnotic Inter-cerebral Control) and EDOM (Electronic Dissolution of Memory). The brain transceiver is inserted into the head thru the nose. These devices are used in the Soviet Union and the United States, as well as Sweden. The Swedish Prime Minister Palme gave the National Swedish Police Board the right (in 1973) to insert brain transmitters into the heads of human beings COVERTLY!

They also developed ELF and EM wave propagation equipment (RAYS) which affect the nerves and can cause nausea, fatigue, irritability, even death. This is essentially the same as Richard Shaver's Cavern "Telaug" Mech. This research into biodynamic relationships within organisms ("BIOLOGICAL PLASMA") has produced a RAY that can change the "genetic structure" and "HEAL." Shaver's Cavern "BEN-Mech" could HEAL!

WARNING: MANIPULATION AND CONTROL - FEAR, FRAUD AND FAVOR...

The Pentagon, the CIA, NSA, DEA, FBI, NSC, etc. seek to capitalize on the Beliefs of the American Public. The Secret Government is getting ready to "stage" a Contact-Landing with "ALIENS" in the near future. This way they can "CONTROL" the release of Alien related Propaganda. We will be told of an Inter-Stellar Conflict.

But... what looks real, may be "FAKE." What is disinformation?

Is your attention being diverted by the Strategy of a "SHADOW PLAN"?

OVERT AND COVERT RESEARCH

As US Energy Secretary, John Herrington named the Lawrence Berkeley Laboratory and New Mexico's Los Alamos National Laboratory to house new advanced genetic research centers as part of a Project to decipher the Human Genome. The Genome holds the genetically coded instructions that guide the transformation of a single cell - a fertilized egg - into a Biological Being.

"The Human Genome Project may well have the greatest direct impact on humanity of any scientific initiative before us today", said David Shirley, Director of the Berkeley Laboratory.

Covertly, this research has been going on for years at DULCE LABS. Level #6 is privately called "NIGHTMARE HALL." It holds the Genetic Labs. Reports from workers who have seen bizarre experimentation are as follows: "I have seen multi-legged 'humans' that look like half-human/half-octopus. Also Reptilian-humans and furry creatures that have hands like humans and cries like a baby. It mimics human words... also huge mixture of Lizard-humans in cages."

There are fish, seals, birds and mice that can barely be considered those species. There are several cages (and vats) of Winged-humanoids, grotesque Bat-like creatures...but three 1/2 to seven feet tall, as well as gargoyle-like beings and Draco-Reptoids.

DULCE WARRIORS

Level #7 is worse, row after row of thousands of humans and human mixtures in cold storage. Here too are embryo storage vats of Humanoids in various stages of development.

"I frequently encountered humans in cages, usually dazed or drugged, but sometimes they cried and begged for help. We were told they were hopelessly insane and involved in high risk drug tests to cure insanity. We were told to never try to speak to them at all. At the beginning we believed that story. Finally in 1978 a small group of workers discovered the truth. It began the 'Dulce Wars,' and a secret resistance Unit was formed." Note: There are over 18,000 "Aliens" at the Dulce Base.

In late 1979, there was a confrontation (over weapons), and a lot of Scientists and Military personnel were KILLED. The Base was closed for a while...But, it IS currently active. Note: Human and animal abductions (for their blood and other parts) slowed in the mid-1980s, when the Livermore Berkeley Labs began production of artificial blood for Dulce.

The late William Cooper stated: "A clash occurred wherein 66 people, of our people, from the National Recon Group, the DELTA group, which is responsible for Security of all Alien-connected Projects, were killed."

The DELTA Group (within Intelligence Support Activity) have been seen with badges which have a black Triangle on a red background.

DELTA is the fourth letter of the Greek alphabet. It has the form of a triangle, and figures prominently in certain Masonic Signs.

*EACH BASE HAS ITS OWN SYMBOL. The DULCE Base symbol is a triangle with the Greek letter "Tau" (T) within it and then the symbol is inverted, so the triangle points down.

* The Insignia of "a triangle and 3 lateral lines" has been seen on "Saucer (transport) Craft," The Tri-Lateral Symbol.

* Other symbols mark landing sights and Alien Craft.

DULCE WARRIORS

INSIDE THE DULCE BASE

Security Officers wear jumpsuits with the Dulce Symbol on the front upper left side. The standard hand weapon at Dulce is a "Flash Gun," which is good against Humans and Aliens. The ID card (used in card slots, for the doors and elevators) has the Dulce Symbol above the ID photo. "Government Honchos" use cards with the Great Seal of the U.S. on it. "The Cult of the All-Seeing Eye" (THE NEW WORLD ORDER) 13, "666" The Phoenix Empire....."9" "Illuminism"... "One out of many."

After the Second Level, everyone is weighed, in the nude, then given a uniform. "Visitors" are given an 'off white' uniform. In front of ALL sensitive areas are scales built under the doorway, by the door control. The person's card must match with the weight and code or the door won't open. Any discrepancy in weight (any change over three pounds) will summon Security. No one is allowed to carry anything into or out of sensitive areas. All supplies are put thru a Security conveyor system. The Alien Symbol language appears a lot at the Facility.

During the construction of the Facility (which was done in stages, over many years) the Aliens assisted in the Design and Construction materials. Many of the things assembled by the workers were of a Technology they could not understand, yet...it would function when fully put together. Example: The elevators have no cables. They are controlled magnetically. The Magnetic system is inside the walls.

There are no conventional electrical controls. All is controlled by advanced Magnetics. That includes a magnetically induced (phosphorescent) Illumination System. There are no regular light bulbs. All EXITS are magnetically controlled. Note: it has been reported that, "If you place a large magnet on an entrance, it will affect an immediate interruption. They will have to come out and reset the system."

THE TOWN OF DULCE

The area around Dulce has had a high number of reported Animal Mutilations. The Government and the Aliens used the animals for Environmental tests, Psychological Warfare on people, etc. The Aliens also wanted large amounts of Blood for Genetic, Nutritional and other reasons.

In the book, *"ETs & UFOs - THEY NEED US, WE DON'T NEED THEM,"* by Virgil "Posty" Armstrong, he reports how his friends (Bob & Sharon) stopped for the night in Dulce and went out to dinner. "They overheard some local residents openly and vociferously discussing Extraterrestrial Abduction of townspeople for purposes of experimentation." The ET's were taking unwilling human guinea pigs from the general populace of Dulce and Implanting Devices in their heads and bodies. The townspeople were frightened and angry but didn't feel that they had any recourse since the ET's had our Government's knowledge and approval.

Recently, participants in a "field investigation" of the area near Archuleta Mesa were confronted by two small hovering "Spheres." They all became suddenly ill and had to leave the area.

"THE MONITORS": ABDUCTIONS

In the Fifties, the EBEs (Greys) began taking large numbers of humans for experiments. By the Sixties, the rate was speeded up and they began getting careless (they didn't care). By the Seventies, their true colors were very obvious, but the "Special Group" of the Government still kept covering up for them. By the Eighties, the Government realized there was no defense against the "Greys." So... programs were enacted to prepare the Public for open contact with non-human "Alien" Beings.

The "Greys" and the "Reptoids" are in league with each other. But, their relationship is in a state of tension. The "Greys" only known enemy is the Reptillian Race, and they are on their way to Earth. (Inside a Planetoid).

Some forces in the Government want the Public to be aware of what is happening. Other forces (The Collaborators) want to continue making "whatever deals are necessary" for an Elite few to survive the conflicts.

The Future could bring a Fascist "WORLD ORDER" or a transformation of Human Consciousness (Awareness). The struggle is NOW...your active assistance is needed. Prepare! We must preserve Humanity on Earth.

MIND MANIPULATION EXPERIMENTS

The DULCE Base has studied Mind Control Implants, Bio-Psi Units, ELF Devices capable of Mood, Sleep and Heartbeat Control, etc., etc.   D.A.R.P.A. (Defense Advanced Research Projects Agency) is using these Technologies to manipulate people. They establish "The Projects," set priorities, coordinate efforts and guide the many participants in these undertakings. Related Projects are studied at Sandia Base by "The Jason Group" (of 55 scientists). They have secretly harnessed the Dark Side of Technology and hidden the beneficial Technology from the Public.

Other Projects take place at "AREA #51" in Nevada..."DREAMLAND"[Data Repository Establishment and Maintenance Land], ELMINT [Electro-Magnetic Intelligence], CODE EMPIRE, CODE EVA, PROGRAM HIS [Hybrid Intelligence System], BW/CW, IRIS [Infrared Intruder System], BI-PASS, REP-TILES.

The studies on LEVEL #4, at DULCE, include Human-Aura research, as well as all aspects of Dreams, Hypnosis, Telepathy, etc.. They know how to manipulate the BIOPLASMIC BODY (of Man). They can lower your heart beat, with Deep Sleep "DELTA WAVES," induce a static shock, and then re-program via a Brain-Computer Link. They can introduce data and programmed reactions into your mind (Information impregnation - the "Dream Library."

We are entering an ERA of the Technological-ization of Psychic Powers. The development of techniques to enhance man/machine communications, Nano-Tech, Bio-Tech Micro-Machines, PSI-War, E.D.O.M. (Electronic Dissolution of Memory), R.H.I.C. (Radio-Hypnotic Intra-Cerebral Control) and various forms of behavior control (Via Chemical Agents, Ultra-Sonics, Optical and other forms of EM Radiation). The Physics of "Consciousness."

We have passed the point of no return in our interaction with the "Alien" Beings. We are guaranteed "A Crisis" which will persist until the final REVELATION (or conflict).

The crisis is here. Global and real. We must mitigate or transform the nature of the disasters to come and come they will. Knowing is half the battle. Read the book, *The Cosmic Conspiracy* by Stan Deyo.

THE GRENADA TREATY

In 1954, the race of aliens, known as Greys, from the Zeta Reticuli area in space, who had been orbiting the equator, landed at Holloman Air Force Base. They stated that their planet was dying and they needed quarters on Earth to conduct genetic experiments that might allow their race to survive; this in exchange for certain technology.

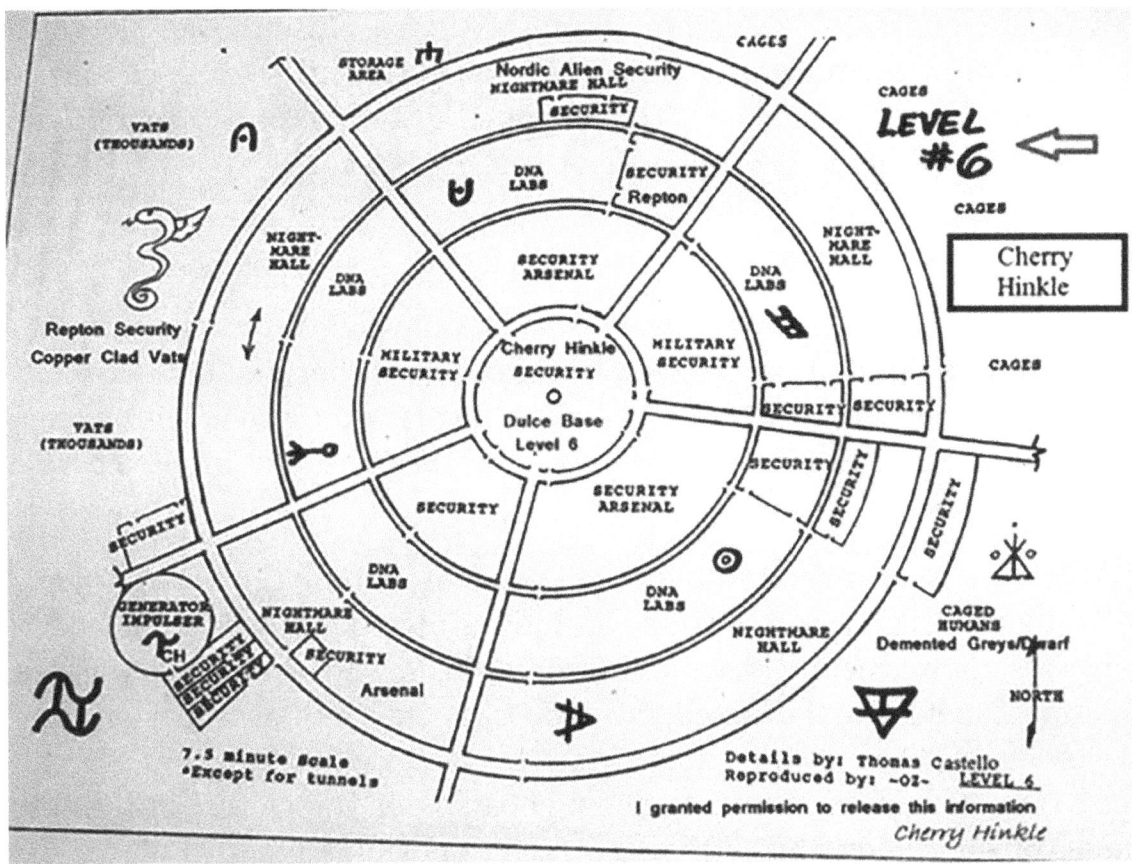

Provided by Cherry Hinkle, illustration allegedly details Level 6 of the Dulce Base.

President Eisenhower met with the aliens and a formal treaty was signed (Grenada treaty). The treaty stated the aliens would not interfere in our affairs and we would not interfere in theirs. We would keep their presence on Earth secret; they would furnish us with advanced technology. They could abduct humans on a limited basis for the purpose of medical examination and monitoring, with the stipulation that the humans would not be harmed, would be returned to their point of abduction, and that the humans have no memory of the event.

It was also agreed the alien bases would be constructed underground, beneath Indian reservations in the 4 Corners area of Utah, New Mexico, Arizona and Colorado. Another was to be constructed in Nevada in the area known as S-4, about 7 miles south of Area 51, known as "Dreamland." A multi-billion dollar secret fund was organized and kept by the Military Office of the White House, supposedly to build secret underground sites for the President and the staff in case of military attacks.

By secret Executive Memorandum, NSC5410, Eisenhower established a permanent committee known as "Majority Twelve" (MJ12) to oversee and conduct all covert activities with the aliens. This included FBI director J. Edgar Hoover and six leaders of the Council on Foreign Relations, known as the "Wise Men" and later others from the Trilateral Commission. George Bush, Gordon Dean, and Zbigniew Brzezinski were among them.

A major finding of the commission was that the aliens were using humans and animals for a source of glandular secretions, enzymes, hormonal secretions, blood and in horrible genetic experiments. The aliens explained these actions as necessary for their survival, saying that if their genetic structure were not improved, their race would cease to exist.

The ruling powers decided that one means of funding the alien project was to corner the illegal drug market. A young ambitious member of the Council on Foreign Relations was approached. His name is George Bush, who at the time was president and CEO of Zapata Oil Co. based in Texas. Zapata Oil was experimenting with offshore oil drilling and it was arranged that the drugs could be shipped from South America to the offshore platforms by fishing boats, then transferred to the U.S. shore by normal transportation, thus avoiding search by customs agents.

The plan worked better than anyone expected, and today the CIA controls all the world's illegal drug markets. The drug money was used to finance the deep underground alien bases.

ANCIENT LEGENDS OF THE REPTILIAN ALIEN GODS

Reptilian - serpent - snake iconography is found throughout the planet in art work and petroglyphs, referring to the spiral of consciousness creation and human DNA. It is laced with metaphors about human origins and destiny.

Several ancient peoples all over the world have described reptilian beings, and some have described reptilian humanoids. Common in numerous mythologies are tales of reptilian creatures (usually not humanoid) who are often, but not always, hostile to human beings.

In Australia the aborigines speak of a reptilian race which lives underneath the surface in caverns. It is said that the ancient cavernous underground chambers under the Black Mountain is such a place.

Yet there is an already-existing ancient cavern system under the Dulce Base.

The Draco (reptilian humanoids) used these caverns and tunnels for centuries. Later, through RAND Corporation plans, it was enlarged repeatedly. The original caverns included ice caves and sulfur springs that the "aliens" found perfect for their needs.

Besides, the Dulce Base seems to be a major "through" point for exterran and subterran reptilian activity, a central "infiltration" zone for surface operatives, as well as an operational base for abduction-implantation-mutilation agendas and also a major convergence for sub-shuttle terminals, UFO ports, and so on.

The origin of these reptilian humanoids:

These Reptilian humanoids are the creation of the Carians, (Bird Headed Beings) their parent race. They evolved on a planet in the Alpha Draconi star system of the Orion Constellation.

The royal lines of reptilians are the Draconians and they have a highly sophisticated knowledge of universal law and are allegedly responsible for the "Mystery School Teachings on Earth."

Now, these reptilians allegedly were given a creational agenda by the Carians. They were to move through the universe and destroy any existing civilization they found along the way, recreating new DNA codes and entities following those codes.

It was part of a Master Plan, a Universal Game, Polarity Integration, reality in conflict, an experiment in emotions, resulting in soul evolution at the end of the cycles of its existence.

Since ancient civilizations have described reptilian beings, it is almost certain that some of these ancient cultures have been in contact with these beings. Otherwise how is it possible that these ancient people, like the ancient Sumer civilization, were able to make such detailed figurines and statues of these creatures?

Finally, myth or not, we should not forget that the NWO elite cooperate with a group of reptilian humanoids in order to establish a global control system and they are the force behind a worldwide conspiracy directed at manipulation and control of humanity through deception, espionage and mind control.

4.

FRENCH SCIENTIST'S DIARY

By Dr. John Gille, Jean-François G. Gille, former theoretical physicist, University of Marseilles, France

Dr. John Gille

French scientist's diary of the 1988 Mount Archuleta expedition, northwest of Dulce, New Mexico.

Thursday, October 6th, 1988, 0645 a.m.:

We arrive, my female companion Elaine A. and I, in Albuquerque, New Mexico, USA, after eighteen hours on the Greyhound.

Elaine A. is a registered nurse from Paris, France.

She had worked in New York, New York, during her twenties, enough time to acquire U.S. citizenship.

I am merely holder of a Green Card since 1986.

Friday, October 7:

I have a short phone conversation with Gabriel Valdez.

Gabriel Valdez, or rather 'Gabe,' is a policeman of the State of New Mexico.

At this time he is in charge of the Bureau of Indian Affairs in the little town (I'd call it a village) of Dulce, a community in the most northern part of the State, quite close to the New Mexico/Colorado State line.

Mr. Valdez invites me to go there and see him without delay.

I had previously obtained Valdez's phone number through William Steinman. (He wrote "*UFO Crash at Aztec*," a book I had read a number of times.

Some Ufologists did not take that book seriously – and I personally would not vouch for the reality of the 'Aztec Crash' itself – but I was interested and moved by the story about Paul F. Bennewitz, of whom I heard for the first time in Steinman's book).
I had recently received in France, where I lived, a few pages called "The Dulce Papers." I had translated into French the John Lear Statement.

Trying to know more and, if possible, beginning to understand not only the How but also the Who and, above all, the Why of the 'Mutes' – the animal mutilations, the paranormal cattle mutilations should we say – were the prime motivation of the whole trip to New Mexico.

Tuesday, October 11:

Driving to Dulce from Albuquerque is a three hours trip.

It's a beautiful landscape, especially for people who love the deserts.

However, as one goes further to the northern part of the State, closer to the Colorado border, the hills and mesas look greener.

Around noon, we meet Gabriel Valdez and his wife, Marge, for the first time, at their home in Dulce.

Mrs. Valdez is a teacher in the village, which is at the limit of the Jicarilla's Indian Reservation.

Gabe and Marge Valdez, and their kids, are quite friendly and straightforwardly/outspoken [See: "*The Dulce Book*," by Branton, chap. 2, available on the Internet with no charge].

Of course Marge sounds a little bit less interested than her husband in the whole UFO stuff.

Some very religious Christians believe that UFOs and their so-called occupants belong rather to negative (i.e. demonic/hellish) spiritual forces than to the natural/material universe/cosmos.

DULCE WARRIORS

Friday, October 14:

I am living now at 1501 Indian School Road, NE, apartment E-309.

The momentous broadcast of "UFO Cover Up - Live" is tonight.

We heard about Falcon and Condor.

We also saw William Moore on the TV set that night.

Wednesday, October 19:

I call Bob Girard, a bookseller specialized in ufology and related domains, who has a "Pop and Mom" business called Arcturus, and sells his books through the mail.

He is at that time located near Atlanta, Georgia.

Friday, October 21:

Sometimes after noon, I call Marge Valdez to arrange details for the trip scheduled to Dulce.

About 7 pm I call at John Lear's place.

Somebody, a polite gentleman, tells me that Mr. Lear will call back in less than two hours...and he did!

John Lear is very friendly, and he invites me to his home in Las Vegas, Nevada.

Unfortunately, at that moment I have not the money necessary for such a trip from New Mexico to Nevada.

Saturday, October 22:

At 9:35 am I receive a call from Gabriel Valdez.

We set up, my companion Elaine and I, for a trip to the town of Dulce, in the north of the State.

The planning is to reckon an area a few miles west of Dulce, an area near Mount Archuleta (8136') where Gabriel and his two sons had been, a number of times, the witnesses of strange phenomenon.

Getting ready for the expedition. Photo courtesy of Edmund Gomez.

Sunday, October 23:

Our party is composed of eight persons: Elaine A., a registered nurse working at Albuquerque Veteran Hospital; Gabriel Valdez, New Mexico State Police; Edmund Gomez, rancher and a friend of Mr. Valdez (he had lost cattle from animal mutilations); "Jack", (not his real name), PhD, a research scientist for a major lab in the US; Manuel Gomez, Jr., younger brother of Edmund Gomez; Greg, son of Gabriel Valdez; Jeff (or rather Geoff), younger son of Gabriel Valdez; John Gille (the author of the present notes).

We left about 2:30 pm in the four wheel drive pick-up of Gabe Valdez.

At about 5:30 pm we arrived at the proposed campsite.

From left to right: Elaine A., Edmund Gomez, Gabe Valdez and William T. McGarity. McGarity, who went by the name of "Jack," was a Los Alamos scientist.

It was on a relatively flat area about 435 yards south-east from the peak of Mt. Archuleta.

At 7:51 pm all eight of us spotted a very bright light coming from the south at a very high rate of speed.

I personally was not able to make out any structure inside that light.

The trajectory was flat, straight, rectilinear and horizontal.

Through the persistence of luminous impression, a standard physiological reaction, it looked like a perfectly straight luminous line, yellowish, and of some thickness, like one which would have resulted from a plane's landing light.

However, it was definitely not a plane.

I used this comparison to give an idea of the luminosity of the trajectory.

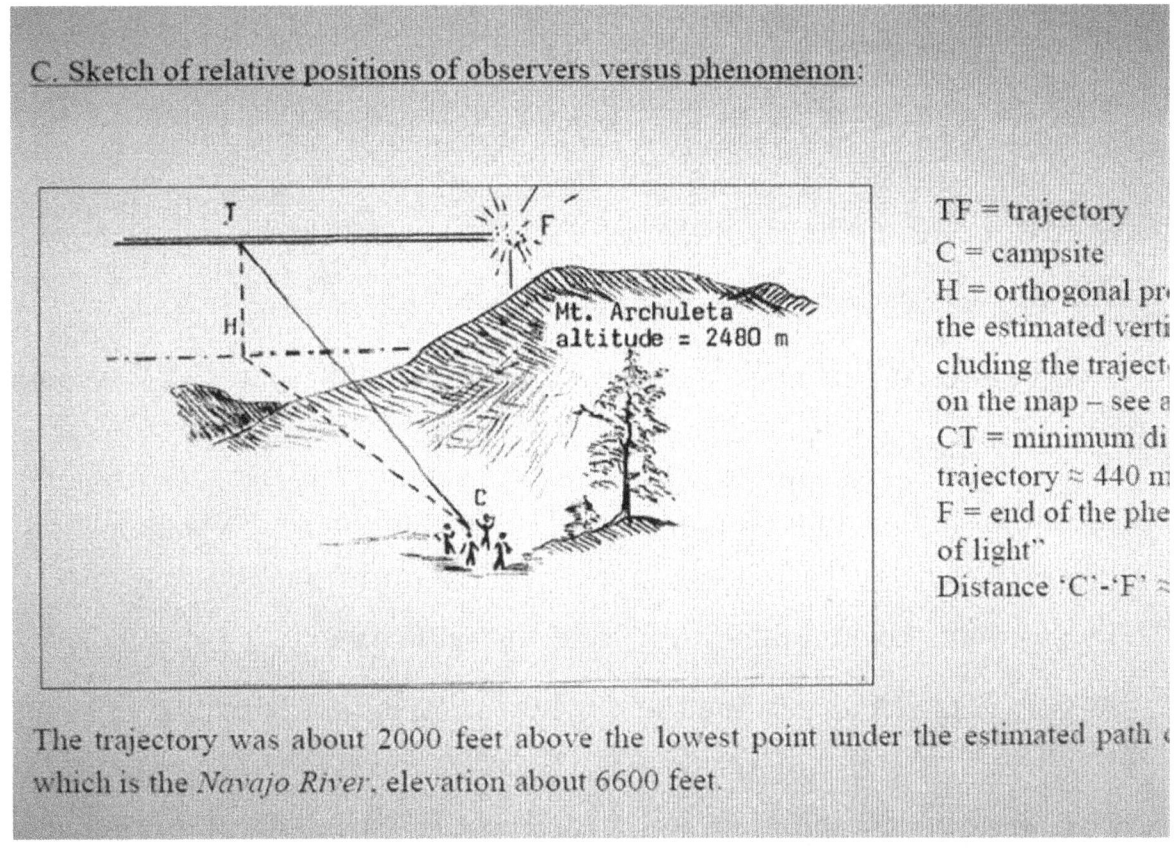

We had seen already a number of shooting stars that night.

The path of the trajectory of our phenomenon was maybe hundreds or thousands of times more luminous than theirs.

There was not any sound coming from the phenomenon.

That fast moving forward light stopped dead on its tracks.

Its trajectory's final spot was very close to the top of Mt. Archuleta, as we saw it from where we were.

At the same time, it became extremely luminous, lighting at least half the sky up.

It looked literally like the blossoming of a flower of light.

There was a "display of gorgeous lights of pure color": yellow, pink, green – enhanced by the center of that luminous phenomenon, giving out a shower of sparks (not unlike portable fireworks mounted on a stick, seen on the 4th of July).

There was kind of a mist, too, around the object's center, at this same moment.

It then sort of "folded on itself", and disappeared, vanished.

There was not anymore anything to be seen.

The duration of the whole phenomenon was no more than 5 or 6 seconds.

Monday, October 24:

After the sighting of yesterday, I tried to sleep under the same small tent as my girlfriend.

I was exhausted, and filled with joy at the same time.

As Mr. Valdez had told me the day before: "You look terrible, but you're not out of shape."

So it was in plain daylight that we climbed to the peak of Mt. Archuleta.

A large landscape filled up our eyes, not with breath-taking high mountains with steep slopes, but a rather monotonous infinity of rolling hills, with vegetation and no human establishment in sight.

We did not see anything out of the ordinary, but for the famous clipped off pine tree that Paul Bennewitz signaled to Gabriel Valdez during their trip together on the same mesa a couple of years ago.

That unfortunate tree was supposedly clipped off by a crashing UFO, a "real-thing" alien UFO, or a poor human-made copy of the same.

We were back, Elaine and I, in Albuquerque the same evening.

Source: April 7, 2021 - CIVILIAN INTELLIGENCE NEWS SERVICE, by Norio Hayakawa.

https://noriohayakawa.wordpress.com/2021/04/07/french-scientists-diary-of-the-1988-mount-archuleta-expedition-northwest-of-dulce-new-mexico/

Much to their disappointment, the expedition failed to uncover any evidence of a secret base at Mt. Archuleta.

5.

GABE VALDEZ CATTLE MUTILATIONS

By Sean Casteel

Gabe Valdez was a state police officer stationed in Dulce, NM.

Before Dulce, New Mexico, was rumored to harbor an underground base occupied by aliens, there was a "real-world" cause for alarm that could be physically documented.

A wave of cattle mutilations began in the area in 1976, and the abandoned carcasses of the unfortunate animals could not be explained away as the fantasies of UFO believers.

In the book *"Dulce Base: The Truth and Evidence From the Case Files of Gabe Valdez,"* author Greg Valdez, the son of the late Gabe Valdez, writes about his adventures with his father going to inspect the scenes of the strangely mutilated cattle.

Gabe was a New Mexico state police officer, and Greg would often ride along in his father's patrol car, accompanying the elder Valdez to car wrecks and bar fights.

"In a weird way," Greg writes, "I guess some of the best times we had in the police car were responding to reports of cattle mutilations. For me, it was an adventure, driving in the middle of nowhere looking for a dead cow, kind of like a treasure hunt. You never knew what you might find when you arrived. And I will never forget the people who would come to our house to talk to my dad for hours and hours about dead cows and mysterious lights. I'll always remember the things I saw with my Dad."

DULCE WARRIORS

THE MUTILATIONS STORY BEGINS

The story of Gabe Valdez and the Dulce cattle mutilations began in June of 1976, when Gabe got a phone call from a local rancher and store owner named Manuel Gomez. The Gomez family had homesteaded and actually named the town of Dulce (the Spanish word "Dulce" translates as "sweet to the taste; soothing, agreeable.") before the surrounding area was officially recognized as belonging to the Jicarilla Apache Tribe.

"In 1887, the federal government had finally given the Jicarilla a reservation and a place to call home," Greg writes. "The tribe relocated from Cimarron, New Mexico, to the current town of Dulce after the Gomez family had been there for several years. The Gomez family had the only privately-owned land within the boundaries of the Jicarilla Reservation."

Gomez told Gabe that he had a very strange problem.

"I hope you can help me," Gomez said. "I don't know who else to call. I was at the ranch down by Mundo Lake and I found one of my cows dead in the pasture."

Gabe responded, "Calm down. I can get a hold of the cattle sanitary board for you if you want since it's only a dead cow."

"I think this involves more resources than the cattle inspector," Gomez replied, "and it is much more than just a dead cow. I wouldn't bother you unless it was important. I need you to see this. I've been ranching all my life and I've never seen anything like this before. I'm afraid no one will believe me if I tell them."

Gomez went on to say that he was checking on his cows that morning when he noticed a dead one lying in the field. When he examined the carcass, it seemed to be cut up in strange ways, and appeared to be mutilated in some manner. He had had cows killed by coyotes and predators, but he was sure that wasn't the case here. The cow was missing its reproductive organs.

"But that is not the only strange part," Gomez continued. "There were three circular impressions in the dirt that looked like some kind of aircraft had landed close by. There was some type of oily substance on the dirt, but I couldn't tell what it was. From the circular imprints, there were smaller imprints that seemed to go up to the cow. Gabe, I hope you don't think I'm crazy, but it was the weirdest thing I've ever seen. Can you help me?"

Gabe told Gomez that he would alert the cattle inspector and would meet him and Gomez at the scene the next morning. If it turned out to be rustlers or poachers, it would be treated as a crime scene and evidence would be collected and processed. The next day they drove out to the location of the dead cow, accompanied by Paul Riley of the New Mexico Cattle Sanitary Board, and began to look around.

The carcass was that of a three-year-old black, white-faced cow. The animal was lying on its side, and its left ear, tongue, udder and rectum had been removed with what appeared to be a sharp, precise instrument. No traces of blood appeared on the cow's skin. The hide on its underside was white, so any spotting of blood would have easily been detected. Other evidence on the cow included a small puncture wound on the brisket.

After trying to process different scenarios to explain what they had witnessed, Gabe said, "You know, I've been getting several reports from people around town saying that they've been seeing a strange light in the sky at night. People say this light is orange and it doesn't fly like a normal airplane or helicopter. They also say they've been seeing the light around Mundo Ridge, which isn't very far from here. I wonder if this has something to do with the cow. I've also been getting reports of unmarked helicopters flying around the area."

The group took photos and collected samples of the animal and the mysterious oily substance. In all their years of ranching, neither Gabe nor Gomez had ever seen anything like this. The cattle inspector was also at a loss. They had never seen predators kill an animal in such a way, and predators didn't explain the circular marks or the oily substance. Gabe considered the possibility of occult worship based on some of his previous experiences with some of the local Jicarilla youth dabbling in devil worship.

The precision and accuracy of the cuts on the animal, in addition to the circular impressions and the remote location of the carcass, ruled out the possibility of local pranksters. Since none of the consumable portions of the cow were removed, they also ruled out the possibility of cattle poachers or rustlers. Later that night, Officer Valdez got in touch with a retired scientist from Sandia National Laboratories named Dr. Howard Burges and told him what had happened.

Three days later Dr. Burges arrived on the scene and tested for radiation exposure. He found that the radiation level in and around the tripod marks was twice the normal background reading. When Valdez asked Burges what was causing the higher level of radiation, Burges said that an aircraft may have landed next to the cow that was nuclear powered. Or whoever killed the cow was using the radiation to intentionally confuse investigators. No nuclear aircraft were known to exist at the time and the answer to what had killed the cow continued to elude the investigating team.

It wasn't long before Gomez reported a second mutilation to Gabe. Gomez eventually lost seventeen animals, including a horse. Investigators would eventually refer to these events as "classic mutilations."

Whether Gabe Valdez wanted it or not, he became one of the leading investigators into the cattle mutilation phenomenon. Throughout northern New Mexico and southern Colorado, numerous reports started coming in about these mysterious deaths – and no one seemed to have an answer. In addition to the routine rape, homicide, car crash, bar fight and domestic violence calls, Officer Valdez was quickly becoming the go-to guy for all things relating to dead cows.

Gabe Valdez inspects the remains of a mutilated steer in the Dulce area.

Although some people viewed the mutilations as merely a bunch of dead cattle, Officer Valdez and the others were fully aware that something other than predators and natural causes was killing these animals. Based on the evidence gathered, it quickly became obvious that some type of higher intelligence was involved with the mutilations.

"In northern New Mexico and other states in the West," Greg writes, "killing a man's cattle was quite frankly still a hanging offense in the eyes of the ranchers who made their living from the cattle they owned. And killing cattle that do not belong to you is still a crime in all the states where the mutilations occurred."

LIGHTS IN THE SKY

In a chapter called "Lights in the Sky," Greg Valdez continues the story.

"By 1978, an estimated ten thousand cattle had been mutilated in the United States," he writes. "Investigators were also receiving numerous reports of sightings of both unidentified aircraft and unmarked helicopters around the same time and locations of the mutilated animals. Investigators were not sure whether the two strange anomalies were somehow connected or merely a coincidence. The unidentified aircraft, more commonly referred to as UFOs, exhibited unique flight capabilities and were routinely viewed by local residents in the town of Dulce."

It became commonplace to views the lights or aircraft, which seemed to have an area called the Mundo Ridge mountain range as a flight path. When Officer Valdez and other locals wanted to view these strange aircraft, they would start by looking at the area around Mundo Ridge.

"Coincidentally – or perhaps not – Mundo Ridge was in close proximity to the Gomez ranch," Greg writes. "People also viewed the aircraft on a fairly routine basis in the area west of Dulce, where several mutilations took place. Four cows owned by the tribal police chief were killed in one night."

On a night of what seemed like endless aircraft sightings, Officer Valdez and officers from the Jicarilla Tribal Police and Jicarilla Game and Fish engaged in a sort of cat-and-mouse game with one of these aircraft.

"The officers from different agencies would call out the location of the strange lights on the police radio," Greg recounts, "and try to pursue the aircraft. They often did this with their headlights turned off, traveling down dirt roads at high speeds at night in attempts to get close to the aircraft and try to identify it."

On this particular night, the officers chased the light, or aircraft, for several hours to no avail. Every time one of the officers would get close and call out his location on the radio, the aircraft would simply disappear into the darkness and reappear in a completely different location, much to the frustration of the chase party pursuing it.

Greg's father finally got on the police radio and told the search party, "This thing is just playing with us. From now on, only speak Apache on the radio and let's see if that helps."

Much to their surprise, it wasn't long before they were able to surround the craft, which was hovering between two tall pine trees. Not quite sure what they were dealing with, and the fact that law enforcement on the reservation was still similar in some ways to the Wild West, Valdez gave the command, "Shoot the thing and try to take it down!"

The light was surrounded by Valdez to the south, two tribal police officers on the east and west, and a tribal game and fish officer to the north. The radio filled with chatter as all the officers began instructing the game and fish officer to shoot the object because they could see it reflecting light over his patrol unit. The game and fish officer couldn't see the aircraft as it slowly flew over him. Much to their disappointment, the officers were not able to shoot down the aircraft that night.

"To add insult to injury," Greg writes, "as Officer Valdez drove back to Dulce after a long night of chasing mysterious lights, his police radio started to squelch loudly at a very annoying pitch and he observed the aircraft approaching him from behind at a very high rate of speed. The aircraft flew directly above and over his unit and quickly disappeared into the night as if to say goodbye and good night to its pursuer. They were never able to identify the aircraft."

[Publisher's Note: If you found the preceding story interesting, you should check out our weighty tome called *"Alien Lives Matter: It's OK To Be Grey"* for more stories of humans taking up firearms against the aliens and the often surprising reactions of the aliens as they respond to the threat of gun-toting UFO witnesses.]

THE MYSTERY CONTINUES

The mutilations started occurring more frequently and Officer Valdez began increasing his nighttime patrols in the area to try to catch the culprits in the act of mutilating a cow. Meanwhile, he did a bit of soul-searching, according to his son.

"What the hell is going on here?" Gabe wondered. "First we find all the dead cows, and now we have these weird lights or aircraft flying around doing things that aircraft are not supposed to be doing. There has to be an explanation. I don't know how I got myself into this mess. Why can't I write tickets like a normal cop, or handle a good old-fashioned bar fight or murder like a regular state police officer? I need some rest."

There is much that would come later in the stories of the Dulce mystery. The tragic victimization of Paul Bennewitz and the mysterious death of Phil Schneider are also related in this book. Perhaps all the differing elements involved will one day be understood and we will know the truth.

But it should be carefully noted that, before the rumors of a joint human/alien underground base in Dulce first began to pique the interest of the UFO community, a long string of cattle mutilations that were physically real and exceedingly strange served as the opening salvos of a war that is still being fought.

While in his book *"Dulce Base: The Truth and Evidence From the Case Files of Gabe Valdez,"* Greg Valdez unequivocally – and frequently – denies the idea of an extraterrestrial presence in Dulce, the history he recounts of mutilated animals and nocturnal visitors in the skies nevertheless offers testimony to that very idea. How to account for all the "high strangeness" reported in Dulce otherwise?

Dulce Base The Truth and Evidence from the Case Files of Gabe Valdez - by Greg Valdez.

6.

MEANWHILE, BACK AT THE (ABANDONED) RANCH

Still unsolved – is an abandoned ranch adjacent to the northern slope of Mt. Archuleta, northwest of Dulce, a former CIA operation?

It has been known by many researchers that the now-defunct National Institute For Discovery Sciences (NIDS, formerly headed by Las Vegas billionaire Robert Bigelow, who presently owns Bigelow Aerospace) reportedly had made an investigation earlier (ca. 1998) regarding this suspicious ranch. This still seems to be unsolved.

This ranch, now totally abandoned (and still off-limits to anyone), has often been associated as part of an alleged Dulce "base," even though there is no evidence so far that a large underground base has ever existed. Such an alleged "base" was rumored to have been located on the northern slope of Mount Archuleta on the New Mexico side, just south of the Redding Ranch. This ranch is not visible from Dulce. In fact, Mount Archuleta itself is not even visible from Dulce. Mount Archuleta is located close to the northwestern portion of the Archuleta Mesa. From Dulce, only the Archuleta Mesa and the Archuleta "Peak" (where the radio towers are located) are visible.

The following report itself made by NIDS regarding this ranch seems to be more suspicious, even now.

(QUOTE, from the original NIDS report).

> It has been reported in the media and on the internet that the Redding War Ranch, located at 37° 2.91' north latitude and 107° 1.44' west longitude (GPS) next to Mt. Archuleta (straddling New Mexico – Colorado border), is rumored to be an undercover facility engaged in secret activity connected with Mt. Archuleta. These rumors further state that the ranch has eight armed guard watch towers (disguised as hunting stands?) scattered along the property.

Hunting stands in disguise? – Photos courtesy of Greg Valdez.

In addition, there is an unusual round steel (and air conditioned) building located behind a ranch entrance gate on the opposite side of the property (37° 6.02' north latitude and 107°2.85' west longitude – GPS).

A metal plaque prominently posted on a watch tower door identified the manufacturer as Houston Blow Pipe & Steel Plate Works (P.O. BOX 1692, Houston, TX 77251-1692).

Having seen the towers and being interested in their origin and purpose, a simple phone call was made to the phone number above.

It was learned during the phone conversation that the President and CEO of the company is Mr. W. A. Redding.

Contrary to the myths that have been perpetuated, a simple explanation was provided by Mr. Redding.

1) Mr. Redding stated that the watch towers are actually hunting stands with the brand name "The Ultimate Hunting Stand." (But are they just disguised as "hunting stands"?)

The hunting stands on the ranch are weatherproof, heavy gauge steel construction (5 feet diameter, 850 pounds est. total weight) equipped with 10 feet high steel angle frame supports, steel ladder or a steel walk-up type stairway with steel pipe hand railing, propane heater and tank, five large one way mirror-pane plate glass (hinged and latched) windows (hunters can see out, but game cannot see inside), swivel chair, and indoor-outdoor carpet on floor and side wall.

Further, the stands are used for photographing game and birds, and hunting of game (deer, elk, javelina, moose, sheep and turkeys).

According to published literature, the stands have been in production since 1963 and employ 75 years of hunting and 60 years of steel fabrication experience in their design for all-weather hunting.

2) The round steel building is a bunk house for ranch hands designed and manufactured by Mr. Redding's Houston steel company. The bunk house design employs the same all-weather heavy gauge steel construction as the hunting stands along with air conditioning and fuel-oil heater.

It is not currently being used.

3) The owner of the Redding War Ranch is Mr. Redding himself. He can be contacted at the phone number given above.

4) The Redding War Ranch is used to raise small herds of "Beefalo."

(UNQUOTE).

IS THERE MORE TO THE REDDING RANCH

Yes, I think so.

Here is what Edmund Gomez from Dulce said about this...and I agree with him.

"Based on the source of research by NIDS, yes, this was their take on the ranch years after the ranch let its defense down and allowed folks to travel through it.

"From the early 1960's to the late 1980's, you could not trespass on the Redding Ranch, not even to retrieve a cow.

"Why?

"That is the million dollar question.

"And, why are all the structures, including the towers, doors and windows in the bunkhouse, constructed of a very heavy gauge steel (making them bulletproof)?

"NIDS continues to provide information (or is it disinformation?) to keep us off track, in my opinion.

"In the fall of 1997, I led Gabe Valdez (the late former New Mexico State Patrol Officer in charge of the Dulce area) and two other scientists from NIDS on the expedition and continued through up to Mt. Archuleta.

"We were able to go directly to the towers, enter, photograph and see the tags with the manufacturer.

"I told them that the glass, doors, shutters and structures were bullet-proof and was going to show them, but inexplicably, Gabe Valdez stopped me.

"I could not get them to go to the 'bunkhouse and hangar' to investigate further.

"Also, I noticed that the airstrip had been plowed and planted with oats.

"But again, no interest was shown by the NIDS folks".

I could not agree more with the above quote from Edmund Gomez. I also never trusted NIDS (National Institute of Discovery Sciences).

By the way, Greg Valdez, in his excellent book *Dulce Base*," mentions that (the late) "Mr. Redding owned Houston Blow Pipe and Steel and was a military contractor providing manufacturing of heavy-duty plate rolling, which was commonly used at the Nevada Test Site for construction of underground tunnels during the testing of nuclear bombs in Nevada.

"Mr. Redding's company also provided air circulation systems (that's one of the services a blowpipe company usually provides, in case you're curious), which would be convenient technology to have for constructing an underground base or tunnel."

Redding Ranch is currently owned by the Southern Ute tribe which purchased it from W.A. Redding on August 16, 2005.

It now seems to be abandoned.

Redding passed away in 2009 in Texas. Redding acquired the property in 1976.

According to Greg Valdez, in his book *Dulce Base*," "The land directly south of the Redding Ranch did not indicate a previous owner.

"The key to this is the fact that the United States government owned all the property prior to 1965 and it wasn't the Forest Service or the Bureau of Land Management.

"When Edmund Gomez looked into the property records during the 1980s, he found fictitious companies listed (a common tactic of agencies such as the CIA) as the owner on record of the Redding Ranch.

"After Edmund's finding of the fictitious companies became public, the ownership records changed back to Mr. Redding."

The big question here is:

Was this some type of a remote test site (such as for small aircraft) operated by the CIA?

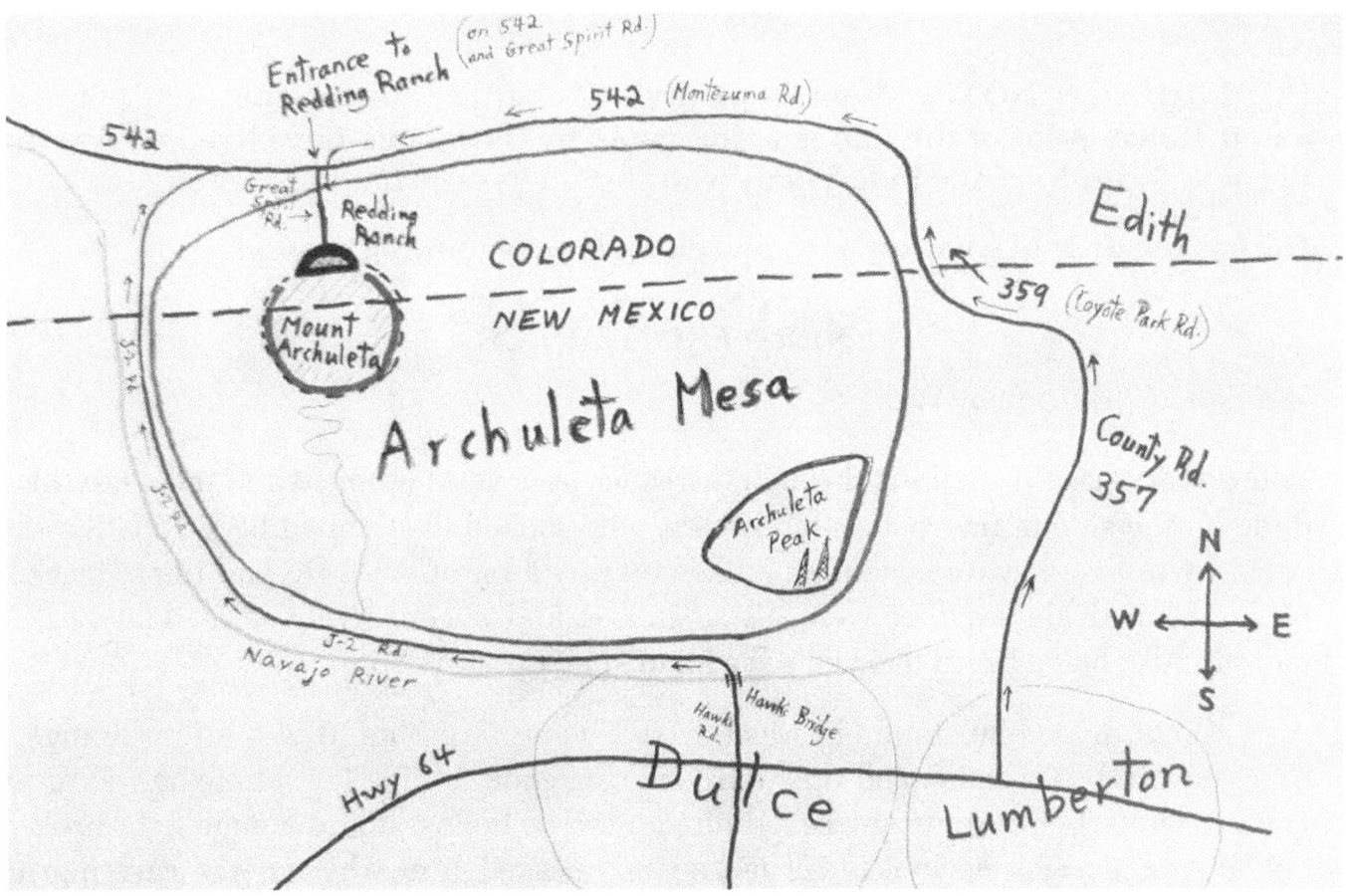

How to get to the now-abandoned Redding Ranch which is still off-limits to anyone. From Lumberton, go north on County Rd. 357, then go to 359 from Edith, then go west on 542.

Source: March 28, 2021, CIVILIAN INTELLIGENCE NEWS SERVICE, by Norio Hayakawa

7.

THE DULCE CHATTER - PUBLIC SCUTTLEBUTT ON A TOP SECRET MYSTERY

PUBLISHER'S NOTE: There is plenty of "chatter" on the message boards about Dulce. A lot of the talk is being made by those who have lived or live in the area – these are the individuals who should know what they are saying.

Here is the drift of what we have picked up from snooping around.

NERD FROM DULCE

[Edit on 26-10-2009 by Well]

A few years ago I was biking through the Dulce area and I stopped and talked to this dude on the side of the road, hitch-hiking, who looked like he had been to hell and back. I was like, hey dude, you look like you saw a lot of s***! He had thick, black, plastic-framed glasses that were all scratched and a conservative, yet laid back, haircut. Also had a beard like you see a lot of spec-ops guys sport.

What made him stand out was this suit he was wearing. It was bright orange, covered with blood stains and this weird looking gooey stuff. He told me he was at a Halloween party but some guy called him a nerd so he lost it and a huge fight broke out and that's why he looked all jacked up. Asked him why he was carrying a crowbar in the desert and he just looked at me with this glare like I've never seen. Then he just slapped his hand with it a few times, gripping it reassuringly and said, "Son, one of these might save your life one day," and walked off, resting it over his shoulder.

It was so-o-o weird. He was very soft-spoken; actually it was hard to get him to say anything. But it was one of those encounters you don't ever forget.

* * * * * * * * *

DULCE WARRIORS

IT'S MY HOME TOWN

What a lot of you people fail to realize is that there are a lot of people on those hillsides every day. Forestry workers, deer/elk hunters, horn searchers and, less importantly, poachers.

I'm from Dulce, and I know people who consistently spend 8 hours a day in those hills. My neighbor was a Game and Fish official in charge of watching for poachers. If there was an obvious entrance, there would have been something said.

After saying that, I know of many people with UFO stories. Hell, I remember seeing lights in the sky and the constant presence of black helicopters (I have pics of copters if requested). I don't think the base is close to Dulce or on the rez. Just across the border into Colorado (literally five miles away) is a different story as it's national forest land and not tribal land.

I would also like to point out the proximity to Sandia National Labs and the "gas buggy project" where nukes were set off underground very close to Dulce. You pass the sign every time you drive to Farmington.

Just my two cents. It's my hometown.

* * * * * * * * *

Hello, everyone. This is my first post on this site and on the subject of Dulce. I live in Dulce. I live with my partner, who was born and raised on the reservation. I thought I would try and clear some confusion up on the subject. Maybe some of these questions have been answered, maybe not. Please bear with me.

Dulce is a very small town. Everyone pretty much knows everyone's business. It is a reservation and the majority of the population is Native American. There is one hotel (Holiday Inn), a grocery store and several small restaurants. Now, since it is a reservation, it is tribal land. Meaning the tribe owns all the land that's part of the reservation. Now, the thing is, if you are not a tribal member, you cannot go onto the tribal owned land. That is, unless you are with someone that is Jicarilla (Apache).

That does not mean that you cannot visit or live on the reservation though. For example, Archuleta is considered tribal land. To even drive up onto Archuleta you have to be from there or with someone that is. For the first time since I have lived there I went atop of Archuleta about a month ago. It's very beautiful. You're surrounded by nothing but trees and fresh air and wildlife.

To drive in that type of terrain, you need to have a truck or some type of SUV that is four-wheel drive. Do not even attempt to drive up in a car. It's very easy to get lost or stuck up there. It's also very confusing and you need to be with someone that knows the land like the back of their hand. Fortunately, I do and, when we drove up Archuleta I experienced several things. The very first thing I noticed was the static electricity. It was crazy! When I touched my seat belt I was shocked. When I picked up my cell phone I got shocked. The people I was with were experiencing the same things.

Another thing was the gas gauge. Before we left we had gotten gas but we ONLY filled up half a tank. I noticed that as we got higher into the mesa the gas had read full. That was really odd for us. The last thing that we experienced was perhaps the oddest. I was kind of nervous to be on top of Archuleta to begin with. We had gotten to a certain point where we had reached a gate. It was more like a rancher's gate but said not to cross, as we were heading into the Ute reservation land which is in Colorado.

So we turned around and as we were heading back down my sister had noticed about 10-15 lights against one of the mountains surrounding us. The position of the lights was VERY similar to the lights that were seen in Arizona some years back. Being that it was already dark we had no way of seeing anything but the lights. I couldn't tell if the lights were in the trees or mountains or even hovering for that matter.

I was getting kind of nervous and I thought that maybe it was a bad idea for us to be there. We continued driving (as fast as you possibly can on a mountain) and I heard my sister say that there were some more lights. By this time we had lost sight of the first set of lights but when I looked to the direction she was talking about there was another row of lights (my right side). It was incredible.

I have never seen anything like this before in my life. As we were watching the lights in awe one huge bright light appeared out of nowhere to my left. We were all speechless. The only way to describe the light was like one huge head light blinking slowly. At that point I just wanted to get off the mountain. So we watched the lights a little longer and continued back down. That was the craziest experience I've ever had and it was beautiful at the same time.

I can't say that what we saw were UFOs but deep down I really believe we saw something out of this world. My only regret was not having a camcorder. The time it took for us get up and down was about an hour and a half. It would be nearly impossible to go up now because of the snow we are receiving. The best time to go exploring for anyone that is planning to go sometime would be during the summer

[Edit on 14-12-2009 by Gazrok]

* * * * * * * * *

IT'S ALL ABOUT MILAB

Now for the Experiments I found this from Lammer MILAB. Bit lengthy, so coffee is a must!!

IV. Tank/tube experiences

Michelle (pseudonym) had her first conscious memory of typical alien abduction experiences with nonhuman beings at the age of eight. She remembers classic alien abduction experiences with three-four feet tall beings with large heads. The following experiences, however, have nothing to do with alien abductions. Michelle had traumatic flashbacks, reality-like dreams and some consciously remembered MILAB events. The memory gaps were investigated by using regressive hypnosis sessions with a professional Ph.D. hypnotherapist who is well known in this field and who is also a MUFON consultant.

Michelle and a boyfriend had a missing time/kidnapping experience during 1970 near a campsite at Ditch Plains in Montauk, New York. She remembers that both were taken by armed military personnel to the now closed Montauk base. They were separated and Michelle was escorted inside an underground facility where she had several frightening experiences. She remembers being in a doctor's examining room, with machines and stainless steel equipment and a table covered in white.

Michelle was placed on the table and strapped down, including her head. After a few minutes a group of five-six people, including one female, came into the room. All of them wore medical cloths white gowns. Surgical masks covering their heads like doctors in a hospital. They turned her head sideways and shaved a small portion of an area behind her right ear. She was completely conscious but immobilized and she could not talk.

Michelle and her boyfriend claim they were abducted and taken to an underground facility at Camp Hero, Long Island.

Michelle remembers that someone was writing something on the skin behind her ear. After this she got an intravenous (IV) injection, she felt a prick in her arm and lost consciousness and awakened with her boyfriend, who was also kidnapped, later on the beach. The next hypnosis session opened further traumatic flashbacks of being in an isolation tank. The following experience was investigated during an emotional hypnotic regression session. Michelle had never had this experience while under hypnosis before. She recalled being in a dark place. She was afraid and floated in something that felt slightly heavier than warm water.

Before this experience she was naked on a table and had wires attached all over her body and her head and she saw a doctor in a white lab coat standing next to her. The next experience was uncovered via a deep trance regression which probed again into the isolation tank experience. Michelle remembered once again that she was in a black enclosed area where she struggled and was afraid of drowning. The experience scared her a lot and she wanted out of the tank. She felt that the liquid was heavier than water, it was warm and she smelled a minty odor. She moved her arms and legs slightly and her head too. She felt the smooth surface of the isolation tank on her right if she stretched her arm. She was completely isolated in the dark tank and had a kind of artificially induced "out-of-body" experience or began to hallucinate.

I researched the literature of sensory deprivation experiments and came across such isolation tanks which were invented by Dr. John Lilly. Dr. Lilly tried to find out how he could isolate the brain and mind. He considered what thought, according to our present scientific consensus, is to stimulate a body. He considered effects of light and its stimulation of the eyes, touch and pressure and their stimulation of the skin and deep-lying organs within the body. He looked at temperature differences, at clothing, effects of gravitation and the effects of heat and cold.

Dr. Lilly visualized a soundproof tank in which the body could be supported in water that would be maintained at the proper temperature to take care of the generation of heat within the body. He found such a tank inside a soundproof chamber in an isolated building near the campus of the National Institute of Health. This tank was constructed during World War II for experiments by the Office of Naval Research on metabolism of underwater swimmers. This was the beginning for research on isolation, including drugs.

It should be noted that Dr. Lilly experimented also with brain implants during the late fifties and early sixties. This was also the period when he was contacted by covert intelligence services and researchers for the Department of Defense (DoD). Dr. Lilly wrote in his book "The Scientist" that while he was at the National Institute of Health, the isolation tank-work, like the brain-electrode work, became subject to the politics. As the isolation tank research became known throughout government agencies, various individuals called him to find out about it. Dr. Lilly claims that among them were researchers working under the auspices of the Army in regard to brainwashing of captured prisoners of war.

He was asked if the isolation tank could be used to change the belief systems of persons under coercion. They wanted to use the isolation tanks and sensory deprivation experiments for brain washing and other mind control experiments. Dr. John Lilly visualized situations in which this method would be used under coercion, by careful control of the stimulation of isolated persons, and that their belief systems could be changed in directions desired by the controlling persons. Dr. Lilly was convinced that the military/intelligence community would use his isolation technique for covert experiments. I think that Michelle's experiences show us that this was true and that there is enough evidence that she is one victim of such a deprivation tank experiment. One should note, however, that this specific experience had nothing to do with aliens, although I don't know how her alien abduction experiences fit in this scenario.

As I noted in my first MILAB paper, the presence of human military personnel inhabiting the same physical reality as alien beings is unbelievable for skeptics and open-minded, serious abduction researchers, too. Although Michelle's before-mentioned experiences were definitely terrestrial, she experienced also a high strangeness close encounter during the same MILAB. She got traumatic flashbacks under hypnosis of a reptilian creature, which was also investigated. She described that she was escorted by military personnel into a dark office-like room where she was raped by a reptilian creature. I don't know what this traumatic experience means. I don't think, however, that the military worked with this reptilian creature. It could be possible that she was drugged with an hallucinogenic and projected the reptilian as a kind of screen memory, although she described the skin and other features of the creature very well. Was this particular experience the product of a mind control procedure? One should consider such procedures first, since her other experiences in the underground facility were completely terrestrial and recent hypnosis sessions performed with Michelle during July 1997 revealed that she may have been used in various mind control experiments during her lifetime.

During a two hour session she remembered being in a room with 2-3 men who were in charge of men in lab coats. Before this she was in some kind of examination room, where someone mounted something on her head. She described silver-colored tongs, pinching at her temples and inducing an intense pain in her head.

This experience reminds me of an artificial stimulation experiment for temporal lobes with magnetic fields. Dr. Michael Persinger, a neuroscientist at Laurentian University of Sudbury, Ontario, showed that one can artificially produce mystical experiences, out of body excursions and other psychic experiences by stimulating the temporal lobes by applying magnetic fields across the brain, since he found that such experiences are linked with excessive bursts of electrical activity in the temporal lobes. A research target would get a helmet or tong-like device on the head and an artificially generated magnetic field would mimic the firing patterns of neurons in the temporal lobes of the brain.

DULCE WARRIORS

Dan Wright, head of the MUFON Abduction Transcription Project, reviewed his records concerning tube or tank experiences of alleged alien abductees. He found several cases in his files in which the abductee saw a tube during her/his experience, but did not identify anything or anyone inside it. In four cases abductees described large clear tubes and recalled either being placed inside it or seeing someone else inside. Two of these four abductees saw an alien creature in the tube. Dan Wright's files reveal three cases in which the abductee was in a tank filled with liquid and in two cases the victim was forced to breathe the liquid. None of the abductees who were placed in a tube or tank reported any unusual mind set (out of body experience, remote viewing, or the like) during their time in these containers. Two of seven tank cases reported military involvement, but not on the same night as the tube or tank episode.

A number of MILAB abductees have reported not only being forced into large tubes filled with liquid, but also seeing people floating in other tubes.

DULCE WARRIORS

MILAB victim Lisa (pseudonym) had similar tank experiences like Dan Wright's alien abductees. She was kidnapped and brought to a military underground facility, where she saw naked humans floating in tubes. Lisa for instance claims that she was forced by humans into some type of pool filled with a golden yellow bubbly fluid, while other humans looked at her. Lisa has traumatic recollections that her kidnappers tried to make her and other victims able to breathe in the liquid. In two of the before-mentioned cases the abductee was forced to breathe the liquid like Lisa. The hypnosis transcripts reveal that the liquid breathing experiences were traumatic for the abductees. Both abductees where totally immersed in the liquid and both reported that they could breathe the fluid.

If one reviews the open scientific literature which is available about fluid breathing, one finds that physically taking fluid into the lungs and breathing liquid instead of air would revolutionize diving. The concept of fluid breathing began in the mid-60s when Dr. J. Kylstra, a physiologist at the State University of New York at Buffalo, realized that salt solutions could be saturated with oxygen at high pressures. Dr. Kylstra worked in a US Navy compression camber and performed experiments on mice. He was able to keep animals alive for up to 18 hours. Since carbon dioxide was not removed fast enough from the system, and quickly built up to near toxic levels, this problem was going to be the stumbling block before his procedure could be used on humans.

The next step in fluid breathing came in 1966, with Dr. Leland Clark's liquid-breathing-mouse experiment. Dr. Clark developed a technique where a mouse survived over 20 hours breathing fluid at 18 degrees centigrade. All animals in the early studies suffered pulmonary damage, but that was due to toxic impurities of the fluorocarbon, chemical interaction of the fluorocarbon with the lung, or some unknown effect that was undetermined. This pulmonary damage mystery as well as the problem of the elimination of carbon dioxide and the fact that the fluorocarbon tended to be retained by body tissues would have to be solved before the process could be attempted on human subjects.

During the following years, the technique of fluid breathing was refined and improved. Liquid ventilation tests of the early 90s proved to be successful. Scientists kept dogs alive in a perfluorocarbon medium for about two hours. After removal the dogs were slightly hypoxic, but returned to normal after a few days. After these tests on animals, the procedure was ready for human subjects used by the medical community for fighting the respiratory distress syndrome, the leading cause of death in premature infants. One could suspect that liquid breathing experiments on adults would be extremely useful for military/Navy/intelligence purposes such as submarine escape and undersea oxygen support facilities.

Alien abductees, such as Betty Andreason, report sometimes that they were put inside a tube filled with liquid for the compensation of large gravity forces during high UFO acceleration periods. One abductee of Dan Wright's files describes such an experience inside such a tube:

"It's like water in there; it's like being in a swimming pool, only I can see through the sides. It feels like we are moving. Where are we going? Whoo, that's fast. Feels like we are moving fast. Oh! And one's standing outside. He's telling me, 'That's why we had to put you in here, because we are moving too fast.' Acceleration. Something about gravity forces too much."

It is interesting to note that under hypnosis this abductee reported how the abductors put something in her nose before they put her in the tube. This means that this abductee was not forced to breathe the liquid. Recent scientific studies of visual and photographic sightings of UFOs carrying out "impossible" high speed maneuvers by Dr. Bruce Maccabee would support such gravity force compensation tube experiences if the abductee was indeed in a real UFO. Dr. Bruce Maccabee stated in his article "Acceleration", that a UFOnaut or abductee inside a UFO accelerating at 500 g's would be pushed by the walls of the craft with a force that would make him seem almost 500 times his weight on Earth. The body of an abductee might be crushed at that acceleration, and the skin might be pulled off the bones, unless the human was suspended in a liquid and the lungs and other body cavities were filled with liquid!

Other alleged alien abductees report that they saw small alien like beings and adult humans in a state of suspended animation inside tube-like incubators. Some of these abductees claim that the humans looked altered like hybrids. These would fit the hypothesis of genetic research done by the "greys." But there are also cases where abductees report human doctors escorting them through underground laboratories where they have seen humans in clear tanks. MILAB victim Christa Tilton described such an experience as:

"I did see what I thought were humans in clear tanks underground. The tanks were leaning about 25 degrees backward until they touched the wall. The room was a regular room...like a laboratory. This was never viewed on a spacecraft. They seemed to be, like I said, in a state of suspended animation. There was a clear liquid filled totally in the tank casing...I believe these humans were being kept alive by some type of tubes behind their head."

Christa Tilton is not alone with such an experience. There are other abductees who claim that they were taken to military underground facilities where they have seen people in such glass or plastic tubes. Some of these MILABs report rows of several identical people, each one in its own tube. One could speculate if someone clones human Dollys in secret. Recently Japanese scientists reported that a goat fetus has survived in an artificial womb for three weeks before its birth. The scientists who designed the womb say that it could help premature human babies to survive. Dr. Yoshinori Kuwabara of Juntendo University in Tokyo and his colleagues removed a goat fetus from its mother 17 weeks into the pregnancy. They placed the fetus in a tank filled with liquid to simulate amniotic fluid. A machine pumped nutrients and oxygen into the animal's blood. Dr. Kuwabara also hopes artificial wombs could one day be used to help fetuses in the final stages of multiple pregnancies when the womb becomes too cramped. However, alien and MILAB abductees claim that they saw small tubes or incubators inside UFOs but also inside terrestrial underground research facilities. Mostly the experiencer describes that these infants look very ill. Alleged alien abductees and abductees with MILAB experiences think that these infants may be hybrids.

It would be logical for someone who is interested in cloning that he develops and uses artificial wombs and incubators filled with nutrient fluid for breeding purposes. Scientists who are working on biotechnology projects claim that cloning "brainless" humans for transplanting organs would be a reality in the future. At this time ethical considerations are against such Frankenstein-like research projects. A more science fiction like purpose would be the creation of a genetically engineered soldier who is immune to biological warfare and possible future genetic warfare attacks. The experiences of some MILAB victims, however, suggest that such projects are indeed going on behind the backs of the official medical research community. Therefore it could be that secret research on artificial wombs and experiments on human fetuses are going on hidden inside black projects.

One can see that alien abductees report similar tank/tube experiences inside alleged UFOs as some abductees in alleged military research facilities. Such similarity was also found in implanting procedures between alleged alien abductees and possible mind control victims.

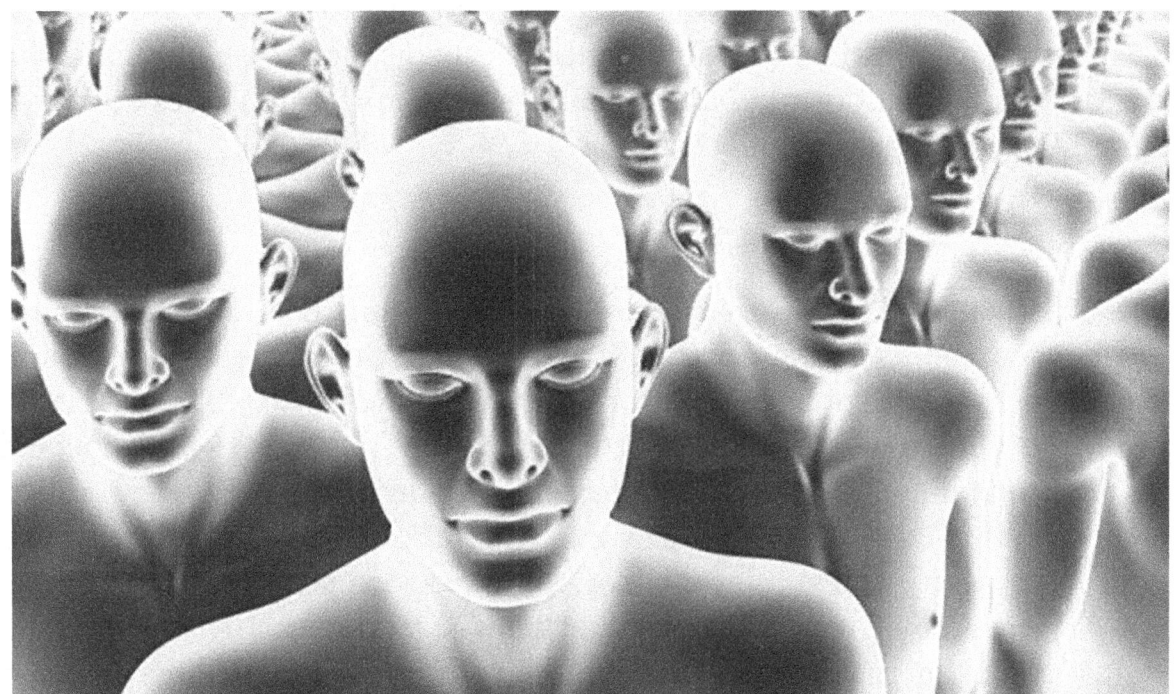

It has been alleged that human cloning experiments were being conducted between Dulce labs and the bio-genetic facility at Los Alamos.

I present now a case where it seems to me that a secretly operating military task force could be in charge of researchers of such a black genetic project. This is one well-investigated case in the MUFON Abduction Transcription Project files where human/military personnel kidnap a woman from her house and drive her to a secret place. She is carried into the building and placed onto an examining table. Her feet are placed into stirrups, what is used for gynecological examinations. A female doctor conducts a gynecological exam. She searches for an embryo but never finds any. The MILAB victim remembers the officer in charge as an older man with silver hair who threatens and interrogates her. She loses consciousness sometime during the examination or on the trip back to her home. Interestingly the military always kidnaps her on the same night or the night after an alleged alien abduction experience.

The activity of this military task force, which seems to be interested in particular alien abductees, would be a logical consequence if their leaders think that some alien abductions are real. As I mentioned above it seems that this group works together with black project scientists who are interested in genetic research. It should be noted that the before-mentioned abductee reported a tube experience but not on the same night as the military kidnapped her. She observed several tubes with different bodies inside and she was placed in front of a tube with a body of a tall blond human woman inside. She described the tube as a glass or Plexiglas cylinder inside a UFO. It should be noted that the above-mentioned abductees are not alone and that their cases represent only examples.

* * * * * * * *

Originally posted by MCory1Preamble: This is a long post. And it intentionally makes no claim one way or another about any of the reported happenings at Archuleta Mesa, more commonly known as the "Dulce Base." This is merely an attempt to determine whether or not it is reasonable to think that an installation could have been built at the time. I apologize for the length, but I could not think of any way to split it up as Gazrok did with Roswell, and while some of it is rather editorial, the majority of it is relevant. Any comments are most welcome; if you find any flaws, please don't hesitate to let me know. I hope that if nothing else this stimulates some more serious thought into the area, and any criticism is appreciated. So, without further ado...

DESERT SECRETS

There's something happening here;

What it is ain't exactly clear...

-Buffalo Springfield, "For What it's Worth"

In the ufology field, like any other research area, the material falls in a large spectrum of publicity. At one end, there's the Roswell incident of July 6th, 1947, where the military allegedly seized a crashed space craft. There's the Travis Walton abduction case, popularized in the 1993 movie "Fire in the Sky." The abduction of Betty and Barney Hill in late 1961 has received lesser fanfare, but is still a favorite among believers. There's the lesser known "Battle of LA," where the military fired on an unknown object in the early morning of February 25th, 1942. At the other end of the spectrum lay the innumerable eyewitness accounts and tales that never receive any attention at all, and often are debunked without more than a cursory glance.

Somewhere in the midst of this spectrum, towards the more quietly spoken end, lies the story of the Archuleta Mesa, commonly referred to as the Dulce Base (due to Dulce, NM being the nearest town.) While a detailed account is beyond the scope of this paper, a brief overview of the story as accounted on AboveTopSecret.com is in order.

Under the Archuleta Mesa in northern New Mexico and southern Colorado, the United States military maintains an extremely confidential, multi-level facility dedicated to research of extraterrestrial beings and technology. A large number of extraterrestrial beings are said to reside in this facility, from various races and worlds. In 1979, there was a revolt of the aliens, and the majority of the human workforce was killed. While the base was closed for a brief period of time, it was eventually reopened and operations recommenced.

Regardless of the validity of the story, it does make for excellent reading. Aliens, government conspiracies, secret bases, it's all the bread and butter of any science fiction writer. Throw into the mix the various accounts of cattle mutilations, mysterious helicopters loitering in the area, and strange lights in the skies. You now have a plot worthy of any Hollywood production team.

While the story of the aliens being held and having a small war is farfetched, prior to dismissing it out of hand one of the more mundane aspects of the story needs to be considered. Is it even reasonable for such a base to have been constructed? In order to determine the plausibility of such construction, there are several variables that must be considered.

The Archuleta Mesa, as stated above, is situated in northern New Mexico and southern Colorado. It is definitely tall enough to maintain a large internal structure, standing at approximately 9,236 feet in elevation. However, the mesa stands on an intrusion of augite andesite (granite) over 300 feet thick. While this in itself does not necessarily preclude an installation being built to any depth below the mesa, it would make for the extension of the base below this sill rather difficult.

Preamble to something and that is clear. Martian Child with John Cusack really a schmuck. The Bear on the Moon and Shangri La might have to wait. Well, I have an ancestor who came over on the Mayflower, so that we came here as refugees from Europe. A pale blue turquoise house, a ghost rider departed across to Tumbola (Gazrok) through the dark veil of rain and fog. According to Time, a magazine with a history of theories of Beast men.

The horror film with Romero the chief shaper. It moves sensationally beyond the limits of all that is hideous, revolting and loathsome. Alien Invasion Imprinting on Fox news, anything green that is good for the cholesterol. The magical sleigh base "recommenced" the government forcing us to learn a foreign language so we can see Star of Bethlehem shows in Dulce Spanish. The physiognomy of the leopard skin creature make it easier to hunt, gave Turtle and skunk "appropriate tails."

Bought on eBay, like my wonderful digital camera and cheap laptop with a crack on the hinge. I like them but they both make sort of a wheezing noise. Down below Archuleta Mesa Multi-level facility you hear wheezing of monstrous Chimera's fire breathing features of a female mixed with a cougar. Or a human baby with Caterpillar features (stomach form of huckleberries) crawls and builds a cocoon turning into a moth. Miniature human hands making a whimpering call.

Only Indians at the top know about it, but they are intimidated by a mastery of "Quark" who will make their life a living hell. I don't even really consider these people anything but more than mirages of this huge clown-like charade. Definitely glad that the Doctor-Professor idea that there are people coming from out in the distance with their dogs. Golden Retrievers security guards at the Rockies, fighting against the aliens (what the puck?)

* * * * * * * * *

I'VE BEEN THERE!

Originally posted by ninjascout -

No there are not a large number of trucks coming in to Dulce every week. There isn't even a Holiday Inn in Dulce. Take the information you hear with a grain of salt.

That's not quite true...

Okay to be fair it's been 10 years since I was last up there and no I don't remember a Holiday Inn but due to a rather prolific oil field industry all around Dulce Highway 64 is a minor truck route. Farmington west of Dulce being the hub of the coal seam gas business... Not only did I grow up in that part of the world I use to work and hunt around those parts.

They were right in that the whole area is crisscrossed with oil field service roads. Real easy to get lost in there, worse when it rains and you have to deal with the red clay that quickly turns into deep mud. Trust me on that one. I stuck a semi in that mud once and it took three tow trucks to pull me loose.

Up in that part of the world it's not UFO hunters anyone worries about, its treasure hunters... There's an old story about a group of Penitents (Los Hermanos de la Fraternidad Piadosa de Nuestro Padre Jesús Nazareno) This happens to be another "secret society" and not well known if you're not from around here...

Anyway the Penitente Brotherhood went around robbing the local ranches and when the officials were called in to investigate they supposedly took mules loaded with treasure up into the hills...One of my duties as a teen was to make sure the treasure hunters weren't digging up the pastures like gophers...

If you're wondering if I have UFO stories, having grown up just south of there, sadly I have to admit no... but I do have a ton of ghost stories and one about a Skin Walker...now that's spooky stuff... :-)

As a side note, as I said, I haven't been up there in a number of years but if anyone did want to go kicking around in the back country I wouldn't mind acting as guide. After all these years I'll probably be as lost as you are

[edit on 15-12-2007 by DaddyBare]

* * * * * * * * *

A STORY THAT IS HARD TO KILL

The Dulce base controversy will never die because rumors are hard to dispel. At first I thought this was some kind of crazy science fiction story made to sell or perhaps a disgruntled government employee trying to get even but unfortunately the more you dig the more you find. It took a great amount of time and effort to assemble the puzzle but in the end I think it was worth it.

Chances are Dulce and many other underground/underwater bases exist in the USA, the Indo-China border, Pacific Islands, the Bahamas area, etc. Do we have proof? Obviously not but that might be a good thing until we, as a human species, are ready to cope with such harsh realities. Perhaps they hide the truth to protect us from going totally ape and society breaking down to chaos. Some people are mature and can handle almost anything but others are not. Just imagine the repercussions if governments were about to disclose everything they knew to us. I remember losing sleep on many occasions just pondering what *could* be true and what that *might* mean for our imminent and distant future.

I could expand this more to general conspiracy discussion but I prefer sticking to the topic at hand. Dulce has been discussed by many people but visual confirmation of the actual base is impossible to get because it is deep underground; probably a mile or two underneath the Archuleta Mesa. Perhaps there are a few clues on the surface but only Native-Americans residing on the reservation will have knowledge and access to them, if any exist. For everyone else the land is STRICTLY OFF LIMITS and people risk getting arrested for trespassing if they ignore the warnings. Don't bother going there!

IMO Thomas Castello and Phil Schneider sounded very convincing discussing what they knew. Thomas Castello had an ultra-7 top secret clearance and was head of security at the time. He described seven levels of which the bottom three housed aliens and important lab work was done. He also mentioned that Dulce was connected to the underground maglev system that interconnected at least a hundred bases throughout the mid and far west. Dulce is probably the central hub of this joint human-alien endeavor.

Phil Schneider was a geologist working on these underground labs/bases and gave many lectures before "committing suicide" in his own house by strangling himself with piano wire (yeah, right). He mentioned conducting all kinds of ground surveys and helped build many of them. While working at Dulce he said he was shot by grey aliens and he returned fire, killing a few.

* * * * * * * * *

DISAPPEARING PLANE

Are you familiar with the disappearing silver cargo plane near Crestone?

I personally interviewed New Mexico State Trooper Cordova. His family had about a dozen head of cattle mutilated just north of Taos. NM trooper Gabe Valdez (RIP) actually called him to assist in the Dulce mutilations. I also interviewed Lt Martinez (ret) of the Taos County Sheriff Department. His story of assisting a fellow Deputy out on the mesa involved a jack-knifed semi and little gray dudes running around the semi.

DULCE WARRIORS

ON MY WAY TO WORK TODAY

Driving to work today, I came upon some road work and had to take another route for a couple of blocks. Hadn't gone this way before, so I was looking around at houses and buildings etc.

While looking at some buildings sitting on lots, etc., I got to thinking, I wonder what's in there. (some of them have no markings, etc.) And then my mind wandered to ATS and Dulce.

What if, I know this is a big IF, but, what if, an entrance to Dulce was right under everyone's noses, right in plain sight?

We get so busy in our everyday lives that we often do not notice or pay attention to that which is right in front of us.

I wonder what kinds of buildings are in or around Dulce that are "empty," just sitting there, that the townsfolk's walk by every day and don't give a second thought to?

What if, one or more of these buildings housed the entrance to Dulce?

The workers (or personnel) walk right up to the building, go in, go over to a secret/hidden control panel, enters the ID or Password or both and the secret entrance opens up and leads maybe to a hallway or elevator or something that eventually leads to the Dulce base?

One other thought is supplies for the base, how do they get there? What if large unused warehouses had the same thing? The trucks drive in, the doors close and unload the supplies into elevators that go below and the supplies then get distributed?

I'd even go as far as to say, these buildings and warehouses that "might" be secret entrances to Dulce, probably are not even near the town of Dulce. Could be a few miles away. Those are my thoughts...yours ?

* * * * * * * * *

DULCE WARRIORS

THE TALL TALE SPIN

The latest spin on the alien phenomenon according to DeLonge and others is that the truth about the aliens is simply too terrible to be told and that the government has been right not to divulge what they know about it.

Which brought to mind the infamous Phil Schneider/Dulce base account...one of the more disturbing alien accounts to come out of the 1990s...and at the end of this account I tie it all together with the recent "tic tac" UFO encounter.

Phil Schneider was a geological engineer who in 1979, according to the story, was contracted by the U.S. military to work construction on a deep underground military base (D.U.M.B.) in Dulce, New Mexico.

And at one point, while excavating a series of large shafts deep into the earth, a problem was encountered and Mr. Schneider went down into the shaft to investigate. It was there that he came face to face with a seven-foot-tall gray alien. He pulled out a pistol he had been carrying and shot and killed the alien as well as killing one other alien before himself being shot by a beam of some sort fired by another of the aliens. This led to a day long battle between U.S. Special Forces and the aliens in which more than 60 people were killed. This incident is now referred to as The Dulce Wars.

And as it turned out, this underground base was a seven-level deep complex, with the upper levels being used by the U.S. military and the lower levels being used by the aliens.

Here the aliens kept abducted humans captive in large, transparent vats filled with liquid. And they kept these humans in order to perform bizarre genetic experiments on them using human and animal DNA. The humans were also kept as a food source for them to feed on which the aliens did by absorbing the human blood through their skin.

And as if all that wasn't bad enough, according to Mr. Schneider there were over 1400 of these D.U.M.B s, all connected by a network of tunnels through which MAG LEV trains traveled at science fiction type speeds.

Of course all that was 40 years ago and it's not hard to imagine that they've improved their technology since then...and perhaps their MAG LEV trains have now been replaced with white, forty foot long, tic tac shaped vehicles that can not only traverse the tunnels but can also travel throughout the earth's atmosphere, as well as through various bodies of water.

****

PUBLISHER'S NOTE: PhantomsAndMonsters.com recently added this bit of chatter from a reader who is familiar with the area around Dulce and the sightings in Kirtland, his mother perhaps being part of military intelligence.

"A side note: My mother was also ex-Navy, as well as a cryptographer, though I have no 'official' confirmation that she was with Naval Intelligence, I can only assume that she based what she told me about some being experimental craft, some not from this earth, on many things she and my father were involved with over the years. Regarding what we saw landing and taking-off from the military airport, although it became more difficult to see as the evening wore on, more often than not I COULD see shapes of craft which were either outlined by lights or had other visible means of delineating the silhouettes. Several times I also saw a triangle-shaped craft which appeared black against the evening sky and had a light at each point of the triangle. Again, experimental U.S. military? Back-engineered? Don't know. They didn't say.

"Other points of which you may or may not be aware: Sandia National Laboratories and Kirtland Air Force Base are located in Albuquerque. Los Alamos National Labs is located approximately 60 miles to the NW of Albuquerque. Dulce/Archuleta Mesa is located in Northern New Mexico, on the Colorado border. There have always been sightings in New Mexico, especially Albuquerque. I've seen many myself. Just recently a young boy on one of the Native American Reservations near Albuquerque was attacked in a parked car by something he claimed was an alien. Whatever the creature was, it grabbed him, leaving claw marks down the boy's arms. Fortunately, his father and a sibling, I believe, heard him yelling, and showed up just in time to scare the creature off. They don't know what it was, but it wasn't anything they'd ever seen and it appeared reptilian/alien.

"Additionally, Albuquerque seems to be the headquarters, or at least very large and critical centers, for several military projects, like Project Pegasus, Project Talent and others."

8.

DULCE MAY EVENTUALLY COME TO A BIG CINEMA SCREEN NEAR YOU

We uncovered a posting regarding a possible feature film on Dulce and assorted topics we would like to see manifest in Imax.

Now, "UMBRA" is to be a Hollywood movie. A paranoid thriller, to be precise, about a man who finds an old cassette tape which reveals a horrifying secret.

Details of this movie first emerged back in 2009, when Roger Donaldson was attached to direct and Nicholas Cage to star, but budgetary concerns about the production – as well as Cage's numerous other movie commitments at the time – meant that it never really got off the ground.

The movie's original screenplay was written by newcomer Steven Karczynski and was leaked online in June 2009 and reviewed by a handful of bemused amateur critics. The consensus was that an intriguing and gripping conspiracy thriller in the vein of Coppola's "The Conversation" was torpedoed in its final act by an unexpected sci-fi twist. The screenplay itself is no longer viewable online, but the reviewers' original comments pointed to the possibility that "UMBRA" is – or, at least, was – a UFO movie.

I can now report that, since posting the above information earlier this year, I have read the original screenplay in its entirety and can confirm that "The UMBRA" (as opposed to just "UMBRA") is indeed a UFO movie, and a damn disturbing one at that. I won't quote from the script directly, nor reveal the intricacies of its plot or broader narrative devices, but here's a brief overview of its UFO/alien-related content, all of which is drawn from preexisting UFOlogical literature and debate:

The script clearly is inspired by the longstanding rumors surrounding the Dulce facility, an alleged deep-underground biogenetic research facility in New

Mexico rumored to be jointly run by human black-ops forces and extraterrestrial entities.

One of the characters in the script is named Michael Lazar, clearly a reference to Bob Lazar of Area 51 fame, although in "The UMBRA" Michael Lazar unmistakably is modeled on Phil Schneider - the self-proclaimed Dulce whistleblower who appeared to have been "suicided" back in 1996. "The UMBRA's" Michael Lazar also attempts to blow the whistle on sinister alien/human activities at the Dulce facility and also is "suicided" (Lazar is not the movie's main character, however. His role is merely functional).

"The UMBRA's" original director - Roger Donaldson - worked closely with the Pentagon on the political thriller "Thirteen Days," and with the CIA on "The Recruit." Donaldson also directed the alien movie "Species." While new helmer Joe Carnahan's production history isn't nearly so interesting as Donaldson's, The UMBRA - if and when it reaches the big screen - is nevertheless certainly one to watch out for. Just don't take your kids to see it.

This is being done for gradual disclosure. IMO, in five years all the truth could be out

A JOURNEY TO "THE UNDERGROUND"

PUBLISHER'S NOTE: And if you can't wait until the blockbuster Hollywood movie finishes production— if it ever does— hey, that's Hollywood— we joyfully recommend a less ambitious project produced/directed by Darcy Weir which you can watch on any of the streaming platforms like Amazon Prime for free (Yes, we said FREE!).

One viewer calls "*The Underground: Director's Cut*," a very good overview, making the case that "the deep state is evil!"

We recently had Darcy Weir on "Exploring The Bizarre," where we grilled him about his Dulce project.

Darcy Weir is a documentarian and filmmaker responsible for such works as "*Volcanic UFO Mysteries*," "*Sasquatch Among the Wild Men*," and "*Occult Journeys*." His series "*Beyond The Spectrum*" looks at subjects such as UFOs, the secret space program, underground bases, Area 51, Phil Schneider's Dulce, New Mexico testimonials, and Jaime Maussan's UFO Files.

DULCE WARRIORS

Weir's films present analysis from a theoretical perspective, showing historical references and facts that surround each mystery. In *"Volcanic UFO Mysteries,"* he talks to pioneers in the field of UFO study, and looks at some of the more unknown UFO activity in Mexico.

His film *"Sasquatch Among Wild Men"* is based on the theory that relic hominids like Sasquatch live in deep wildernesses all around the world. He uncovers interesting scientific evidence and the connections between sightings in China, Russia, and the United States.

After reading this "teaser interview" below here that concentrates on the Dulce aspects of our questioning, if you wish to hear the entire show you may find it at:

https://kcorradio.com/Library/archive/exploring-the-bizarre/2021/february/darcy-weir-and-stephen-bassett.mp3

"Exploring The Bizarre" co-host Tim Swartz opens up the discussion with Weir on the subject of his film about Dulce.

SWARTZ: Okay, Darcy, I wanted to ask you a question - and you've touched on this briefly in the first segment - but this concerns your earlier film about Phil Schneider. Now, his case has always been fascinating to me. I communicated with his wife quite a bit early on, not too long after he was "suicided." And for those in our audience who may not be familiar with this gentleman, can you give us just like a brief explanation on who he was and what your film was about?

WEIR: Sure. The film is really about underground bases and the deep history of underground bases, or, for lack of a better explanation, the existence of beings - crypto-terrestrials - that may exist on different planes of the planet. So, not on the surface, but underneath the surface. There have been many accounts of people, even abductees, saying that they've been taken to under the ocean, to underwater bases and underground bases when they had their abduction experiences,

But with this documentary we really wanted to go about it by talking about cultures and their history of underground bases, what they think has happened on this planet, historically. But then, on top of that, the Phil Schneider testimony, how he worked on an underground base, the Dulce, New Mexico, underground base. Some others call it DS3, which is reported in Anthony Sanchez's book *"UFO Highway."*

Phil Schneider is a really incredible character, because he came out very early on in the 90s talking about his involvement in building the Dulce, New Mexico, base and other bases. He talked about how the military/industrial complex had been using government funding. And, in that regard. public funding, to build clandestinely these underground facilities to house and develop and research exotic technologies and keep these out of the sight and sound of the public. To have command and control and security over these projects so they could never see the light of day.

And, you know, people say he killed himself, people say he was "suicided." I think the most interesting thing about his story is just the fact that he was such a sort of heroic character when it came to doing his lectures in the early 90s until he passed in 1996. And just how much people were attracted to his charisma and the story of underground bases. And that's the real showstopper there, in my opinion. The fact that there ARE underground bases, there ARE secret facilities, and there possibly IS an extraterrestrial presence here on Earth and around Earth that has been here for a long time and still continues today.

Darcy Weir is a producer and director, known for "Being Taken - Director's Cut"(2021) (2018), "Beyond The Spectrum" (2017) and "The Underground" (2021).

DULCE WARRIORS

DULCE - A COMEDY OF HORRORS

Eric Hollerbach is a stand-up comedian and actor who says that he has become obsessed with the book *"The Dulce Wars,"* written by Branton and Commander X. His obsession led him to write a screenplay called "Dulce," which seeks to humanize and dramatize the operations of a worldwide, all-encompassing, alien conspiracy. Though originally conceived as a motion picture, Hollerbach's aspirations grew to where he saw —"foresaw?" – his creation becoming a series you can binge watch on "Netflix" or "Hulu."

Hollerbach started doing stand-up open mics at 16 in NYC. He did some training with the Upright Citizens Brigade Improv Theater, and a week before he graduated from Eugene Lang College; he was performing on the UCB Main Stage.

In 2009, Eric moved to Los Angeles, where he continued to perform Improv and stand-up comedy while working on reality shows such as "Shark Tank," "Amazing Race," Hulu's "If I Can Dream," and many more.

In Los Angeles, Eric produced a few of his own projects including the pilot "Damien Shadows PI: Psychic Investigator" and the web series "Here Comes Godot." He's also produced, and hosted the feature-length short-horror-film anthology "Theater of the Deranged II." (Out on DVD, Blu Ray, & VOD with Troma.)

Hollerbach obtained his MFA in Screenwriting from the University of New Orleans in 2017. In 2020, he dropped three stand-up specials on YouTube. "Conspiracies and Dick Jokes," "Fart Porn in Beer Halls," and "It's a Medical Device."

He currently lives in Austin, TX, and performs stand-up comedy full-time.

And while Hollenbach's script is top secret "for executive eyes only," he did give permission to snoop around a bit and offer a tad bit of his series plot.

****

"Tone: Sci-Fi Mystery Dulce" is a suspenseful hour-long science fiction series. Elements of dark comedy keep the bad-guys more interesting.

SEASON ONE - EPISODE ONE - DESCRIPTIONS

Columbus, Ohio (1990)

DULCE WARRIORS

"The Best Fish in the Pond" (65 Min) SEAN is a fetus in an incubator, in a secret government laboratory under Dulce, NM, in 1984. In this facility, the US Military secretly works with Draconian Aliens, who supply them with them higher technology. In exchange, the US Government allows Dracos to abduct a certain amount of American citizens for experimentation and food. Sean has been created by Dr. Green and Father Murphy, who congratulate each other on a successful human-alien hybrid. Sean also had a successful brain-chip implantation.

"Father Murphy petitions Dr. Green for foster parents to adopt Sean as well as half this 'batch' of hybrids as soon as possible. Father Murphy wants to experiment by allowing a certain number of foster parents to adopt these cloned children. He believes traditional families may foster better, more creative, scientists in the future. Dr. Green, a man who likes to have more control on test subjects, brings up security and secrecy concerns, but slowly relents. After tests and experimentation, we meet the Wessell family. A dopey all-American family from outside Columbus, Ohio. Gary (33), a-Marine-turned-hardware store owner is having trouble conceiving with his wife Olivia (26).

"Dr. Green, slides into the role of their local fertility specialist and suggests adopting Sean. He lies, saying Sean was left on the doorstep of Father Murphy's church. A church where Gary and Olivia are parishioners. Father Murphy and Dr. Green perform more tests, on Sean who is eventually given to the Wessell family. Sean, (6 for the rest of the season in 1990) starts to showcase incredible abilities. Olivia takes him to a local Chinese Restaurant, Peking Wok, where he speaks fluent Chinese with the cook. Sean attends Saint Catherine's Academy for first grade, run by Father Murphy. There, he meets his love interest, Victoria Marlow (6) an orphaned clone living at Saint Catherine's. Again, half the batch live on campus of Saint Catherine's.

"In class, Father Murphy projects different Catholic Bishops on the wall, and the students learn the art of MAPPING. They successfully pin photos of the Bishops to a cork-board world-map to match the Bishop to the correct diocese. They use natural psychic abilities with the coaching of Father Murphy. Captain Mark Richards (39), an Air Force Intelligence Officer, uses Sean and Victoria's mapping skills to locate his friend lost in Afghanistan. During a camping trip Gary nearly tells Sean about his adoption. Olivia loudly interrupts him. At the end of the episode the Wessell family invites Victoria over for dinner. After Victoria shares the fact that she's an orphan, living at Saint Catherine's, Gary shares the fact that Sean is too. Sean has a hard time dealing with this news.

* * * * * * * * *

We recently welcomed Eric on "Exploring The Bizarre," where he not only revealed plans for his Dulce series but spoke about secret societies in general and the Masonic Order in particular, as well as telling us about an "old friend" of his who might have a bit of reptilian blood running through his "veins" (if reptilians have veins of course?).

You don't have to be scared - though maybe you should be! – But in any regard check the show out in this archived presentation on KCORradio.com

https://kcorradio.com/Library/archive/exploring-the-bizarre/2021/april/eric-hollerbach.mp3

Stand-up comedian Eric Hollerbach appeared on "Exploring the Bizarre" to discuss his obsession with the Dulce mystery.

Eric Hollerbach said he became obsessed with Dulce after reading Branton's *"The Dulce Wars."* His obsession led him to write a screenplay called "Dulce," which seeks to humanize and dramatize the operations of a worldwide, all-encompassing alien conspiracy.

SECTION TWO

The Faces Behind Dulce

9.

ENIGMATIC PERSONALITIES BEHIND THE INITIAL DULCE BASE RUMORS

When it comes to the "Dulce base" topic, it is really not about the "base" itself ....(since, apparently and evidence-wise so far, it does not seem to exist), but rather about the various personalities that have initially promoted this myth.

Let's examine some of the enigmatic personalities, how it all started (from around 1979 to 1983), etc. and how, ultimately, deluded con artist Phil Schneider took advantage of the Dulce base myth.

PAUL BENNEWITZ

Owner of Thunder Scientific Corporation (contractor to Kirtland Air Force Base), located right next to the entrance of Kirtland AFB in Albuquerque, NM, presently operated by his sons.

DULCE WARRIORS

From around 1979 Paul Bennewitz began to witness some strange lights hovering over Manzano underground nuclear storage area, not too far from his residence in the Four Hills area of Albuquerque.

Some researchers (such as Greg Bishop) theorize that he was looking at some tests of Project Starfire (laser-based optical tracking system being developed at that time by Sandia Laboratories next to the Manzano base) or possibly some tests of prototypes of remotely-controlled aerial platforms (present-day UAVs) possibly being independently developed by Sandia Laboratories at that time.

Paul Bennewitz later became convinced that those objects were somehow related to an underground base in northern New Mexico near Dulce, a suggestion seemingly pushed then by a Richard C. Doty of AFOSI at Kirtland Air Force Base.

Articles on Bennewitz soon began to appear in newspapers such as the Albuquerque Journal and Albuquerque Tribune.

Paul Bennewitz began to suffer from paranoia and was later institutionalized.

It is quite possible that Paul Bennewitz had long only pretended that he had been "brainwashed" by some within the AFOSI, while he continued to conduct his own investigations into Dulce.

Another possible scenario may have been that there was a dissension among the AFOSI and an element among the group may have accidentally provided Bennewitz with some crucial information on an alleged crash of a U.S. military's prototype stealth aircraft near Mount Archuleta.

He passed away in 2003. His remains are buried in Veterans Cemetery in Santa Fe.

Paul Bennewitz' sons refuse to be interviewed, the main reason being that Thunder Scientific Corporation still does business with Kirtland AFB. They sell military grade humidifiers and calibration instruments, many of which were developed, modified and improved by the late Paul Bennewitz.

Paul Bennewitz' wife, Cindy Bennewitz, still lives at the residence, which is located close to the original Manzano underground nuclear storage facility (which allegedly was closed down in 1992) in the Four Hills area of Albuquerque.

DULCE WARRIORS

MYRNA HANSEN

In 1980 she claimed to have been abducted near Cimarron, NM and claimed to have been taken to an unknown underground location.

She was at that time a resident of Eagle Nest, New Mexico.

Paul Bennewitz interviewed her at his house, together with Leo Sprinkle who did a hypnotic regression.

Paul Bennewitz later on decided that she must have been taken into the Dulce base.

This was allegedly only after Bennewitz begun to suspect that there was a base in Dulce.

Later on, a Richard C. Doty (who was with AFOSI Kirtland AFB at that time) suggested to her that she might have been taken to an underground weapons storage facility in northern New Mexico.

TOM ADAMS

He was investigating cattle mutilations in the late 1970s.

Tom Adams first heard about the Dulce base from reading Paul Bennewitz' article in the newspaper and other sources from around 1981.

It is alleged that Tom Adams knew "Ann West".

"ANN WEST"

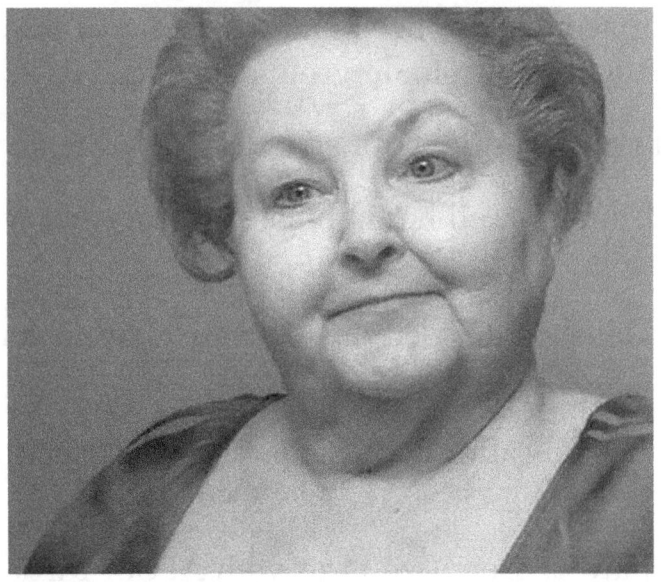

Her true identity was not initially confirmed, although it was Tal Levesque who claimed that she had been on Facebook with a different name (Cherry Hinkle, who claimed that her "half-alien" cat has lived for 29 years).

She was said to have been an acquaintance of Tom Adams.

"ANN WEST" (Cherry Hinkle) claimed to have drawn the initial pictures of the vats of the Dulce base in 1987, yet claimed to have never heard of Paul Bennewitz before.

She allegedly knew Tal Levesque.

She also claims to have known a "Thomas Edwin Castello."

Tal Levesque claims that she visited him and his wife and also "Thomas Edwin Castello" in Santa Fe.

Tal Levesque claims that Ann West is dangerous and is part of the "invisible government."

However, Levesque's claim (that Ann West is part of the "invisible government") ...sure sounds like lunacy.

JOHN LEAR

Lear heard about Dulce allegedly from "Ann West."

Lear befriended TAL through John Grace (a.k.a. Val Valerian).

According to Tal Levesque, John Lear retouched the Dulce drawings of "Ann West" that he received in 1987.

Lear first came up with his *Hypothesis* in 1988 about Dulce and also about Area 51.

On December 29, 1987, Lear released a "Public Statement" (revised on March 25, 1988), claiming that his contacts in intelligence, investigating the allegations that the executive and military-industrial branches of the United States "government" knows about, and colludes with, alien forces.

Lear claims that the U.S. has a treaty with aliens that allow them to establish bases, with the help of humans, at secret locations throughout the country…Dulce being one of these bases.

John Lear has never been taken seriously by the UFO community.

Some people suspect that John Lear purposely throws in some ridiculous-sounding items as part of PSYOPS.

He recently claimed that there are cities on the back side of the moon.

TAL LEVESQUE, a.k.a., TAL or Jason Bishop

(The enigmatic Jason Bishop, a.k.a., TAL Levesque when he appeared on a Japanese Nippon TV special two-hour program on Area 51 and Dulce in March of 1990).

His real name is Thomas Allen LeVesque ("Le Vesque" in French means "The Bishop", thus his a.k.a.).

TAL Levesque claimed that he worked in Santa Fe as a security person for a private company around 1980 or 1981.

He claimed to have begun contact with "Thomas E. Castello" who, Tal Levesque claims, worked in the same company in Santa Fe.

"Thomas E. Castello" allegedly revealed his secrets to Tal -- (the secret was that there was an underground U.S./alien bio-lab under Archuleta Mesa, next to Dulce and that he had worked as a security person at that facility).

But before coming out with this "Thomas Edwin Castello" story, Tal Levesque also seems to have heard initially about the Dulce base rumors from reading about Paul Bennewitz.

Tal Levesque claimed that he was visited by a tall Reptoid at his home in Santa Fe in 1979. He currently lives in Mariposa, California.

It was Jason Bishop (a.k.a., TAL Levesque) who originally came out with the so-called underground tunnel systems map with Dulce, New Mexico as its central hub.

(A few years ago I had corresponded with Jason Bishop's relative Carolyn LeVesque of Arroyo Grande who told me that he has always had some type of psychological problem (i.e., a form of mental "delusion"), to put it mildly – probably from indoctrination from reading too many SHAVER MYSTERY science fiction novels of the 1950s that dealt with underground civilizations).

"THOMAS EDWIN CASTELLO"

Of course, there are many persons with the same name.

However, an "alleged" retired Air Force Colonel who claimed that he was involved in Dulce, claimed that there has never been a Thomas Edwin Castello that was ever employed as security personnel in Dulce.

(The late Gabe Valdez also stated that there was never such a person connected to the alleged Dulce base).

CHRISTA TILTON

Some researchers seem to say that she came to the scene slightly after "Ann West."

They say that Christa Tilton and Tom Adams were initially partners and that she was in touch with Myrna Hansen.

According to Tim Beckley, Christa Tilton later on got together with Wendell Stevens.

Christa Tilton was said to have distributed her manuscript, *"The Bennewitz Papers"* in 1987.

She claimed that she was in touch with a Richard C. Doty (formerly with AFOSI at Kirtland AFB in Albuquerque).

Christa Tilton was featured on a Japanese TV program about the Dulce base back in 1989 and 1990. Christa Tilton flew over the Archuleta Mesa and over Soldier Canyon with Junichi Yaoi of Nippon TV in 1989.

She appeared on Japanese TV a couple of times and claimed to have taken a photo of a circular structure over Soldier Canyon, which is slightly SW of Dulce.

Tilton, in her manuscript *"The Bennewitz Papers"* expressed her belief that the whole "Thomas E. Castello" story was a fabrication.

"Ann West", in turn, reportedly claimed that Christa Tilton's information was nothing more than disinformation of the highest degree.

BRANTON – a.k.a., Bruce Walton, a.k.a., Alan B. de Walton

Beginning in the early 1990s, "Branton" compiled a book called the "*DULCE BOOK*," and also "*THE DULCE WARS*."

Walton allegedly got most of the information from TAL...some from John Lear, some from Val Valerian (John Grace).

Branton's earliest writings were articles for the fanzine "The Hollow Hassle," dealing with underground mysteries and lost civilizations.

Branton is the author of a number of books such as "*A Guide to the Inner Earth*", "*The Omega Files*", and "*Reptilian Humanoids [Homo-Subterreptus] Case Files.*"

In May 2001, Branton was struck by a car while riding his bicycle in Provo, Utah. He was flown by a LifeFlight helicopter to the LDS Hospital in Salt Lake City in critical condition. He sustained injuries to his head and had several broken bones in his face. His family said that due to his head injury, Branton's recovery was slow and he suffered from continuing cognitive problems.

Tal Levesque reported that Branton was incarcerated in 2009 in Utah for felony charges. He was later released after serving two years in prison.

GABE VALDEZ

The late Gabe Valdez was a retired New Mexico State Patrol Officer who was in charge of the Dulce area for many years (from the early 1970s to the late 1980s).

He passed away on August 6, 2011 at his residence in Albuquerque.

Valdez claimed that the government was most likely responsible for the cattle mutilations which started happening from around 1975.

He claimed that the government may have begun to periodically monitor the radiation levels of certain cattle some years later, after the 1967 underground nuclear explosion (Project Gasbuggy) which took place about 22 miles southwest of Dulce.

Valdez also stated that the government "staged" several UFO incidents in the Dulce area (Archuleta Mesa, etc.) by use of high tech equipment such as prototypes of holographic image projections as well as unmanned aerial vehicles or remotely-controlled platforms that were made to resemble "flying saucers."

Valdez believed that bio-warfare experiments were conducted at Dulce and that "UFO/alien" stories were concocted by the government as cover stories to conceal various Black Projects in the area.

WILLIAM "BILL" MOORE

It was Moore who first propagated (or "revived") the story about Roswell in 1980 when he (together with Charles Berlitz) published the book "*INCIDENT AT ROSWELL*" (until this book came out, most Americans had no interest or knowledge about the Roswell incident since it was long forgotten and dismissed as misidentification by the U.S. Army in 1947).

He claimed that around the same time that he began to propagate the Roswell story, he was working with Richard C. Doty of Kirtland AFB and participated in a disinformation ploy to saturate Paul Bennewitz (who was pursuing his independent investigations on Dulce) with false information on the Dulce base.

This he claimed in a 1989 MUFON Conference that took place in Las Vegas, Nevada.

However there is no verifiable documentation whatsoever that Moore participated in such disinformation ploy in any official capacity except for his verbal "confession" that he made at a 1989 MUFON conference in Las Vegas, Nevada.

RICHARD C. DOTY

Initially with Kirtland Air Force Base AFOSI around 1979, 1980 and 1981 in Albuquerque, New Mexico. He was not a high-ranking officer.

He claimed that he participated in disinformation in official capacity, along with Moore.

Again, there is no documentation that he participated in such disinformation ploy at Kirtland AFB AFOSI in any official capacity, even though Paul Bennewitz' name and Doty's name appear on one or two Kirtland OSI documents because Kirtland AFB invited Bennewitz to testify to what he allegedly was seeing over the Manzano storage areas.

Later on Richard C. Doty became a promoter of the SERPO PROJECT (which some researchers seem to describe as being a total fabrication).

Project Camelot seems to have bought Doty's story hook, line and sinker. Presently he is working as New Mexico Highway Patrol Officer, just about to retire soon.

PHIL SCHNEIDER

Phil Schneider was never a part of the initial Dulce base rumors.

Apparently he must have read many articles concerning the alleged Dulce Base by the time he came out into the scene in 1995 and started giving lectures.

It was only in 1989 that Bob Lazar first came out with the story that there was an altercation between the U.S. military and "alien entities" in an underground installation. Lazar never specified any location. Phil Schneider also heard about the Bob Lazar story.

Apparently, knowing that no one had yet come up with any claim of personal involvement in the alleged 1979 "altercation", he conveniently cast himself into the scene, claiming that he was a survivor of the Dulce "Wars."

Schneider died in 1996, apparently by suicide, but there were some inconsistencies with the police and coroners reports that led some to believe that Schneider could have been the victim of foul play.

Source: August 29, 2016 - CIVILIAN INTELLIGENCE NEWS SERVICE, by Norio Hayakawa.

10.

JOHN LEAR'S INCREDIBLE DULCE THEORIES—AND BEYOND — WAY BEYOND!

PUBLISHER'S NOTE: John Lear always seemed comfortable talking about UFOs, no matter how strange and bizarre the topic got. He showed up several times at our UFO conferences and held the audience spellbound. Some of the subjects he covered were so bizarre I had a hard time giving them credibility, but Lear is Lear and he has been a controversial figure in the field for quite a few years. He was one of the original backers of the Dulce base, and added bases on the moon, which were also under the greys' control. Here are his views in a - pardon the expression - "nut shell."

* * * * * * * * *

John Lear, a captain of a major U.S. Airline, has flown over 160 different types of aircraft in over 50 different countries. He holds 17 world speed records in the Lear Jet and is the only pilot ever to hold every airman certificate issued by the Federal Aviation Administration. Mr. Lear has flown missions worldwide for the CIA and other government agencies. He has flown clandestine missions in war-zones and hot-spots around the world, often engineering hairs'-breadth escapes under dangerous conditions. A former Nevada State Senatorial candidate, he is the son of William P. Lear, designer of the Lear Jet executive airplane, the 8-track stereo, and founder of the LEAR Siegler Corporation.

John Lear became interested in the subject of UFOs 13 months prior to the date given below, after talking with a friend in the United States Air Force by the name of Greg Wilson, who had witnessed a UFO landing at Bentwaters AFB, near London, England, during which three small "grey" aliens walked up to the Wing Commander. Since then Lear has tapped his contacts in intelligence, investigating the allegations that the executive and military-industrial branches of the United States "government" knows about, and colludes with, alien forces. Lear no longer suggests the following scenario is a "possibility" - he emphatically states that the aliens are here and that many of them bode us ill.

"It started after World War II," he begins.

"We [the Allied forces] recovered some alien technology from Germany. Not all that they had; some of it disappeared. It appears that sometime in the late '30s, Germany recovered a saucer. What happened to it we don't know. But what we did get was some kind of ray gun..."

* * * * * * * * *

The following is a "Public Statement" released by John Lear on December 29, 1987, and revised on March 25, 1988. It was originally sent to some of Lear's personal friends and research associates, who in turn put pressure on the Ace Pilot to release this information publicly. The first version of the statement was apparently meant for the "inside" crowd of researchers with whom Lear associated, whereas the following revision contains the same information as the first edition, yet is directed towards the public in general:

NOTE TO THE PRESS:

"The government of the United States continues to rely on your personal and professional gullibility to suppress the information contained herein. Your cooperation over the past 40 years has exceeded OUR wildest expectations and we salute you.

"'The sun does not revolve around the Earth.'

"'The United States Government has been in business with little grey extraterrestrials for about 20 years.'

"The first truth stated here got Giordano Bruno burned at the stake in AD 1600 for daring to propose that it was real. THE SECOND TRUTH HAS GOTTEN FAR MORE PEOPLE KILLED TRYING TO STATE IT PUBLICLY THAN WILL EVER BE KNOWN. (Note: emphasis here and throughout this section is ours. - Branton)

"But the truth must be told. The fact that the Earth revolves around the sun was successfully suppressed by the [Roman] church for over 200 years. It eventually caused a major upheaval in the church, government, and thought. A realignment of social and traditional values. That was in the 1600's.

THE HORRIBLE TRUTH

"Now, about 400 years after the first truth was pronounced, we must again face the shocking facts. The 'horrible truth' the government has been hiding from us for over 40 years. Unfortunately, the 'horrible truth' is far more horrible than the government ever imagined.

"In its effort to 'protect democracy,' our government sold us to the aliens. And here is how it happened. But before I begin, I'd like to offer a word in defense of those who bargained us away. They had the best of intentions.

"Germany may have recovered a flying saucer as early as 1939. General James H. Doolittle went to Norway in 1952 to inspect a flying saucer that had crashed there in Spitzbergen.

"The 'horrible truth' was known by only a very few persons: They were indeed ugly little creatures, shaped like praying mantises... Of the original group that were the first to learn the 'horrible truth,' SEVERAL COMMITTED SUICIDE, the most prominent of which was Defense Secretary [and Secretary of the NAVY] James V. Forrestal, who jumped to his death from a 16th story hospital window.

(Note: William Cooper, a former member of a Navy Intelligence briefing team, insists that Forrestal was in fact murdered by CIA agents who made his death look like a suicide. Based on sensitive documents Cooper claims to have read, two CIA agents entered the hospital room, tied a bed sheet around Forrestal's neck and to a light fixture, and threw him out the window to hang. The bed sheet[s] broke and he fell to his death, screaming on his way down according to some witnesses "We're being invaded!" - Branton).

"Secretary Forrestal's medical records are sealed to this day.

"President Truman put a lid on the secret and turned the screws so tight that the general public still thinks that flying saucers are a joke. Have I ever got a surprise for them!

"In 1947, President Truman established a group of 12 of the top military scientific personnel of their time. They were known as MJ-12. Although the group exists today, none of the ORIGINAL members are still alive. The last one to die was Gordon Gray, former Secretary of the Army, in 1984.

"As each member passed away, the group itself appointed a new member to fill the position. There is some speculation that the group known as MJ-12 expanded to at least seven more members.

"There were several more saucer crashes in the late 1940's, one in Roswell, New Mexico; one in Aztec, New Mexico; and one near Laredo, Texas, about 30 miles inside the Mexican border.

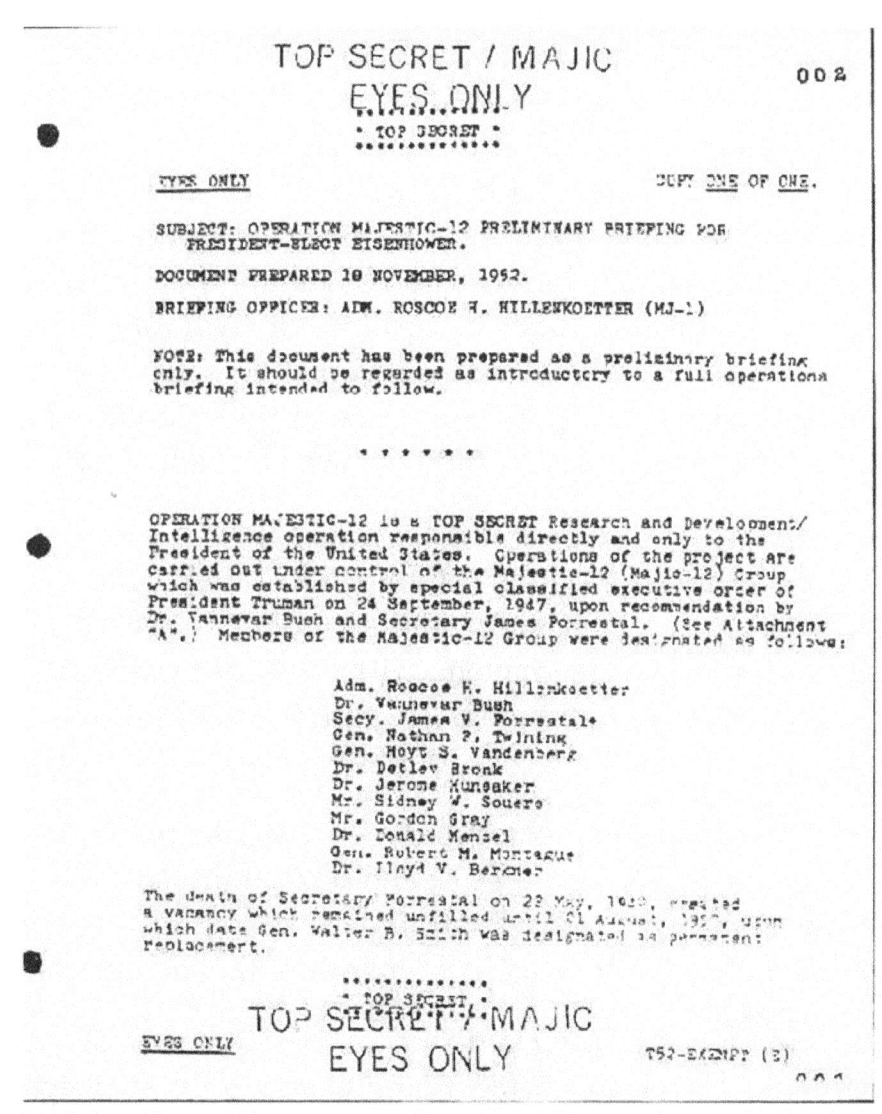

"Majestic-12" document dated November 19, 1952.

DULCE WARRIORS

WHY THE COVER-UP?

"Consider, if you will, the position of the United States Government at that time. They proudly thought of themselves as the most powerful nation on Earth, having recently produced the atomic bomb, an achievement so stupendous, it would take Russia four years to catch up, and only with the help of traitors to democracy. They had built a jet aircraft that had exceeded the speed of sound in flight. They had built jet bombers with inter-continental range that could carry weapons of enormous destruction. It was the post war era, and the future seemed bright. Now imagine what it was like for those same leaders, all of whom had witnessed the panic of Orson Wells' radio broadcast, 'The War of the Worlds,' in 1938. Thousands of Americans panicked at a realistically presented invasion of Earth by beings from another planet. Imagine their horror as they actually viewed THE DEAD BODIES OF THESE FRIGHTENING LITTLE CREATURES WITH ENORMOUS EYES, REPTILIAN SKIN AND CLAW LIKE FINGERS. Imagine their shock as they attempted to determine how these strange 'saucers' were powered and could discover no part even remotely similar to components they were familiar with: no cylinders or pistons, no vacuum tubes or turbines or hydraulic actuators. It is only when you fully understand the overwhelming helplessness the government was faced with in the late 40s that you can comprehend their perceived need for a total, thorough and sweeping cover-up, to include the use of 'deadly force.'

"The cover-up was so successful that as late as 1985 a senior scientist with the Jet Propulsion Laboratory in Pasadena, California, Dr. Al Hibbs, would look at a video tape of an enormous flying saucer and state for the record, 'I'm not going to assign anything to that [UFO] phenomena without a lot more data.' Dr. Hibbs was looking at the naked emperor and saying, 'He certainly looks naked, but that doesn't prove he's naked.'

"In July 1952, a panicked government watched helplessly as a squadron of 'flying saucers' flew over Washington, D.C., and buzzed the White House, the Capitol Building, and the Pentagon. It took all the imagination and intimidation the government could muster to force that incident out of the memory of the public.

"Thousands of sightings occurred during the Korean War and several more saucers were retrieved by the Air Force. Some were stored at Wright-Patterson Air Force Base, some were stored at Air Force bases near the locations of the crash site.

"One saucer was so enormous and the logistic problems in transportation so enormous that it was buried at the crash site and remains there today. The stories are legendary on transporting crashed saucers over long distances, moving only at night, purchasing complete farms, slashing through forests, blocking major highways, sometimes driving two or three lo-boys in tandem with an extraterrestrial load a hundred feet in diameter. (It is alleged that ALPHA or BLUE Teams out of Wright-Patterson AFB were the ones who were most often mobilized to carry out "crash-retrieval" operations. - Branton)

"On April 30, 1964, the first communication [occurred] between these aliens and the 'U.S. Government.' (Others claim that there was an even earlier contact-communication in 1954 during the Eisenhower administration. - Branton)

THE SANCTIONING OF ALIEN ABDUCTIONS

"During the period of 1969-1971, MJ-12, representing the U.S. Government, made a deal with these creatures, called EBEs [Extraterrestrial Biological Entities, named by Detley Bronk, original MJ-12 member and 6th President of John Hopkins University]. The 'deal' was that in exchange for 'technology' that they would provide to us, we agreed to 'ignore' the abductions that were going on and suppress information on the cattle mutilations. The EBEs assured MJ-12 that the abductions [usually lasting about 2 hours] were merely the ongoing monitoring of developing civilizations.

"In fact, the purposes for the abductions turned out to be:

"(1) The insertion of a 3mm spherical device through the nasal cavity of the abductee into the brain [optic and/or nerve center]. The device is used for the biological monitoring, tracking, and control of the abductee.

"(2) Implementation of posthypnotic suggestion to carry out a specific activity during a specific time period, the actuation of which will occur within the next two to five years.

"(3) Termination of some people so that they could function as living sources for biological material and substances.

"(4) TERMINATION OF INDIVIDUALS WHO REPRESENT A THREAT TO THE CONTINUATION OF THEIR ACTIVITY.

Did the U.S. government make a "deal with the devil" with extraterrestrial visitors in order to obtain alien technology in exchange for human victims?

"(5) Effect genetic engineering experiments.

"(6) Impregnation of human females and early termination of pregnancies to secure the crossbreed infant.

(Note: Or perhaps a better term for it would be a "genetically altered" infant, since there has been no evidence forthcoming that an actual 'hybrid' between humans and the 'EBE' or 'Grey' species has been successful. In other words, the offspring would tend to fall to one side or the other, a 'reptilioid' or 'grey' entity possessing no 'soul-energy-matrix,' or a humanoid being possessing such a matrix or soul although somewhat altered genetically in its outward physical appearance or characteristics. - Branton).

"The U.S. Government was NOT initially aware of the far reaching consequences of their 'deal.' They were led to believe that the abductions were essentially benign and, since they figured that the abductions would probably go on anyway, whether they agreed or not, they merely insisted that a current list of abductees be submitted, on a periodic basis, to MJ-12 and the National Security Council. Does this sound incredible? An actual list of abductees sent to the National Security Council? Read on, because I have news for you...

"The EBEs have a genetic disorder in that their digestive system is atrophied and not functional... In order to sustain themselves they use enzyme or hormonal secretions obtained from the tissues that they extract from humans and animals.

"The secretions obtained are then mixed with hydrogen peroxide [to kill germs, viruses, etc.] and applied on the skin by spreading or dipping parts of their bodies in the solution. The body absorbs the solution, then excretes the waste back through the skin. (Urine is also excreted through the skin in this manner, which may explain the ammonia-like stench that many abductees or witnesses have reported during encounters with the grey-type 'aliens'. - Branton).

"The cattle mutilations that were prevalent throughout the period from 1973 to 1983 and publicly noted through newspaper and magazine stories and included in a documentary produced by Linda Howe for Denver CBS affiliate KMGH-TV, were for the collection of these tissues by the aliens. The mutilations included genitals taken, rectums cored out to the colon, eyes, tongue, and throat all surgically removed with extreme precision. In some cases the incisions were made by cutting between the cells, a process we are not yet capable of performing in the field. In many of the mutilations there was no blood found at all in the carcass, yet there was no vascular collapse of the internal organs.

HUMAN MUTILATIONS

This has also been noted in the human mutilations, one of the first of which was Sgt. Jonathan P. Lovette at the White Sands Missile Test Range in 1956, who was found three days after an Air Force Major had witnessed his abduction by a 'disk shaped' object at 0300 while on search for missile debris downrange. His genitals had been removed, rectum cored out in a surgically precise 'plug' up to the colon, eyes removed and all blood removed with, again, no vascular collapse. From some of the evidence it is apparent that this surgery is accomplished, in most cases, while the victim, animal or human, is still alive.

(Note: According to former Green Beret commander Bill English, this incident was also mentioned in the Above-Top-Secret *"GRUDGE/BLUE BOOK REPORT NO. 13"* which was never released with the rest of the innocuous and voluminous "Project Blue Book" reports. The "Blue Teams" who were sent on crash-retrieval operations were reportedly working on behalf of the covert branch of the Blue Book operations, and Ufological legend has it that a secret warehouse with multiple underground levels exists at Wright Patterson AFB in Ohio, one which is literally packed with alien craft, hardware, and even alien bodies 'on ice'. Wright Patterson was - and is? - the headquarters of Project Blue Book. - Branton)

"The various parts of the body are taken to various underground laboratories, one of which is known to be near the small New Mexico town of Dulce. This jointly-occupied [CIA-alien] facility has been described as enormous, with huge tiled walls that 'go on forever.' Witnesses have reported huge vats filled with amber liquid with parts of human bodies being stirred inside.

BROKEN BARGAINS

"After the initial agreement, Groom Lake, one of the nation's most secret test centers, was closed for a period of about a year, sometime between about 1972 and 1974, and a huge underground facility was constructed for and with the help of the EBEs. The 'bargained for' technology was set in place but could only be operated by the EBEs themselves. Needless to say, the advanced technology could not be used against the EBEs themselves, even if needed.

"During the period between 1979 and 1983, it became increasingly obvious to MJ-12 that things were not going as planned. It became known that many more people [in the thousands] were being abducted than were listed on the official abduction lists. In addition, it became known that some, not all, but some of the nation's missing children had been used for secretions and other parts required by the aliens.

"In 1979, there was an altercation of sorts at the Dulce laboratory. A special armed forces unit was called in to try and free a number of our people trapped in the facility that had become aware of what was really going on. According to one source, 66 of the soldiers were killed and our people were not freed.

"By 1984, MJ-12 must have been in stark terror at the mistake they had made in dealing with the EBEs. They had subtly promoted 'Close Encounters of the Third Kind' and 'E.T.' to get the public used to 'odd looking' aliens that were compassionate, benevolent and very much our 'space brothers.' MJ-12 'sold' the EBEs to the public, and were now faced with the fact that quite the opposite was true. In addition, a plan was formulated in 1968 to make the public aware of the existence of aliens on earth over the next 20 years to be culminated with several documentaries to be released during 1985-1987 period of time. These documentaries would explain the history and intentions of the EBEs. The discovery of the 'Grand Deception' put the entirety of the plans, hopes and dreams of MJ-12 into utter confusion and panic.

"Meeting at the 'Country Club,' a remote lodge with a private golf course, comfortable sleeping and working quarters, and its own private airstrip built by and exclusively for the members of MJ-12, it was a factional fight of what to do now. Part of MJ-12 wanted to confess the whole scheme and the shambles it had become to the public, beg their forgiveness and ask for their support. The other part [the majority] of MJ-12 argued that there was no way they could do that, that the situation was untenable and there was no use in exciting the public with the 'horrible truth' and that the best plan was to continue the development of a weapon that could be used against the EBEs under the guise of 'SDI,' the Strategic Defense Initiative, which had nothing whatsoever to do with a defense for inbound Russian nuclear missiles. As these words are being written, Dr. Edward Teller, 'father' of the H-Bomb, is personally in the test tunnels of the Nevada Test Site, driving his workers and associates in the words of one, 'like a man possessed.' And well he should, for Dr. Teller is a member of MJ-12 along with Dr. Kissinger, Admiral Bobby Inman, and possibly Admiral Poindexter, to name a few of the current members of MJ-12.

BILL MOORE'S PART OF THE PICTURE

"Before the 'Grand Deception' was discovered, and according to a meticulous plan for metered release of information to the public, several documentaries and videotapes were made. William Moore, a Burbank, California, based UFO researcher who wrote *'The Roswell Incident'* - a book published in 1980 that detailed the crash, recovery and subsequent cover-up of a UFO with four alien bodies - has a videotape of two newsmen interviewing a military officer associated with MJ-12. This military officer answers questions relating to the history of MJ-12 and the cover-up, the recovery of a number of flying saucers and the existence of a live alien [one of three living aliens captured and designated, or named, EBE-1, EBE-2, and EBE-3, being held in a facility designated as YY-II at Los Alamos, New Mexico. The only other facility of this type, which is electromagnetically secure, is at Edwards Air Force Base in Mojave, California]. The officer names those previously mentioned plus a few others: Harold Brown, Richard Helms, Gen. Vernon Walters, JPL's Dr. Allen and Dr. Theodore van Karman, to name a few of the current and past members of MJ-12.

Bob Lazar took John Lear's advice and applied for a job with a government agency and claims he ended up working at Area 51.

"The officer also relates the fact that the EBEs claim to have created Christ. The EBEs have a type of recording device that has recorded all of Earth's history and can display it in the form of a hologram. This hologram can be filmed but because of the way holograms work does not come out very clear on movie film or videotape. The crucifixion of Christ on the Mount of Olives (this actually took place on the hill Calvary, not the Mt. of Olives - Branton) has allegedly been put on film to show the public. The EBEs 'claim' to have created Christ, which, in view of the 'Grand Deception,' could be an effort to disrupt traditional values for undetermined reasons.

"Another videotape allegedly in existence is an interview with an EBE. Since EBEs communicate telepathically (via psionic crystalline transceiver-like implants that link the Greys together into a mass collective-hive-mind – Branton), an Air Force Colonel serves as interpreter. Just before the recent stock market correction in October of 1987, several newsmen, including Bill Moore, had been invited to Washington D.C., to personally film the EBE in a similar type interview and distribute the film to the public. Apparently, because of the correction in the market, it was felt the timing was not propitious. In any case, it certainly seems like an odd method to inform the public of extraterrestrials, but it would be in keeping with the actions of a panicked organization who at this point in time doesn't know which way to turn.

"Moore is also in possession of more Aquarius documents, a few pages of which leaked out several years ago and detailed the super-secret NSA project which had been denied by them until just recently. In a letter to Senator John Glenn, NSA's Director of Policy, Julia B. Wetzel, wrote, 'Apparently there is or was an Air Force project with the name [Aquarius] which dealt with UFO's. Coincidentally, there is also an NSA project by that name.' NSA's Project Aquarius deals specifically with 'communications with the aliens' [EBEs]. Within the Aquarius program was 'Project Snowbird,' a project to test-fly a recovered alien aircraft at Groom Lake, Nevada. This project continues today at that location. In the words of an individual who works at Groom Lake, 'Our people are much better at taking things apart than they are at putting them back together.'

"Moore, who claims he has a contact with MJ-12, feels that they have been stringing him along, slipping him documents and providing him with leads, promising to go public with some of the information on extraterrestrials by the end of 1987.

"Certain of Moore's statements lead one to believe that Moore himself is a government agent working for MJ-12, not to be strung along, but to string along ever hopeful UFOlogists that the truth is just around the corner. Consider...

"1. Moore states emphatically that he is not a government agent, although when Lee Graham [a Southern California based UFOlogist] was investigated by DIS [Defense Investigative Service] for possession of classified documents received from Moore, Moore himself was not.

"2. Moore states emphatically that the cattle mutilations of 1973-1983 were a hoax by Linda Howe [producer of 'A Strange Harvest'] to create publicity for herself. He cites the book 'Mute Evidence' as the bottom line of the hoax. 'Mute Evidence' was a government sponsored book to explain the mutilations in conventional terms.

"3. Moore states that the U.S.A.F. Academy physics book, *'Introductory Space Science'*, vol. II chapter 13, entitled 'Unidentified Flying Objects', which describes four of the most commonly seen aliens [one of which is the EBE] was written by Lt. Col. Edward R. Therkelson and Major Donald B. Carpenter, Air Force personnel who did not know what they were talking about and were merely citing 'crackpot' references. He, Moore, states that the book was withdrawn to excise the chapter.

"If the government felt they were being forced to acknowledge the existence of aliens on Earth because of the overwhelming evidence such as the October and November sightings in Wytheville, Va., and recently released books such as *'Night Siege'* [Hynek, J. Allen; Imbrogno, Phillip J.; Pratt, Bob, Ballantine Books, Random House, New York], and taking into consideration the 'Grand Deception' and the obviously hostile intent of the EBEs, it might be expedient for MJ-12 to admit the EBEs but conceal the information on the mutilations and abductions. If MJ-12 and Moore were in some kind of agreement, then it would be beneficial to Moore to toe the party line. For example, MJ-12 would say... 'Here are some more genuine documents... but remember...no talking about the mutilations or abductions.' This would be beneficial to Moore as it would supply the evidence to support his theory that E.T.'s exist but deny the truths about the E.T.'s. However, if Moore was indeed working for MJ-12, he would follow the party line anyway... admitting the E.T.'s but pooh-poohing the mutilations and abductions. If working alone, Moore might not even be aware of the 'Grand Deception.'

"Time will tell. It is possible that Moore will go ahead and release the video interview with the military officer around the first of the year, as he has promised. From MJ-12's point of view, the public would be exposed to the information without really having to believe it because Moore is essentially not as credible a source as, say, the President of the United States. After a few months of digestion and discussion, a more credible source could emerge with a statement that, yes, in fact the interview was essentially factual. This scenario would cushion somewhat the blow to the public. If, however, Moore does not release the tape by, say, February 1 of 1988, but comes instead with a story similar to: 'MJ-12 has informed me that they are definitely planning a release of all information by October of 88... I have seen the plan and have seen the guarantee that this will happen, so I have decided to withhold the release of my videotape at this time as it may cause some problems with MJ-12's plans.' This would in effect buy more time for MJ-12 and time is what they desperately need.

"Now you ask, 'Why haven't I heard any of this?' Who do you think you would hear it from? Dan Rather? Tom Brokaw? Sam Donaldson? Wrong. These people just read the news, they don't find it. They have ladies who call and interview witnesses and verify statements on stories coming over the wire [either AP or UPI]. It's not like Dan Rather would go down to Wytheville, Virginia, and dig into why there were four thousand reported sightings in October and November of 1987. Better Tom Brokaw or someone else should risk their credibility on this type of story. Tom Brokaw? Tom wants Sam Donaldson to risk his credibility. No one, but no one, is going to risk their neck on such outlandish ideas, regardless of how many people report sightings of 900 foot objects running them off the road. In the case of the Wytheville sightings, dozens of vans with NASA lettered on the side failed to interest newsmen. And those that asked questions were informed that NASA was doing a weather survey.

THE FAILURE OF SCIENCE

"Well then, you ask, what about our scientists? What about Carl Sagan? Isaac Asimov? Arthur C. Clarke? Wouldn't they have known? If Carl Sagan knows then he is committing a great fraud through the solicitation of memberships in the Planetary Society, 'to search for extraterrestrial intelligence.' Another charade into which the U.S. Government dumps millions of dollars every year is the radio-telescope in Arecibo, Puerto Rico, operated by Cornell University with - guess who? - Carl Sagan. Cornell is ostensibly searching for signals from outer space, a sign, maybe, that somebody is out there. It is hard to believe that relatively intelligent astronomers like Sagan could be so ignorant.

(Note: Also, even if 'they' did find evidence of extraterrestrial life, do you think that SETI and similar government-sponsored projects would tell US about it? Let's just take a look at some actual statements from those involved with these projects.

The following is a quote from Matt Spetalnick's article "IS ANYBODY OUT THERE? NASA LOOKS FOR REAL ET'S", in *Reuters Magazine,*" Oct. 5, 1992: "At least 70 times scientists have picked up radio waves that bore the marks of communication by beings from other worlds, but they were never verified, [Frank] Drake said." And researcher John Spencer, in a reference to Dr. Otto Strove, tells how this astrophysicist assisted Frank Drake in establishing Project OZMA, and it's very mysterious conclusion: "...the project began its search by focusing on the star TAU CETI. According to claims made at the time, as soon as the project got underway strong intelligent signals were picked up, leaving all the scientists stunned. Abruptly, Dr. Strove then declared Project OZMA had been shut down, and commented that there was no sensible purpose for listening to messages from another world." [*The UFO Encyclopedia*]. (So then, these 'insiders' will accept all of our hard-earned tax dollars to finance their radio projects - if not their underground bases and covert space operations. Yet cursed be any 'mere mortal' for having the audacity to actually insist on having access to the products of their 'financial investments'! - Branton)

"What about Isaac Asimov? Surely the most prolific science fiction writer of all time would have guessed by now that there must be an enormous cover-up? Maybe, but if he knows he's not saying. Perhaps he's afraid that 'Foundation and Empire' will turn out to be inaccurate.

"What about Arthur C. Clarke? Surely the most technically accurate of science fiction writers with very close ties to NASA would have at least a hint of what's really going on. Again, if so, he isn't talking. In a recent science fiction survey, Clarke estimates that contact with extraterrestrial intelligent life would not occur before the 21st Century.

SETI radio telescopes scan the skies for possible extraterrestrial signals. Have such signals already been detected, but kept secret from the public?

"If the government won't tell us the truth and the major networks won't even give it serious consideration (Note: This was written before such programs as SIGHTINGS, ENCOUNTERS, UNSOLVED MYSTERIES, CURRENT AFFAIR, MONTEL WILLIAMS, STRANGE UNIVERSE and other TV news digests and talk shows DID begin dealing with the UFO phenomena, abductions, and so on in much greater depth - not to mention the X-FILES, DARK SKIES and other TV series'. - Branton), then what is the big picture, anyway? Are the EBEs, having done a hundred thousand or more abductions [possibly millions worldwide], built an untold number of secret underground bases [Groom Lake, Nevada; Sunspot, Datil, Roswell, and Pie Town, New Mexico, just to name a few] getting ready to return to wherever they came from? Or, from the obvious preparations, are we to assume that they are getting ready for a big move? Or is [it] the more sinister and most probable situation that the invasion is essentially complete and it is all over but the screaming?

"A well planned invasion of Earth for its resources and benefits would not begin with mass landings or ray-gun equipped aliens. A properly planned and executed invasion by a civilization thousands [of] years in advance of us would most likely be complete before a handful of people, say 12?, realized what was happening. No fuss, no muss. The best advice I can give you is this: Next time you see a flying saucer and are awed by its obvious display of technology and gorgeous lights of pure color - RUN LIKE HELL!

- June 3, 1988 Las Vegas, NV"

[The following was an addendum to the above that was included with later copies of John Lear's 'statement']:

"In 1983, when the 'Grand Deception' was discovered, MJ-12 [which may now be designated 'PI-40'] started work on a weapon or some kind of device to contain the EBEs who had by now totally infested our society. This program was funded through SDI, which, coincidentally, was initiated at approximately the same date. A frantic effort has been made over the past four years by all participants. This program ended in failure in December of 1987.

(Note: British Ufologist Timothy Good claimed that over 22 British scientists - who were working on the U.S. SDI program for British Marconi and other Aerospace companies - had all mysteriously died or 'committed suicide' within the space of a few years. Could this have had anything to do with this 'failure'? Apparently

someone 'out there' was intent on sabotaging the SDI/STAR WARS project. Also there are reports that several of our 'defense satellites' have been destroyed as well.
- Branton).

"A new program has been conceived but will take about two years to develop. In the meantime, it is absolutely essential to MJ-12 [PI-40], that no one, including the Senate, the Congress or the citizens of the United States of America [or anyone else for that matter] become aware of the real circumstances surrounding the UFO cover-up and the total disaster it has become.

"Moore never did release the videotapes but claims he is negotiating with a major network to do so...'soon'."

Another source added the following statements in regards to Lear's claims:

"Area 51... and a similar setup near Dulce, New Mexico, may now belong to forces not loyal to the U.S. Government, or even the human race. 'It's horrifying to think that all the scientists we think are working for us [in the joint-interaction bases] are actually controlled by aliens.'

"...SDI, regardless of what you hear, was completed...to shoot down incoming saucers. The mistake was that we thought they were coming inbound - in fact, they're already here. They're in underground bases all over the place. It seems that the aliens had constructed many such bases without our knowledge, where they conduct heinous genetic experiments on animals, human beings, and 'improvised' creatures of their own devising.

"Thus was born PROJECT EXCALIBUR. Press reports described EXCALIBUR as a weapons system designed to obliterate deeply-buried Soviet command centers, which the Reagan administration hypocritically characterized as destabilizing. We have exactly similar centers. Lear claims the weapon was actually directed toward the internal alien threat. Unfortunately, the 'visitors' have invaded us in more ways than one.

"Millions of Americans have been implanted. There's a little device that varies in size from 50 microns to 3 millimeters; it is inserted through the nose into the brain. It effectively controls the person. Dr. [J. Allen] Hynek estimated in 1972 that one in every 40 Americans was implanted; we believe it may be as high as one in ten now. These implants will be activated at some time in the near future, for some unspecified alien purpose."

When Lear was pressed to disclose some of his sources, he stated that his anonymous intelligence informants "go right to the top." He did however mention some of the names in not-so-sensitive intelligence positions from whom he has also gathered information. Many of these names may be familiar to veteran Ufologists. These include:

* Paul Bennewitz, director of Thunder Scientific Laboratories [a New Mexico-based research facility with government contract ties], who claims to have gained access to and 'interrogated' an alien computer system via a radio-video-computer setup of his own invention.

Is John Lear UFOlogy's man with the tin foil hat or is he a straight shooter?

* Linda Howe, the television documentarian responsible for "Strange Harvest" (a program about cattle mutilations), who received astonishing 'leaks' from a special intelligence officer, Colonel Richard Doty, formerly of Kirtland AFB, a name noted in aerial research circles.

* Robert Collins [code-named 'Condor', according to Lear] who has secured numerous official documents relating to UFOs.

* Sgt. Clifford Stone, premiere collector of UFO related Freedom of Information Act or FOIA documents.

* Travis Walton, professed UFO abductee whose experience inspired the movie "*Fire In The Sky.*"

THE ALIEN/CIA CONNECTION

In a relatively brief period, William Cooper has surfaced as one of the all-time controversial figures in UFO research. Cooper is, however, the first to point out that he is not primarily a UFOlogist, but a government "whistleblower," whose purpose it is — he feels — to bring the truth to the public about not only any possible alien Intervention in our society, but the very existence of the so-called "Secret Government" that is behind everything from the Kennedy Assassination to international drug trafficking, MJ-12, Armageddon, the Men-in-Black, and a variety of other conspiracies that all tie-in with a continuing disinformation program that molds our thinking on just about every subject.

PUBLISHERS NOTE: William Cooper, who wrote the book "*Behold a Pale Horse,*" hosted a shortwave radio show, "The Hour of the Time," from a studio in his house atop a hill in the town of Eagar, Arizona. By the late 1990s, Cooper talked less about UFOs, and concentrated more on his beliefs towards militias and the anti-government movement. In July 1998, he was charged with tax evasion and an arrest warrant was issued. However, Cooper eluded law enforcement and in 2000, he was named a "major fugitive" by the United States Marshals Service.

Cooper repeatedly said that if anyone tried to arrest him "...I will try to kill as many as I can before they kill me."

On November 6, 2001, Cooper shot a sheriff's deputy who was trying to arrest him on charges of aggravated assault with a deadly weapon. The charges

stemmed from disputes with local residents who were threatened by Cooper in July and September.

After shooting the deputy, Cooper ran from his truck to the house, but was killed by multiple shots from other officers before he made it inside.

John Lear was one of many UFO "whistle-blowers" who claimed the U.S. had allowed extraterrestrials to abduct humans for study and horrific experimentations.

11.

UFOLOGISTS' LIVES MATTER – BILL COOPER SPEAKS FROM THE GRAVE
By Timothy Green Beckley

The long blue arm of the law extended its mighty fist and gave Bill Cooper a mighty "gut punch," which cut him down outside his home.

Depending upon which side of the "blue line" you are on, you might want to refer to this as a "murder."

The truth is, Cooper was a volatile guy.

He was a large, husky, and very determined man who never seemed to let anything get in his way. Even though he only had one leg he was a pillar in every sense of the word. He did have a "rough side" to his personality, which came out sometimes when he drank, but he was mostly a friendly sort, kind of like a big bear ready to give you a huge hug if he liked you. If he didn't, he might try to pull off his prosthetic leg, having he lost one in the Vietnam war, and try to clobber you with it as he once tried to do in a donnybrook with Bigfoot-ologist Eric Beckjord.

In a relatively brief period, Cooper rose to be one of the all-time controversial figures on the conspiracy fringe scene of the UFO movement. He was, however, the first to point out that he was primarily a UFOlogist, but also a government whistleblower, whose purpose it was to bring the truth to the public about a series of events which included a possible alien intervention in our society, but also involved the most controversial of chatter on secret governments behind everything from the Kennedy assassination to international drug trafficking, MJ 12, Armageddon, Men-in-Black and a wide variety of other creepy conspiracies that all tie in - or so he said - with a continuing disinformation program that molds our thinking on just about every topic - and for which some say he died trying to expose.

Bill Cooper and I had a relationship that lasted several years. He was the top draw at my conspiracy and UFO conferences, talking nonstop for hours about such events in his own life as the time an unexplainable object came up out of the water and flew low over the bow of a ship he was stationed on while in the Navy. He also claims to have seen Top Secret documents which revealed an agreement between the U.S. government and extraterrestrial forces.

I know, some individuals accused Bill of being anti-Semitic, but he always told me that he thought those who controlled the world wanted to pit one group against another, using politics, religion and economics to build walls around all of us so that we could be more easily controlled. I once organized a mini-conference with Cooper as the only speaker at the Little A'Le'Inn located at the end of the Extraterrestrial Highway far out in the Nevada desert, but very close to Area 51. We had a great weekend of sky watching and conversation. One of the subjects he loved to talk about was the existence of Secret Societies.

"History is replete with whispers of secret societies, accounts of elders or priests who guarded the forbidden knowledge of ancient peoples. Prominent men, meeting in secret, who direct the course of civilization, are recorded in the writings of all people." As most everyone who is into conspiracies realizes, Bill was shot to death in November of 2001 in a wild west-style rumble with the sheriff's department in Apache County, AZ. Local law enforcement officials apparently felt it necessary to spring into action on trumped-up charges under the cover of darkness and in plainclothes, because they considered Bill to be a threat to the community. Indeed, Cooper was recognized as a rebel rouser who in general was known for defying officialdom, including the IRS, who claimed he owed the government back taxes. Bill strongly held to his belief that the IRS was an unconstitutional collection agency who should NOT possess such devastating power over hard working Americans.

Time passes rapidly, and little by little we began to put the shooting between Cooper and the law out of our mind. We had stated our feelings in a book we published shortly after Bill's unwarranted – we felt – demise. In *"Death of a Conspiracy Salesman,"* we presented all sides of the William Cooper story from every possible angle. Those who respected him had their final say, while those who were opposed to what he stood for also got in a word or two edgewise.

Conspiracy Expert Maintains Life on Earth Could Be Doomed By 1999!
WILLIAM COOPER ON EARTH CHANGES

Unlike many "doom and gloom" soothsayers, William Cooper, author of the conspiracy thriller **BEHOLD A PALE HORSE**, doesn't see the Earth coming to an end through a natural disaster such as the popularly predicted polar shift. Instead, the controversial lecturer who has appeared before large crowds all over the country, maintains if there is an end to civilization, it may be because "Big Brother" had a hand in it.

"There is a rocket on the way to Jupiter right now—due to arrive in 1999—with enough platinum on it to blow up the planet. I think elements of the 'secret government' are planning to make a new sun in our solar system in order to prevent an Ice Age, which seems to be on the horizon."

According to Cooper, this new ice age could come about rather quickly and "furthermore, we are being tricked into believing that there is a mass global warming taking place, when the exact opposite is really the case."

Cooper says that we should learn to become more self-sufficient, in case a global event of this magnitude does take place, because it will put officialdom into turmoil and in essence it will be "everyone for themselves" all over the land.

Cooper has become a popular figure at previous conferences put on by Inner Light and his appearance at the 3 Annual National New Age & Alien Agenda Conference in Phoenix is sure to be eye-opening. "I'll be covering some new material in relation to the CIA and the alien agenda that is going to be affecting us all," Cooper notes, "as well as covering material on the New World Order and related matters such as the hostage for arms situation and the Farm Credit Bureau rip off which could lead to a lot of good folks unnecessarily going broke."

While in Naval Intelligence, Cooper saw documents regarding an agreement made between the ETs and the government to exchange alien technology for abducting humans, a practice which, as far as he knows, is still going on!

Cooper will be lecturing as part

BILL COX TO MAKE "UNSEEN KINGDOMS" VISIBLE!

The author of one of Inner Light's most popular books, **UNSEEN KINGDOMS**, researcher Bill Cox is convinced that there are many realms and dimensions around us which are vibrating to higher frequencies than most of us can normally see or sense, but that sometimes this "doorway" opens and we receive knowledge and information which can be useful. As part of his globe-trotting adventures, he has traveled many a dusty trail in search of hidden civilizations, the occupants of which used modern forms of technology, though they vanished from the face of the planet centuries ago. In South America, he's penetrated the deepest jungles, while in Egypt he has explored the secret chambers of mighty high priests.

As a result of his investigations, he is convinced we are in the midst of a psychic explosion and that beings of super intelligence are starting to walk the Earth again. As part of his lecture—and in more detail in his workshop—he will explore what he has found and how it can be applied to everyday life to benefit us all. He will also expose the secrets of dowsing and how to tell if a UFO contact or encounter is authentic. His lecture will be held during the Saturday morning session with a full workshop-seminar scheduled for Sunday, September 8th at 12:30 PM.

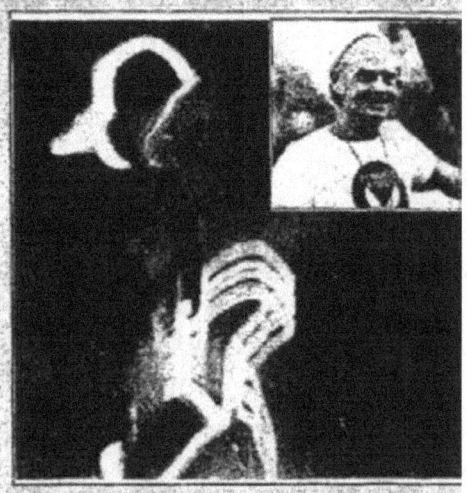

"Spacemen" living amongst us have the ability, says Cox, to distort their image on film and to take upon other likenesses.

Article about Bill Cooper from Timothy Green Beckley's "UFO Universe" magazine.

OUT OF NOWHERE, JESSICA COOPER APPEARS

Boom! I didn't see it coming. Late one evening while I was hunkered down over my lap top, I received a totally unexpected email from one of Bill's children, a daughter by the name of Jessica, who was asking for help in finding out more about her father, whom she had met only once since her parents were separated when she was three years old.

She longed to know about her father's work and had been turned off by some of his "close associates," who seemed anxious for her to be removed from the picture. A lively and energetic woman of 27, Jessica had only visited with her dad once and it was not under the best of circumstances. Federal Marshals, she told me, wanted her to set up her own father so that he would come down off his mountaintop retreat and they could arrest him without a potential shoot out. When "Wild Bill" heard about this, he went absolutely ballistic.

In our possession is a copy of one of Cooper's "Hour of the Time" shortwave broadcasts in which he threatens what amounts to an all-out war with anyone who dares try to compromise his love for his family and put them in harm's way. His comments are blistering, but in this case well-deserved. Obviously, we were anxious to speak with Jessica at length to share with her any information we could about her father, and to find out what she might know about his life and knowledge of esoteric matters that was not public knowledge.

It was at about this time that we had started to re-edit the transcripts to several major symposiums that we had organized under the collective title of *The Alien Agenda and Cosmic Conspiracies Conference*. Held in Phoenix and San Diego, the seminars covered a multitude of controversial topics and featured a parade of speakers that included John Lear, Jordan Maxwell, Alexander Collier, Philadelphia Experiment survivor Al Bielek, Sean David Morton, Vladimir Terzinski – and yes, even Bill Cooper.

In order to pay homage to those researchers who have over the years freely devoted their lives to the study of that which might place them in life threatening situations, we asked Jessica Cooper if we could possibly record an interview with her and include it in what we were hoping would be a major work, something her father certainly deserved to be a key part of. Jessica agreed, and so with associate Sean Casteel we set up a date and proceeded to tape an eye popping conversation which we truly believe the majority of our readers will find of immense significance. If you are at all fascinated with the legacy of William Cooper, the Kennedy Assassination, Secret Societies, MJ12 and all those secrets Uncle Sam would rather have you forget about, we highly recommend *"William Cooper Death of a Conspiracy Salesman."*

SO WHAT EXACTLY DID COOPER HAVE TO SAY ABOUT ALIENS?

This statements can be attributed to Cooper before he became more "political," my feeling being that he realized that UFOlogists were not about to give up their hard-earned income, unlike the right wing community who had invested in gold and were digging underground shelters for "security reasons," be there an alien, or a "socialist," takeover. Readers can assert their own independent thinking on Cooper. Thousands saw him as a "savior," while others wish he had never appeared on the UFO scene to "muddy the waters."

ALIENS: There were four types of aliens mentioned in the papers. A LARGE-NOSED GREY, with whom we have the treaty, the GREY reported in abductee cases that works for the LARGE- NOSED GREY, a blond human-like type, described as the NORDIC, and a red-haired human-like type called the ORANGE.

The homes of the aliens were described as being a stars in the Constellation of Orion, Barnards star, and Zeta Reticuli 1&2. I cannot remember even under hypnosis which alien belongs to which star.

EBE is the name or designation given to the live alien captured at the 1947 Roswell crash. He died in captivity.

KRLL OR KRLLL OR CRLL OR CRLLL pronounced Crill or Krill, was the hostage left with us at the first Holloman landing as a pledge that the aliens would carry out their part of the basic agreement reached during that meeting.

KRLL gave us the foundation of the yellow book which was completed by the guests at a later date. KRLL became sick and was nursed by Dr. G. Mendoza, who became the expert on alien biology and medicine. KRLL later died. His information was disseminated under the pseudonym O.H. Cril or Crill.

GUESTS were aliens exchanged for humans who gave us the balance of the yellow book. At the time I saw the information there were only three left alive. They were called Alien Life Forms.

Bill Cooper broadcasting his radio show, "Hour of the Time," from his home studio.

RELIGION: The aliens claim to have created Homo sapiens through hybridization. The papers said that RH-blood was proof of this. They further claimed to have created all four major religions. They showed a hologram of the crucifixion of Christ which the government filmed. They claim that Jesus was created by them.

ALIEN BASES exist in the Four Corners area of Utah, Colorado, New Mexico, and Nevada. Six bases were described in the 1972 papers, all on Indian reservations and all in the Four Corners area. The base near Dulce was one of them.

MURDER: The documents stated that many military and government personnel had been terminated (murdered without due process of law) when they had attempted to reveal the secret.

CRAFT RECOVERIES: The documents stated that many craft had been recovered. The early ones from Roswell, Aztec, Roswell again, Texas, Mexico, and other places.

GENERAL DOOLITTLE made a prediction that one day we would have to reckon with the aliens, and the document stated that it appeared that General Doolittle was correct.

ABDUCTIONS were occurring long before 1972. The document stated that humans and animals were being abducted and/or mutilated. Many vanished without a trace. They were taking sperm and ova samples, tissue, performed surgical operations, implanted a spherical device 40 to 80 microns in size near the optic nerve in the brain and all attempts to remove it resulted in the death of the patient.

The document estimated that one in every 40 people had been implanted. This implant was said to give the aliens total control of that human.

CONTINGENCY PLAN: SHOULD THE INFORMATION BECOME PUBLIC OR
SHOULD THE ALIENS ATTEMPT A TAKEOVER? This plan called for a public announcement that a terrorist group had entered the United States with an atomic weapon. It would be announced that the terrorists planned to detonate the weapon in a major city. Martial law would be declared and all persons with implants would be rounded up along with all dissidents and would be placed into concentration camps. The press, radio, and TV would be nationalized and controlled. Anyone attempting to resist would be arrested or killed.

CONTINGENCY PLAN TO CONTAIN OR DELAY RELEASE OF INFORMATION: This plan called for the use of MAJESTIC TWELVE as a disinformation ploy to delay and confuse the release of information should anyone get close to the truth. It was selected because of the similarity of spelling and the similarity to MJ-12. It was designed to confuse memory and to result in a fruitless search for material that does not exist.

SOURCE OF MATERIAL CONTAINED IN THE DOCUMENTS WHICH I SAW: The source of the material was an Office of Naval Intelligence counter-intelligence operation against MJ-12 in order for the Navy to find out the truth of what was really going on. The Navy (at that time or at least the Navy that I worked for) were not participants in any of this. The different services and the government conduct this type of operation against each other all the time. The result of this operation was that the Navy cut themselves in for a piece of the action (technology) and control of some projects. As you can see, this file is only a little different from my previous file. Only some names were scrambled previously to confuse the government long enough for someone to verify that what I have said is the truth. I have added information in this file that puts me in absolute danger.

I have sent a copy of this file to people all over the country and will continue to do so. Please get this file into as many hands as you can and maybe that will protect me, but I doubt it.

HISTORY WILL BE THE JUDGE OF ME AND THIS INFORMATION, AND I HAVE NO FEAR OF THAT JUDGEMENT.

I SWEAR THAT THIS INFORMATION IS TRUE AND CORRECT TO THE BEST OF MY KNOWLEDGE.

Even though he died in 2001, William Cooper's conspiracy theories continue to resonate with militia, Qanon and other right-wing, fascist groups in the United States and throughout the world.

DULCE WARRIORS

I wish to thank all those people who have aided me in reaching this point and for their patience and understanding. I owe you all more than I can ever repay.

Finally, it does not matter who is right and who is wrong or if a project name is in the wrong place. It does not matter who is working for whom or what is really what. It should be obvious by now that something sinister and terribly wrong is going on involving the government and the UFO phenomenon.

We must all band together and expose it now. I have done my part in the best manner that I could. I can add nothing else except my testimony in Congress or a court of law that what I saw and have written in this file is true and that I saw it.

Everything in my previous file that does not conflict with this file is true and correct to the best of my knowledge and some of it is from sources and research. You may combine the files to get the entire picture. Throw out only that information that conflicts with that contained in this file.

There will be no further additions or corrections to this information either now or in the future. My file is complete and stands to be judged by history. Sometime in the future the exact papers that I saw will surface, and you will all see this exact information contained within them.

Milton William Cooper

Jan. 10, 1989

* * * * * * * *

Those wishing to experience an enlightening William Cooper update should proceed to the following online report posted by the "Arizona Central" (azcentral.com).

"How William Cooper and his book '*Behold a Pale Horse*' planted seeds of QAnon conspiracy theory," by Richard Ruelas and Rob O'Dell.

12.

THE MYSTERIOUS JASON BISHOP III
(a.k.a, Tal Levesque, a.k.a., TAL)

Jason Bishop III (a.k.a., Tal Levesque, a.k.a., TAL), was one of the original promoters of the "Dulce Base" myths.

This photo of Jason Bishop III was taken in 1990 in Los Angeles when he was filmed by Nippon Television for a program dealing with Area 51 in Nevada and Dulce, New Mexico.

The interview with Nippon Television took place at my residence in Gardena, California, where I was living at that time.

The two-hour program was shown only in Japan on March 24, 1990. He requested that his face be blacked out for the program.

In the early 1990s, Jason Bishop III visited with me many times at my residence, even after I moved to Torrance, California. Apparently, at that time, he was living in Redondo Beach, California. It is not an exaggeration to say that more than 90% of the original information that one reads on Dulce originated from Jason Bishop III.

(Until recently I was not aware of his passing. From what I heard, he died on December 21, 2018, in California, at the age of 69, presumably in Mariposa where he was thought to be residing at that time. My belated condolences. Without him, I would never have known about the origins of the fascinating Dulce base rumors.)

Jason Bishop III claimed he worked with a Thomas E. Castello when he was living in Santa Fe, New Mexico (1978, 1979) working in security for a private company.

It was there that Bishop claimed to have befriended the alleged Castello.

Jason Bishop III reportedly gave the impression that he was present at the 1988 Mount Archuleta expedition (alongside Gabe Valdez, Edmund Gomez, Jeff and Greg Valdez, French physicist Dr. John Gille, Manuel Gomez, Jr., Elaine A. and a scientist from Los Alamos).

Dr. John Gille denied that Jason Bishop III was even present at that expedition.

(I had the honor of getting together with Dr. Gille in France in the spring of 2016).

I am sure that Jason Bishop III's influence extended widely, probably affecting people such as Alan B. de Walton (BRANTON), and even Phil Schneider, who must have certainly read Jason Bishop III's writings.

To know more about BRANTON (a.k.a., Alan B. de Walton), author of *"The Dulce Book,"* and *"The Dulce Wars,"* read the article: *"Who was Branton, author of the Dulce Book and the Dulce Wars?"*

https://noriohayakawa.wordpress.com/2016/08/29/who-was-branton-author-of-the-dulce-book-and-the-dulce-wars/

It was Jason Bishop III who devised the so-called "underground tunnels" connection map of the U.S. centering in the American Southwest, through the so-called Dulce "hub."

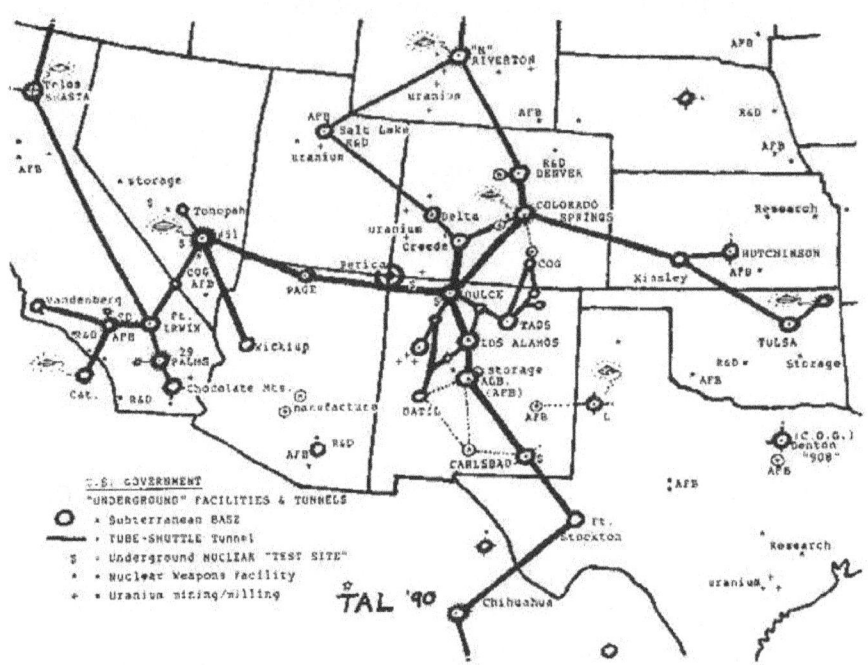

Jason Bishop's "Underground Facilities and Tunnels" map allegedly showing the immense, secret tunnel system, located in the southwest United States.

Jason Bishop III's extensive writings can be found at the BLUE PANET PROJECT: www.bibliotecapleyades.net/vida_alien/blueplanetproject/blueplanetproject.htm, a book heavily promoted by a TV program entitled: *Unsealed Alien And Conspiracy Files.*

In January of 2009, Jason Bishop III became quite infuriated when I told him that I was organizing the first-time ever "underground base" conference in Dulce, New Mexico.

He warned me not to have such a conference in Dulce. Nevertheless, I went forth with the conference, which was held on March 29, 2009, in Dulce.

The conference, open to the public, was entitled: "THE DULCE BASE: FACT? OR FICTION?"

It was a historic and successful conference in many senses of the word (even though nothing conclusive had come out of it) and was attended by more than 140 persons from all over, including many local residents.

Just prior to the conference date, Jason Bishop III became quite upset with me because I had not invited a John Rhodes, his protégé, to speak at the conference.

John Rhodes claimed that he was an expert on "reptilians."

Jason Bishop III was one of the many avid readers of the original SHAVER MYSTERY in the early 1950s. He was deeply influenced by the SHAVER MYSTERY.

According to Wikipedia: "Richard Sharpe Shaver (1907 - 1975) was an American writer and artist. He achieved notoriety in the years following World War II as the author of controversial stories which were printed in science fiction magazines (primarily AMAZING STORIES), in which he claimed that he had had personal experience of a sinister, ancient civilization that harbored fantastic technology in caverns under the Earth.

The controversy stemmed from the claim by Shaver, and his editor and publisher Ray Palmer, that Shaver's writings, while presented in the guise of fiction, were fundamentally true. Shaver's stories were promoted by Ray Palmer as THE SHAVER MYSTERY."

Like I said, Jason Bishop III was an avid reader of the SHAVER MYSTERIES in the early 1950s. A couple of years ago, I received a letter from Jason Bishop III's sister Carolyn LeVesque of Arroyo Grande, confirming to me about his long-term "condition," i.e., some form of mental, "delusional" illness. Also a few years ago, a friend of mine, C. Gilbert Wright, told me that coincidentally he had corresponded with the brother of Phil Schneider who told him that Phil was also suffering from a certain long-term "condition," i.e., some form of mental, "delusional" illness.

Source: November 27, 2016 CIVILIAN INTELLIGENCE NEWS SERVICE, by Norio Hayakawa.

13.

THE FASCINATING LIFE OF CHERRY HINKLE - HER STORY OF DULCE

PUBLISHER'S NOTE: Recently we were discussing the subject of the greys and Dulce on "Exploring the Bizarre," and during a "coffee break," KCOR's producer, Tina Marie Caouette, mentioned that I should probably contact a Facebook acquaintance of both of ours. Apparently, Cherry Hinkle, of Henderson, Nevada, had been undergoing experiences that could be related to the underground world at Dulce, and, besides, she was a close friend of the late Tom Castello, who apparently no one knew better than Cherry did. Tina warned that Ms. Hinkle was about to dissolve her contact network on acebook because of her current health crisis. So we decided that it was "now or never," and put together this material, with her permission, and share it with one and all at this inopportune of opportune times.

Just by "coincidence," the interview with Cherry was conducted by our friend and fellow compatriot in UFO arms Adam Gorightly, the self-described "crackpot historian." Adam Gorightly's articles have appeared in nearly every 'zine, underground magazine, counter-cultural publication, and conspiratorial website imaginable. Bringing a mischievous sense of Prankster-Discordianism to the zany world of fringe culture, once Gorightly connects his dots, readers are plunged into alternative universes that forever alter their view of "reality." Adam is the author of such books as *"Historia Discordia," "Caught in the Crossfire: Kerry Thornley, Oswald and the Garrison Investigation," "A is for Adamski,"* along with Greg Bishop. And his latest *"Saucers, Spooks and Kooks."*

* * * * * * * * *

QUESTION: Cherry, maybe we could start with your earliest experiences with UFO's and ET's. I understand these experiences started in the early 1960s.

ANSWER: I have been a contactee since a preschool child. Beings contacted me every two years; no matter if I lived in the United States or elsewhere. At the age of 8, I was reading the works of Madame Helene Blavatsky, and understanding the occult. The unusual and the paranormal was my average day. By the early 1960s I had already experienced enough unusual events that I felt confident I would never be unnerved by a strange event. But I was mistaken.

I experienced a strange event on the way to shopping one evening. I am sure you understand the confusion when you experience a medical-type exam by small greys with large golden eyes - large enough to have their elongated eyes "wrap" around the temple? Their flat faces, tiny mouths and large lumpy domed heads didn't frighten me as much as their method to take me. I couldn't move, couldn't scream for help. I was totally paralyzed; only my thoughts were still active.

When an alien wearing a black robe touched my shoulder and placed a coin-like disk on my forehead, I relaxed and no longer feared them. Since the 1962 event several people have seen or met "Jahel," the alien in black robes. All four of my children experienced events with Jahel, and at least a couple of visiting missionaries from the Mormon Church got the shock of their life when Jahel suddenly appeared in my living room. That was hard to explain, and the missionaries certainly left in a hurry. I have enjoyed a fascinating life and experienced many other events since that 1960s encounter.

QUESTION: It is interesting that you mentioned the occult. My research has led me to suspect that the UFO phenomena seems to be highly associated the occult, and that many of these encounters may be the result of magic rituals conducted either wittingly or wittingly on the part of the observers/witnesses. In other words, UFO witnesses may play a large role in this experience, in terms of "calling down" the phenomena/craft and of making these entities appear, whatever they may be. Your thoughts?

ANSWER: There are certain things I am not at liberty to freely discuss regarding the occulted aspects of Dulce Base, but I'll at least mention a few items. However, I believe I can freely mention my great-uncle William Wynn Westcott, my paternal grandmother's uncle. W.W. Westcott founded the famed organization known as "Golden Dawn." Since it is a family tradition I do understand the practices in Golden Dawn, as well as other secretive mystery schools such as the Rosicrucians.

DULCE WARRIORS

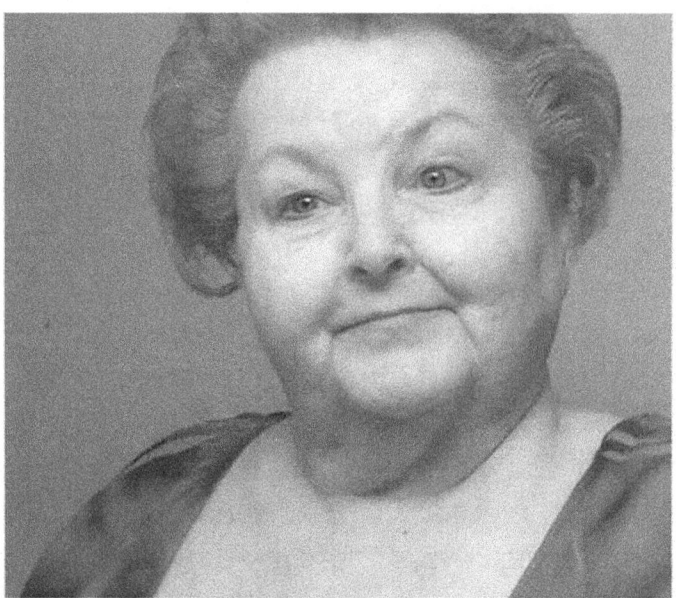

Cherry Hinkle

I am sure you are familiar with the dark side of the alien story and that high strangeness smacks of ritualistic magical acts during the so-called alien abductions. Items such as the nude physical examination while the human is strapped on the table/altar surrounded by the instrument-carrying aliens. Usually one unique being stands aside, merely watching the procedures. I must admit it does sound very much like the highest magical rituals. No one could deny the parallel courses of high magic and alien abduction.

The modern practice of the "calling down" of the alien craft is very much like a primitive ritual, not too different than the ancient rituals used by the African Dogon tribe to communicate with the space beings from Sirius; some things never change. I wouldn't be shocked to discover the Dogon shared an interest in the biblical Enoch and his fascinating books. Nor would I be surprised to find they have a basic understanding of the works of Dr. Wilhelm Reich. They might have different terms for Orgone Energy in Africa, but the same effects are unchanged.

QUESTION: Since you mentioned Dulce, let's talk about that a bit. How did you come to know Thomas Castello, and what information did he pass on to you about the Dulce Base?

ANSWER: Back in 1962, Tom Castello was in the Air Force, and stationed at Nellis Air Force Base in Las Vegas, Nevada. Tinkering on his 1950 Packard car became his hobby, and in the process of ordering handcrafted modified car parts, he met my father, Charlie, a master machinist. Tom and Dad shared the same fascination with UFOs, and spent hours debating all aspects of the unidentified flying objects. Within a few months Dad introduced Tom to me, and he became a family friend.

Tom and I quickly became close friends - no romance, just friends; I stood up for him when Tom married Cathy. We started investigating UFO cases together and submitted the reports to a secretive UFO group known as the Central Unit. Then Tom left the Air Force and accepted work with the Rand Corporation in California. Within a few months he transferred to Los Alamos - and Dulce Base. He worked as the head of security in Dulce Base for two years, until in October 1979, when there was a fatal conflict inside the seven-leveled genetic facilities. The day after the conflict, Tom reentered the Base through an air ventilation shaft in one of the ice caves in New Mexico. When he left Dulce Base, Tom brought out photos, documents, diagrams and his spare flash-gun, an awesome weapon.

Ultimately Tom asked me to help him find a safe place to hide the items he gathered. I knew the exact place – a rugged mountain in Arizona, a place my son and I have visited a few times. That mountain was remote and difficult to climb. Together Tom and I buried a box of the materials, confident no one would accidentally stumble across the box. By then, Tom was on the run, trying to stay one step ahead of the group that was determined to reclaim the missing materials and capture or kill him.

Cherry Hinkle claims to have been close friends with the mysterious Thomas Castello.

DULCE WARRIORS

In 1987 Tom asked me to find a trustworthy person to help expose Dulce Base and the horrid experiments going on in that underground place. I tried a lot of people, but finally the best person was the well-known John Lear, here in Las Vegas. Starting with a few sketches and a one page description of the items in the buried box, John did an exceptional job of getting the material out in a short period of time. I will always hold John Lear in high regard for his exceptional work in exposing Dulce Base. Those few pages - with the sketches - comprise *"The Dulce Papers."*

The last time I saw Tom, in late 1990, he asked me to promise I would complete his work for him, if something happened to him. I suggested he find someone else, because I am reclusive and he needed someone more aggressive, more outgoing. But he insisted he trusted me and knew I wouldn't let him down. I promised I'd never give up and keep trying to expose Dulce Base.

In April 1991, Tom was living in Costa Rica, working in an underground facility near the border of Panama, when a 7.5 earthquake devastated the area. Since that day, I've never heard from Tom. I have all his letters, my hand-written notes regarding the box and materials buried in Arizona, and a determination to fulfill my promise to my best friend. I've ignored the snide remarks, the personal death threats, and have a strong will power to do what is right, at any cost.

QUESTION: Are you at liberty to tell us what agency Castello worked for when he served as head of Security at Dulce? I was also under the understanding that Castello lived in Santa Fe during the period of the Dulce conflict. If he did indeed live in Santa Fe at the time, is it possible he gained access to the Dulce Base through an entrance in Santa Fe? The reason I'm curious about this is due to the difficulty people have had finding an actual entrance to the Dulce Base in the area of Archuleta Mesa on the Jicarilla Apache Indian Reservation. This, in addition to rumors I have heard that there actually is an entrance to Dulce in Santa Fe.

ANSWER: You are correct, Adam. When the Dulce conflict occurred Tom lived in Santa Fe, and traveled through Los Alamos to Dulce Base. With no exception, all workers entered Dulce Base through the underground shuttle terminal at Los Alamos. I'm certain you are familiar that Santa Fe and Los Alamos are close by, roughly a short 30 minute drive apart, and many of the workers carpool. Although a few people visit the town of Dulce, New Mexico, hoping to find the few ventilator shafts down to Dulce Base, their chance of finding these vents is next to impossible. Determined searchers that stumble across the vents would be surprised to find security cameras to Dulce Base, not to mention the motion sensors - followed by angry armed guards.

In 1987-1988 I posted instructions to five entrances to the vents I heard from Tom. But I'm sure those entrances were blocked or sealed shortly after I posted them. These people intend to keep the Base secret - by any methods required.

For several years, I have considered sharing the information found in that buried box in Arizona with the right person or group of people - those people must have the natural intelligence to make sure the box of material and proof goes to the right research team. The "right" people must make sure Tom's Flash Gun does not fall into the wrong hands. That weapon has incredible power; on the highest setting the Flash Gun can totally disintegrate any human, animal, plant or other object in its path, leaving only a minimum residue to mark its original position. The weapon vaporizes anything, a human, a car, anything, with no limits. According to Tom Castello, the only exception is certain forms of quartz. Tom passed away before he could fully explain that exception, and why quartz is powerless against the Flash Gun.

The documents, diagrams, letters and photographs include undisputed proof of living aliens that co-inhabit planet Earth, and I consider it vital that information like that needs to remain free information, and must not be blocked or sold to any one person or country. Regarding certain occult information in Dulce Base, I must be very careful here, due to an oath I signed to never reveal sensitive classified information, under the penalty of incarceration or death.

Although they used coercion to gain my signature, the document remains a binding legal document. I signed that oath in 1980, and, since that date, I've been very careful not to risk breaking that oath. With that in mind, I can only state that in Dulce Base there is a strong occult connection that affects the highest governmental offices in every country, worldwide. The Dracon Leaders are master occultists, and to the average 'man-on-the-street' on the surface of planet Earth, the Leaders are real magicians or more like the Magi. They have mastered atomic material, and can walk through walls, levitate and can use bi-location at will. Aside from that, I can't offer a better explanation. But if you are wise, you can read my message and understand a hidden message.

14.

PHILIP SCHNEIDER - MYSTERIOUS DEATH OF A DULCE WHISTLE-BLOWER

By Tim R. Swartz - With Assistance From Cynthia Drayer

Al Pratt suspected something was wrong with his friend Philip Schneider. For several days in a row, Al had gone to Phil's apartment, in Willsonville, Oregon, saw his car in the parking lot, but received no answer at the door.

Finally, on January 17th, 1996, Al Pratt, along with the manager of the Autumn Park Apartments and a detective from the Clackamas County Sheriff's office, entered the apartment. Inside, they found the body of Philip Schneider. Apparently he had been dead for five to seven days. The Clackamas County Coroner's office initially attributed Philip Schneider's death to a stroke. However, in the following days disturbing details about his death began to surface, leading some to believe that Philip Schneider had not died from a stroke, but had in fact been murdered.

Philip Schneider's life was certainly as controversial as his death. He was born on April 23, 1947, at Bethesda Navy Hospital. Philip's parents were Oscar and Sally Schneider. Oscar Schneider was a Captain in the United States Navy, worked in nuclear medicine and allegedly helped design the first nuclear submarines. Captain Schneider was also part of OPERATION CROSSROADS, which was responsible for the testing of nuclear weapons in the Pacific at Bikini Island.

In a lecture videotaped in May 1996, Philip Schneider claimed that his father, Captain Oscar Schneider, was also involved with the infamous "Philadelphia Experiment." In addition, Philip claimed to be an ex-government structural engineer who was involved in building underground military bases (DUMB) around the country, and to be one of only three people to survive the 1979 incident between the alien greys and U.S. military forces at the Dulce underground base.

DULCE WARRIORS

Philip Schneider's ex-wife, Cynthia Dryer, believes that Philip was murdered because he publicly revealed the truth about the U.S. government's involvement with UFOs. For two years prior to his death, Philip Schneider had been on a lecture tour talking about government cover-ups, black budgets, and UFOs. Philip stated in his lecture that in 1954, under the Eisenhower administration, the federal government decided to circumvent the Constitution and form a treaty with extraterrestrials. The treaty was called the 1954 Grenada Treaty. Officials agreed that, in exchange for extraterrestrial technology, the greys could test their implanting techniques on select citizens. However, the extraterrestrials had to inform the government just who had been abducted and subjected to implants. Slowly over time, the aliens altered the bargain, abducting and implanting thousands of people without reporting back to the government.

Phil Schneider with his wife Cynthia and daughter Marie.

THE DULCE CONNECTION

In 1979, Morrison-Knudsen, Inc. employed Schneider. He was involved in building an addition to the deep underground military base at Dulce, New Mexico. The project at that time had drilled four holes in the desert that were to be linked together with tunnels.

Philip's job was to go down the holes, check the rock samples, and recommend the explosives to deal with the particular rock. In the process, the workers accidentally opened a large artificial cavern, a secret base for the aliens known as greys.

In the panic that occurred, sixty-seven workers and military personnel were killed, with Philip Schneider being one of only three people to survive. Philip claimed that scars on his chest were caused by his being struck by an alien weapon that would later result in cancer due to the radiation.

If Philip Schneider's claims are true, then his knowledge of the secret government, UFOs and other information kept from the public could have serious repercussions to the world as we know it. In his lectures, Philip spoke on such topics as the Space-Defense-Initiative, black helicopters, railroad cars built with shackles to contain political prisoners, the World Trade Center bombing, and the secret black budget.

The quotes below are from a lecture given by Philip Schneider in May 1995, at Post Falls, Idaho.

RAILROAD CARS

"Recently, I knew someone who lived near where I live in Portland, Oregon. He worked at Gunderson Steel Fabrication, where they make railroad cars. Now, I knew this fellow for the better part of 30 years, and he was kind of a quiet type. He came in to see me one day excited, and he told me 'They're building prisoner cars.' He was nervous. Gunderson, he said, had a contract with the federal government to build 107,200 full-length railroad cars, each with 143 pairs of shackles to hold prisoners down and against the walls. There are 11 sub-contractors in this giant project. Supposedly, Gunderson got over two billion dollars for the contract. Bethlehem Steel and other steel outfits are involved. He showed me one of the cars in the rail yards in North Portland. He was right. If you multiply 107,200 times 143 times 11, you come up with about 15,000,000. This is probably the number of people who disagree with the federal government."

"STAR WARS" AND THE ALIEN THREAT

"Sixty-eight percent of the military budget is directly or indirectly affected by the black budget. 'Star Wars' relies heavily upon stealth weaponry. By the way, none of the stealth program would have been available if we had not taken apart crashed alien disks. None of it. Some of you might ask what the space shuttle is 'shuttling.' Large ingots of special metals that are milled in space and cannot be produced on the surface of the Earth. They need the near vacuum of outer space to produce them. We are not even being told anything close to the truth. I believe our government officials have sold us down the drain - lock, stock and barrel. Up until several weeks ago, I was employed by the U.S. government with a Rhyolite-38 clearance factor - one of the highest in the world. I believe the 'Star Wars' program is there solely to act as a buffer to prevent alien attack - it has nothing to do with the 'Cold War,' which was only a ploy to garner money from all the people. For what? The whole lie was planned and executed for the last 75 years."

BLACK HELICOPTERS

"There are over 64,000 black helicopters in the United States. For every hour that goes by, there is one being built. Is this the proper use of our money? What does the federal government need 64,000 tactical helicopters for, if they are not trying to enslave us? I doubt if the entire military needs 64,000 worldwide. There are 157 F-117A stealth aircraft loaded with LIDAR and computer-enhanced imaging radar. They can see you walking from room to room when they fly over your house. They see objects in the house from the air with a variation limit of one inch to 30,000 miles. That's how accurate that is. I worked in the federal government for a long time, and I know exactly how they handle their business."

TERRORIST BOMBINGS

"I was hired not too long ago to do a report on the World Trade Center Bombing (February 26, 1993). I was hired because I know about the 90 some odd varieties of chemical explosives. I looked at the pictures taken right after the blast. The concrete was puddled and melted. The steel and the rebar were literally extruded up to six-feet longer than its original length. There is only one weapon that can do that - a small nuclear weapon. A construction-type nuclear device. Obviously, when they say that it was a nitrate explosive that did the damage, they're lying 100 percent, folks. I want to further mention that with the last explosion in Oklahoma City, they are saying that it was a nitrate or fertilizer bomb that did it.

"First, they came out and said it was a 1,000 pound fertilizer bomb. Then, it was 1,500, then, 2,000 pounds. Now it's 20,000. You can't put 20,000 pounds of fertilizer in a Rider Truck. Now, I've never mixed explosives, per se. I know the chemical structure and the application of construction explosives. My reputation was based on it. I helped hollow out more than 13 deep underground military bases in the United States. I worked on the Malta project in West Germany, in Spain and in Italy. I can tell you from experience that a nitrate explosion would have hardly shattered the windows of the federal building in Oklahoma City. It would have killed a few people and knocked part of the facing off the building, but it would have never have done that kind of damage. I believe I have been lied to, and I am not taking it any longer, so I'm telling you that I have been lied to.

Black helicopters are part of a conspiracy theory that claims that special silent running helicopters are used by the military, the federal government, or secret agents of the New World Order.

"Right now, I am dying of cancer that I contracted due to my work at Dulce for the federal government. I could live six months. Eleven of my best friends have been murdered in the last 22 years. Eight of their murders were called "suicides." Before I went to speak in Las Vegas, I took a friend to Joshua Tree, near 29 Palms. I drove through the mountains, in California, and I was followed by two government E-350 moving cars with G-14 plates, each with a couple of occupants, one of whom had an Uzi. I knew exactly who they were. I have spoken 19 times and have located 45,000 people probably. I am going to upload 140,000 pages of documentation to the Internet about the structure of the government and the entire plan. I have already started that task."

PHILIP SCHNEIDER, ACCORDING TO HIS EX-WIFE

In 1987 Philip married Cynthia Marie Drayer Simon. The two had met in June of 1986 at a meeting of the Oregon Agate and Mineral Society. As Cynthia put it years later, "He had so many interesting stories, so much information to share, we bonded and love began to bloom."

Philip and Cynthia would later have a daughter, Marie Schneider. Unfortunately their marriage had difficulties. According to Cynthia, health problems contributed to their break up. Philip had multiple health concerns, many of which could have killed him. He had chronic lower back pain that never went away, even after a back operation. He had multiple Sclerosis, which was chronic and progressive. Occasionally he had to use crutches, a body brace, leg braces, bladder bag, catheter, diapers, and a wheelchair. He often had to sleep in a hospital bed with railings, a helmet, and body braces. When Cynthia first met him he was taking Dilantin for seizures, and almost died three times from this medication due to an allergic reaction.

Philip also had Brittle Bone Syndrome (osteoporosis) and cancer in his arms. He had hundreds of shrapnel wounds, a plate in his head with a metal fragment in his brain, fingers missing from his left hand. There was a scar that ran down from the top of his throat to below his belly button, and another scar that ran from just under his ribs, side to side.

Cynthia would later state: "Philip was a complex person. He had brain damage after a bomb was dropped on him while working as a civilian structural engineer for Morrison-Knudsen in Vietnam. He had a Rhyolite clearance. He was learning disabled, brilliant in some areas, yet unable to fill out a form in the doctor's office. Able to create time travel formulas, but unable to budget money; he had to file bankruptcy one year. I now believe that he had been 'deprogrammed' so that he could not remember most of his 'past' life. But something began to happen shortly after we first met. Perhaps because of the seizures, or because he changed his medication, or because he now had another person to talk to that was interested in what he had to say, he began to remember the old days.

"Being the scientific, logical minded person I am, I listened intently to his stories with a grain of salt, waiting for additional information to verify them. I can still remember the night he began to talk in some foreign language (sounded like Chinese and another night in what sounded like French.) Philip told me he knew 11 languages before the brain damage. After the space shuttle, Challenger, exploded, I visited Philip in his apartment. He had a large chalk board with complicated formulas which proved that a 'Cosmosphere' had shot down the space shuttle."

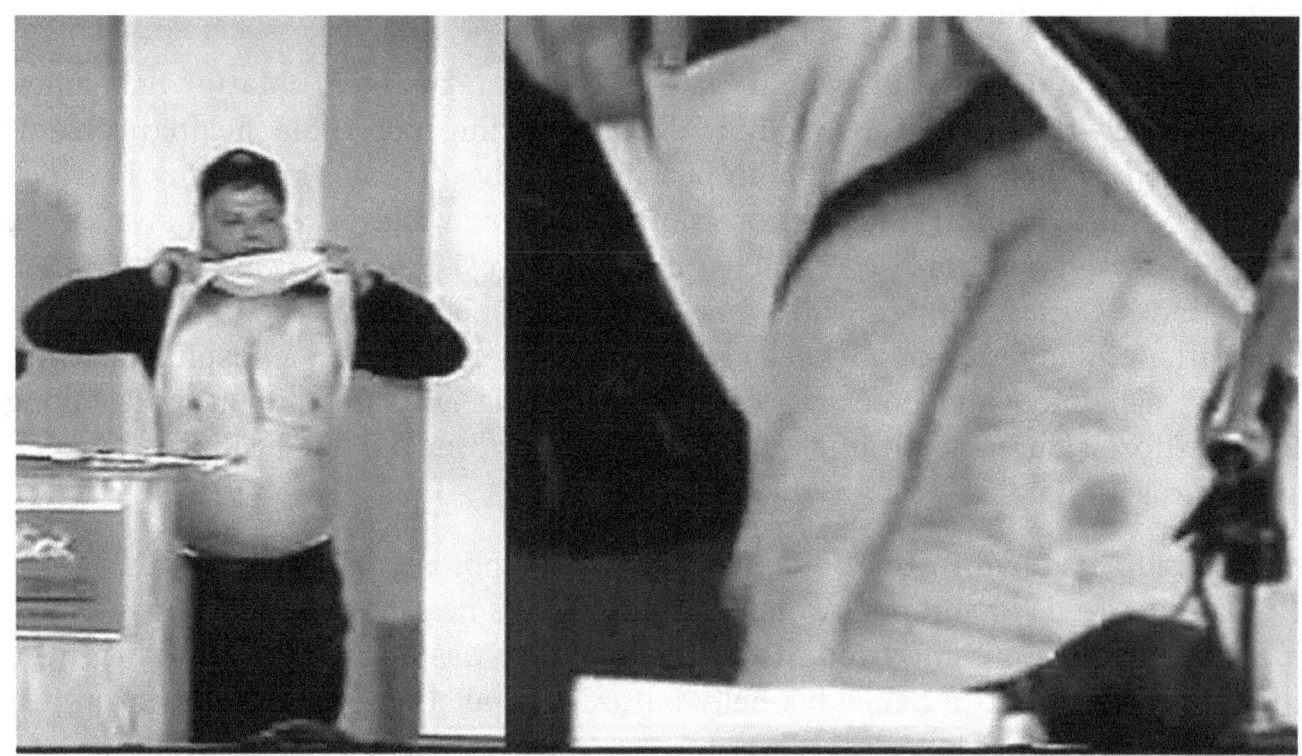

During his lectures, Phil would show the audience the numerous scars on his chest that he claimed were caused by an alien weapon.

Cynthia also said, "It was a difficult marriage for both of us, which was complicated by a failed self-employed business selling rocks, minerals, and antiques. His re-constructive surgery on scars on his chest, my gall-bladder surgery and the birth of our daughter, all within a one-year period. The pressures of our new family, failed business, and physical problems culminated in our divorce in 1990. Philip was an emotional abuser and could be very mean and abusive. He was a complex person, part genius and part paranoid schizophrenic. We had a bad marriage but developed it into a great friendship."

THE PHILADELPHIA EXPERIMENT

One of Philip's more amazing stories was his father's alleged involvement with the "Philadelphia Experiment." When Philip's father, Captain Oscar Schneider (Navy Medical Corp.) died in 1993, Philip discovered original letters in his basement.

According to Philip, the letters were evidence that the Philadelphia Experiment actually existed, and that Oscar Schneider had been a participant in it after the crewmembers had been quarantined in a Virginia psychiatric ward. Captain Schneider supposedly autopsied the bodies of the crew members as they died, and found alien implants in their arms, legs, behind their eyes, and deep inside their brains.

Captain Schneider was confused by these implants, so they obviously were not military. They had to have been alien in nature, and the small "transistor" like item was discovered before transistors had been invented. Here was evidence that either by accident, or on purpose, aliens were involved with the Philadelphia Experiment, and were probably responsible for its failure.

Also discovered in Oscar's basement were photographs taken during Operation Crossroads, in which a nuclear device was used on Bikini Island. Authentic military photos taken from an airplane showed UFOs raising up from the lagoon and flying through the mushroom cloud. These photos, however, mysteriously disappeared from Philip's apartment at the time of his death.

Some investigators in Philip Schneider's mysterious death have had problems believing some of the incredible claims he made before he died. Even those who knew Philip when he was alive didn't always accept the validity of his stories. Cynthia Schneider noted that when Philip was under crisis or pressure, he would tell people that he had been arrested, or that people from the sheriff's office or government had been at his door. This was the way he expressed his crisis. Unfortunately, she claims, sometimes it was true, like "the little boy who cried wolf." His friends became numb to his reports.

SUICIDE OR MURDER?

Despite the fact that Philip's claims seemed too wild or disturbing to be true, he obviously believed in what he was saying. Philip claimed that his life was in danger because he was revealing the truth, a truth that some would kill to keep secret. He borrowed a gun from his friend Ron Utella, stating that he felt he needed protection and that there had been several attempts to have his car run off the road. In the end, though, Philip's safeguards were not enough to save his life. On either January 10 or 11, 1996, Philip Schneider died under mysterious circumstances.

After the initial cause of Philip's death was listed as a stroke, Cynthia asked to see the body before it was to be prepared for cremation. The funeral director who felt that the body's advanced state of decomposition would be too traumatic dissuaded her. However, she could not shake the feeling that something was wrong.

The next day Cynthia was contacted by Detective Randy Harris who said that "something was wrong" – that there were marks on Philip's neck. Philip Schneider's body was removed from the funeral home and autopsied by Dr. Karen Gunson, Medical Examiner for Multnomah County, Oregon. The autopsy revealed that Philip had in fact died as a result of having a rubber hose wrapped three times tightly around his neck and tied in a knot. The conclusion from the autopsy was that he had committed suicide. He had wrapped the tubing around his neck, tied it in a knot, blocked the flow of blood to his head, became unconscious and finally died.

More surprising was Cynthia's discovery that Philips lecture material, unknown metals, military photographs, and all notes for his unwritten book on UFOs were missing from his apartment. However, money and other valuables were left untouched.

When he was found in his apartment, Philip's body was in an unusual position. His feet were under the bed, his head was in a wheelchair seat, at an unusual angle, and the rest of his body was on the floor, hands by his sides. There was blood found on the floor near the wheelchair, but no blood was found on the wheelchair. There were no apparent wounds on Philip's body to account for the blood.

No sample of the blood was taken due to the initial belief that Philip had died of natural causes. No suicide note has ever been found. In fact, Mark Rufener, a longtime friend of Philip, said, "I saw Philip the weekend of January 6 and 7th 1996. We were going to buy land in Colorado. We were excited because he was going to hire me to help write a book about his knowledge on UFOs and aliens, the One World Government, and the Black Budget. He did not commit suicide. He was murdered and it was made to look like a suicide."

When he was alive, Philip enjoyed eating out at the 76 Truck Stop in Aurora, Oregon. A waitress named Donna remembered his stops when they would talk about his work. Philip mentioned to her that there had been 19 attempts to stop him from talking. Donna states that Philip said: "If they ever say that I have committed suicide, you will know that I have been murdered." She said that Philip believed he had a mission to talk about a government cover-up about aliens and UFOs, and that there were forces out to stop people who talked.

Phil Schneider with his daughter Marie.

MYSTERIOUS FIGURES SURROUND SCHNEIDER'S DEATH

Was Philip Schneider murdered? His ex-wife Cynthia believes this to be the case. She thinks that someone met Philip whom he knew and injected him with a drug in order to incapacitate him. The assailants then wrapped the rubber hose around his neck, asphyxiating him. In fact, shortly after Philip's death, several friends told Cynthia that they had seen Philip with an unknown blond woman several weeks before he died.

During the course of the meeting, Cynthia noticed a longhaired blond woman in a car, watching the meeting through the window with a pair of binoculars. When they tried to approach the car, the woman quickly sped away. Cynthia later traced the license plate number and it turned out to be from a truck, with the plate reported as stolen. Cynthia thinks the reports of women with blond hair is significant because Cynthia's mother, through a channeling session, had told her that a woman wearing a blond wig was involved in Philip's death.

Despite the fact that officials have closed the case as a suicide, Cynthia has not stopped in her efforts to discover the truth in her ex-husband's death. She says that she knows in her heart and soul that Philip would not have committed suicide willingly, and she still hopes that Philip's blood and urine can be relocated by the Multnomah County Medical Examiner's Office and examined for traces of drugs that would not normally be there.

However, as the days go by, the reality for such tests grows smaller. She still hopes that someone will come forward with pertinent information to help her find justice for Philip's death. Until that time comes, Cynthia Drayer will continue her task, perhaps putting her own safety at risk. That prospect doesn't frighten her anymore, "I just want people to know the truth about Philip Schneider, a person who died trying to expose the difficult truths of this world."

One of the more persistent rumors surrounding the Dulce mystery is that there is a secret tunnel system throughout the U.S. constructed with the help of nuclear powered tunneling machines.

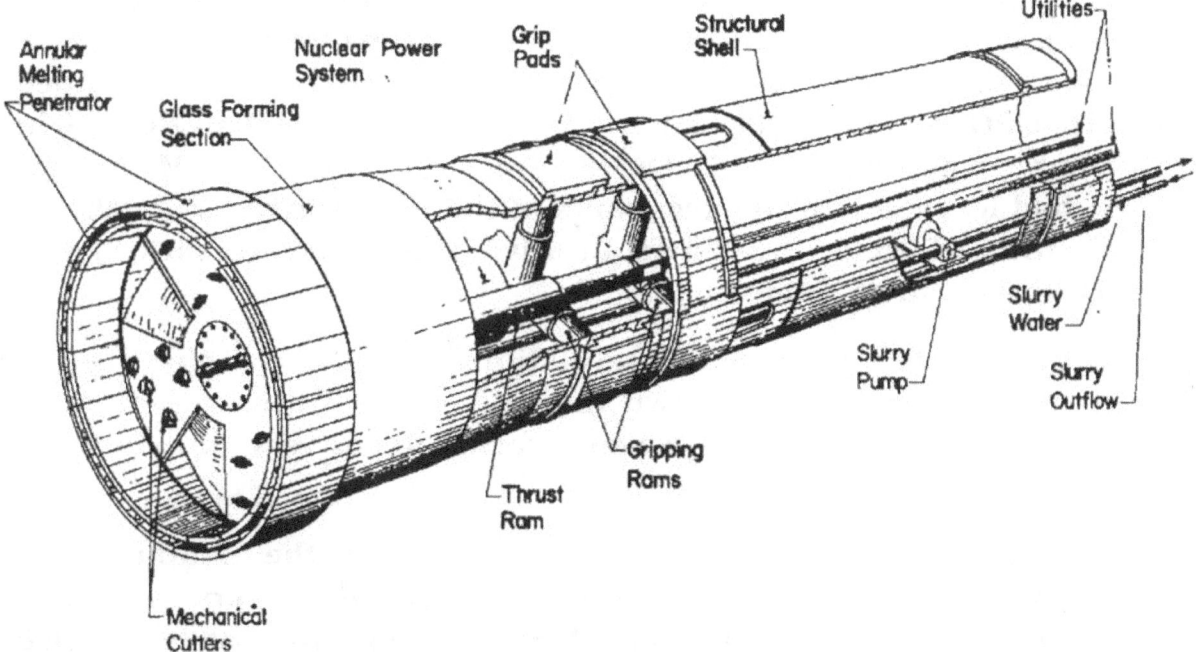

Fig. 1. Conceptual design of Type-I NSTM with peripheral kerf-melting penetrator and mechanical central-face cutter.

15.

BIRTH OF AN ALIEN HYBRID - THE CHRISTA TILTON STORY

PART ONE

PUBLISHER'S NOTE: She was a fascinating lady, but I never really knew what to make of her. Christa Tilton was somewhat of a fixture in the UFO field, though an enigmatic one. She had been married to animal mutilation researcher Tom Adams and, after they split, she hooked up with veteran UFOlogist Wendelle Stevens and tied the knot with him.

She was bright, attentive and attractive. Men thought she had a magnetic personality - and I would guess the aliens thought so as well.

I corresponded with Christa Tilton over a period of years, met her at a UFO conference and spoke to her in private. Before she vanished from the field we published a book containing a goodly quantity of material she had submitted for publication. Christa's book *"Underground Alien Bio Lab At Dulce: The Bennewitz UFO Papers"* dealt with a man by the name of Paul Bennewitz who claimed to have photographed UFOs that appeared over a New Mexico military base. He had learned that the occupants of these craft had established a base under the town of Dulce (located on a Native-American reservation) and were generally thought to be "up to no good."

As verification of Mr. Bennewitz's revelations, Christa says she was taken to the same bunker seven levels down into the Earth and was impregnated by extraterrestrials, which came in several forms, from very human looking to the often dreaded greys.

Christa's ongoing series of encounters begins in the summer of 1962. According to a lengthy account published in the now defunct newsletter CRUX, which her husband Tom Adams published, "At dusk, 10-year-old Christa was looking for rocks in the desert of suburban Tucson. After watching a 'fireball' land or crash, she was approached by a 5-foot-tall gray being who traded rocks with her, then took her on board a craft. She was examined physically and to alleviate her fears was told that they were 'planting a garden.' On board she met a more human-appearing being she would come to think of as the 'Doctor' and would see him several times in future experiences."

This "Doctor" was what is often referred to as a Nordic - a space being said to be very Aryan in appearance.

Several other instances are reported in that same publication:

Tulsa, Oklahoma - Fall 1971:

Grey aliens took her from apartment and onto their craft, where she was implanted with fertilized ovum.

New Orleans - Early winter 1971:

Hypnotic regression disclosed that grey aliens took her again, this time extracting the fetus prematurely; something had gone wrong. There was a taller gray that seemed to be in charge; about 5 feet tall, like the one in Tucson in 1962. This was the most disturbing, most traumatic of Christa's experiences. She was shown stacks of incubators containing fetuses. She saw what was apparently a hologram of a human child, a girl of about ten years old. She was told this was the daughter she would give birth to in the future. Also on board was the human-like alien, the "Doctor."

Tulsa - February 1976:

Following a long period of no sexual activity, Christa was suddenly pregnant. Regression disclosed implantation of another fertilized ovum. She would later meet the father. The pregnancy resulted in the birth of a daughter who, at the age of ten, looked identical to the child she had seen in the hologram in 1971.

In an interview I did for *"UFO Universe Magazine,"* Christa described in intimate detail one of her traumatic experiences which she believes took place deep underground.

Christa Tilton

TAKEN CAPTIVE

By Christa Tilton

My experience happened in July of 1987. I had about a three hour missing time episode in which later, under hypnosis, I relived a most harrowing night. I remember driving to a deserted area, north of Tucson, Arizona, in the middle of the night. I saw a craft sitting up on a small hill and it was then I saw two aliens approach my car. I panicked and locked my doors. When they got closer, I heard a click and it was then I noticed my door had just opened. I began fighting off the two entities and, after laying me on my back, one grabbed one of my arms and the other did the same and they actually pulled me over the rocky terrain up to the craft. When on board I was given something to drink. The next thing I realized I was being led off the craft and I noticed I was in a different area than where I had been abducted. I looked around and noticed the craft was sitting next to an opening in the mountain. I saw what looked to be a tunnel that led into the side of the mountain. This time I was accompanied by a human who wore a type of military uniform like what a test pilot would wear. He was to be my guide for the rest of the trip.

We entered the tunnel and I soon noticed the tunnel was illuminated with some type of artificial lighting. Another human with the same type of uniform approached us. I noticed he was wearing a strange looking weapon on the side of a large black belt. I also saw a strange symbol worn on a patch on his chest.

The guard did not seem friendly at all and, when I tried to ask questions, I was told not to speak. The guard asked me to step on something that looked like a large scale. I saw what looked to be a large computer screen in front of me and two cameras were visible at that checkpoint. I was then told to clip on some type of identification card with holes punched in it. It seems as though they had me change into some type of uniform, but I do not consciously remember all the details.

It was at that time I saw a huge elevator that had no door. I heard strange tones inside this area and noticed strange symbols on the walls. There was a time in which my guide explained to me that we had just entered LEVEL ONE of the facility. I asked him what kind of facility this was and he replied that I would soon see.

It was like an underground city. I was amazed at what I saw there. We rode in some strange transit car that was rounded and looked as though it was connected someway to the side of the cavern. I noticed other people walking by and none of them even glanced my way. Some wore white uniforms and lab coats and others had the military-type of jumpsuits on. As I said before, the lighting was very strange. I could not find a source for it.

After exiting the vehicle, I was taken to a large area. So large that it looked as though a jet plane could fly and land there. It was then I saw the small alien craft parked to the sides. I noticed a large number of scanning cameras. They made me very nervous because I felt as if I was being monitored everywhere I went. I was taken down a long hall where I viewed huge computers and heard strange tones and frequencies. I saw cubicle areas where others worked. It was like a factory atmosphere. At times I thought that is where I was, but I would soon find out it was not a factory!

THE TANKS

The whole time I felt as though I was taken on a special tour, as if I was meant to be there for a specific reason. My guide argued with some guards at one point. They kept looking over at me, but I could not hear what all the arguing was about. It was at this point I was taken down on the elevator once again. It seemed like it took forever, but we arrived and when I stepped into the secured area a different set of guards approached us immediately. They were not friendly at all.

All of a sudden, an extreme sense of fear overcame me. My guide explained that as long as I was with him I would not be harmed. The guards were issuing orders right and left. My guide swiftly walked me down a long hallway. I heard a humming sound like a generator. We passed an area in which I felt as if I were going to be physically ill. I saw huge tanks with gauges hooked to them and an arm-like device was extending down into the tanks. They looked to be around four to five feet in height and just as I started to go see what was in the tanks I felt my guide quickly grab my arm and lead me out of this huge area.

I was told that it would only complicate matters if I knew what was being kept in those tanks; I became very scared at this point. At this point if I had known what was in store for me, I probably would have started screaming and run for my life! I was led into what only looked to be a laboratory. I saw the back of a small alien's head as he was working diligently at a counter. I heard the clinking of metal and it was then that I remembered my training in the operating room in the late 1970s. I was beginning to get very frightened until I saw a man in a white lab coat turn around to greet us. He smiled and shook hands with my guide.

I remember it being very cold in this room and I started to shake. My guide smiled and patted me on the back and said he would be just outside and told me to relax and I would be finished in no time. I began to cry. I cry when I am terribly scared. The man was a doctor and he called for an assistant to come and help. This is when I saw the grey alien come in. The next thing I knew, I was very drowsy. I was told to lie on the table and I felt as if I were dying. My legs were positioned and I realized that I was being examined internally. The "doctor" rubbed something clear and cool on my abdomen and it seemed to calm me and make the pain subside. I could not believe this was happening to me all over again and in such a strange place. I felt more alone than I ever had in my life. I felt like a guinea pig and after I left this lab I became very silent. I was angry at this man for allowing this to happen to me. He told me it was necessary and told me to forget.

How could I ever forget?

Artist's rendering of "The Doctor," who has been a part of Christa Tilton's life since the age of ten.

THE FACILITY

The most bizarre part of this facility was an area we approached in which I saw the strangest thing. I saw what looked to be people of all different races standing up against the wall inside a clear chamber. I went up to one and touched it. It felt ice cold. The people looked like wax figures ... not real. I also went past some small cages in which I saw animals in a similar state of what I could only guess was suspended animation. I think the animals were alive though. For some reason seeing the animals upset me more than seeing humans in the chambers. And every so often we would pass other technicians working. Never once did they turn around to acknowledge my presence. They looked almost like robots doing their menial tasks in an emotionless manner. It was all very disturbing to me.

It became very apparent that this facility was not run by just aliens, but a form of military also. The security was very high and it was impossible for us to get to LEVEL SIX. I was told that this level contained some things that might be upsetting and it would be something, at this time, that I would not be able to comprehend. It was then we started our assent back up.

I was returning that evening to the area in which my car was parked. I walked back to my car and drove back to my aunt's home. I was still wearing my dirty night shirt I had left the house in and must have immediately fallen asleep in my room, not waking my best friend. In the morning my friend saw huge long red scratches on my back and it was then that I realized something very strange had occurred the night before. It was too bizarre to believe.

MILAB INTERVENTION

EDITOR'S NOTE: At this point Christa begins to bring in the weird but ever prevalent relationship between the military and the aliens. Dubbed MILAB, numerous abductees who have been taken to their "chambers" say they have been molested and harassed by an unknown branch of what appears to be the government. Many times these agents show up later and continue to bombard the experiencers with their negativity.

Christa continues:

Many people report abduction experiences, but there is an aspect of my account which is not common to most. Most abductees, whether they experience isolated or repeated incidents, are left to fend for themselves, often with no one with whom to candidly discuss their experiences. This often occurs without anyone offering corroboration or supporting evidence for their accounts, for whatever consolation that would be (and in most cases that would be substantial, trauma-dispelling corroboration). In the past few years of my own investigation into my own abductions, I have had communication by phone and in person with a military man who not only exhibits intimate knowledge of my abductions, but also my life in general. He is - or claims to be - an agent of the federal government. I refer to him as John Wallis.

The first inkling I had that the government was involved in my abductions is when I began to receive strange phone calls while I was staying at researcher Wendelle Stevens' home in Tucson in August of 1987. At first the man would tell me he knew all about my experiences and then he would tell me that it would be a good idea if I were to move back home and forget I ever had these experiences. Alarmed by these calls, Wendelle Stevens encouraged me to "keep the faith" and he continued to help me sort through all the details of what had happened to me. The next week I received a visitor at Wendelle's home and when I opened the door, the man flashed what looked to be an official government card and asked if I would mind if he came in to ask me a few questions. Startled by his urgency, I said it was alright.

He stayed for approximately one hour and in that time he seemed to indicate to me that his agency was concerned about me and he wanted to warn me not to marry a certain researcher. I was shocked at his insistence. I asked him why the government would care about what I do. He stated that it was his business to know every detail of my experiences. He told me there was a government listing of people who had been abducted. I laughed and told him that our government could care less. He stated that that was not the case as many people think. I asked him if he could show me any documentation about my abductions and he said the papers were in a file and it was all kept in confidence.

A few months later, he showed up on my doorstep in Tulsa, Oklahoma. This really frightened me. We had a rather heated conversation about my trip to New Mexico. He wanted to know every detail about what I saw,

What was really fantastic about the Tulsa visit is John Wallis' knowledge of the abduction I had in Tucson in July, 1987. He claimed there was a video tape of the incident and also photos taken. I was horrified! I demanded to know why he did not try to help me and he stated that they were aware of where I would be taken and knew I would be safe. I couldn't believe my ears! I made a note of the date and later was told by a man that worked in the Sheriff's office that a UFO was spotted in that very area that same night. I also found out later through hypnosis that in the facility they had removed another fetus from me.

There were discussions about emotions, hormones, and a chemical imbalance in my brain. And what was strange is that John Wallis had even admitted to me that he was present. Then I began to remember.

Whatever the reason, John Walls has maintained contact with me since 1987 and has not only asked information of me, but also volunteered prudent information to me. There seems to be an exchange program of some kind, but it is a mutual one. I do not believe John Wallis has been sent to do me any harm. He may be a pawn also in this game the aliens are playing with us.

EDITOR'S NOTE: When asked if she ever was able to find out where the man who questioned her lived or is stationed, Christa said yes, she did! "He is stationed at a major military installation – one of the most sensitive in this country– and he has been there for quite a while. I know he feels it is his duty to keep these secrets (about MILAB). He is a very patriotic man. Be he has told me that there are several alien factions on Earth and that some of them can pass for human. I spoke for a UFO group in Dallas and he was there in the audience. He was simply monitoring what information I was giving out to the public."

HER DAUGHTER'S ABDUCTION

For what seemed like ages, I tried to keep the pregnancy which resulted in the birth of my daughter a secret. But eventually the cat came out of the bag (or the alien in this instances I suppose you could say) as we had a sighting together in May, 1986.

The craft was wobbling back and forth. I was sure it was going to crash and it was at that time a black unmarked helicopter appeared and began circling the UFO at a close range. I told my daughter to stay and watch as I ran into the house to grab our binoculars. I was only gone a few seconds, and when I returned she told me the object just disappeared into thin air and the helicopter dashed off in the other direction.

The only thing I could move was my head. I could move my head from side to side. As I did so, I saw a figure standing in a doorway. It was the young man I had seen in the record store once again. It had been exactly a year before. He was wearing a uniform like the others on board. I then looked over to the being that has always dealt with me. He is not one of the little grays. He appears to perhaps be a hybrid himself, although he is not as human in appearance as the young man from the record store. I had always thought of this being as "The Doctor." I telepathically cried out to him. I guess, wanting to know what the hell was going on. He told me that, yes, my suspicions were correct - that this young man whose name was Aaron was indeed the father of my daughter. I remember a surge of energy in which I found that I was able to get up off the table. I was confused and enraged. I was ready to fight them all. They shot some kind of blue beam at me and I fell to the floor, paralyzed again. Right before this, the "Doctor" looked over at Aaron and telepathically instructed him to leave the room that he and I were to have no contact. I was told, however, that I would be able to meet with him one more time at some point in the future.

EDITOR'S NOTE: As is highly unusual in abduction scenarios, a man, a total stranger, came forward to verify Christa Tilton's story because he insists he saw here in the underground facility while he was being examined and mistreated there. The South Carolina man was taken by a group of ETs where a series of bizarre experiments were conducted on him and during the process a small "tattoo" was even placed on the base of the abductee's back.

We published this testimony initially in "UFO Universe," but the case has since been covered by other media.

THE TESTIMONY OF A MAN NAMED MASTERS

The Christa Tilton story also involves the participation of a man named Donavan Masters.

Masters admits he had a longtime interest in UFOs and had sightings that verified his beliefs. His wife thought him a bit odd, but didn't push the issue until one day she was in the market and someone approached her and said he knew her husband and wanted to know what Mrs. Masters thought of her husband's UFO fascination. The woman wanted to know how this complete stranger would know of her husband's "hobby." She was told, "We know a lot about him. He isn't crazy, even if you think he is, and at the right time all will be revealed to him."

VIEWING CHRISTA UNDERGROUND

The following is, I feel, a very real experience, which I believe ties in with the experiences of Christa Tilton.

Three of my friends and I were taken to what I perceived to be some type of underground installation or UFO base. I say "friends" because that is how I perceived them, although I had not met them at the time. I remember feeling as though I had been drugged, as if everything was kind of going in slow motion. We were placed on and strapped to a conveyor belt by our wrists and ankles. The conveyor was activated, and as it began to move, our bodies were passed through blocks of pure intense light. These blocks of light (perhaps laser scanning devices) were either green or blue in color. At each block there was what I perceived to be a robot controller. They also were either blue or green in color. Their color corresponded to the color of the light in front of which they stood.

There were no distinguishable human characteristics. Along the wall in the first room were barrels of some substance which had a very pungent odor. These barrels were stacked one on top of the other.

Suddenly we were on a different conveyor belt or at the end of the first one. As the belt moved around a circular console, it stopped. There were two men, human in form and characteristics, seated at the console. One assisted the other. One of them picked up what I thought was a razor and shaved an area on my back left side, just below the waist line. I remember the spot bled considerably. I was released and then I observed them carrying out the same procedure on my friends. I remember thinking over and over, "What is happening to me?" Then I heard a reply from one of the aliens. "You have just been implanted with your government control extension number." I remember looking into a mirror and looking at the area that bled. The number "04" was there.

In a very upset manner I turned to a woman in a uniform and exclaimed, "You can't do this to me!" Incidentally, all the personnel in this facility wore uniforms. I then ran back to the console where they allowed me to leave. By that time, my friends had been released also. I hurriedly told them what I had discovered about what was happening to us. As I was speaking, the two men at the console were gathering materials in a great hurry, in what seemed to me like an attempt to escape. In particular, I remember the man that had implanted the number on me had a computer print-out list. He protected that list with his life as my friends and I ran after him and another humanoid. They escaped through a set of double doors.

This is what is strange...that during the time I was there I sincerely believe I saw Christa Tilton in this same facility. I also do not think it was our first meeting.

Like Christa, I also have been plagued by intense, repetitive dreams of meetings and communications with what appear to be non-human, otherworldly beings. I am also continually frustrated by my inability to learn the truth about my experiences. Also, like Christa, I suffer from insomnia and the fear of what might happen if I fall asleep. I believe that I have been abducted countless times and it was one of those vivid times when I am sure I saw Christa aboard a craft.

DULCE WARRIORS

I remember walking around a circular corridor; just sort of checking things out unattended, when I came upon an open door. I walked just inside the door and there she was, just lying there on what seemed to be an examination table. She was surrounded by light grey alien beings, 1/2 to four-feet-tall. They were wearing what looked like close-fitting coveralls, almost like a second skin. I was then told telepathically that I was not to enter that area or to ever contact her. I was not only asked to leave, but also escorted out of the room and down the corridor. At that very moment things became very hazy and I fainted. That is all I can recall from this experience.

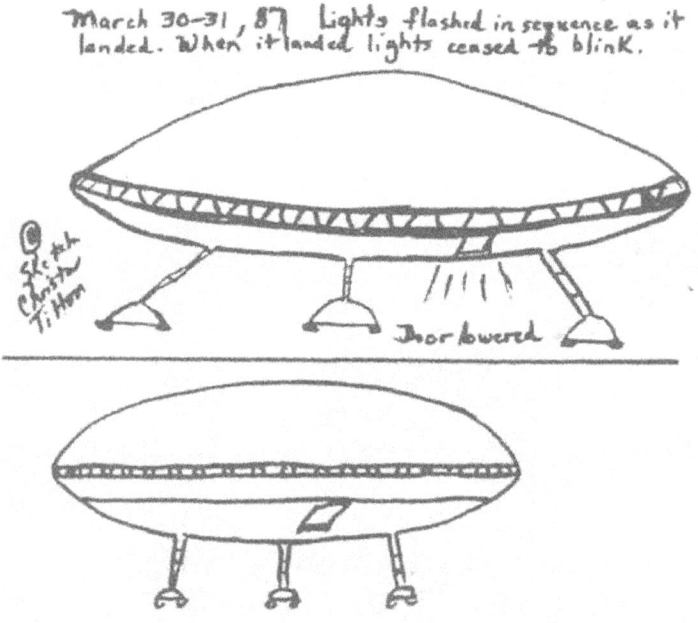

TOP: Craft seen by Christa in the early morning of March, 31, 1987, 28 miles south of Tulsa. BOTTOM: Compare to the landed UFO reported by Nebraska policeman Herbert Schirmer in the fall of 1967.

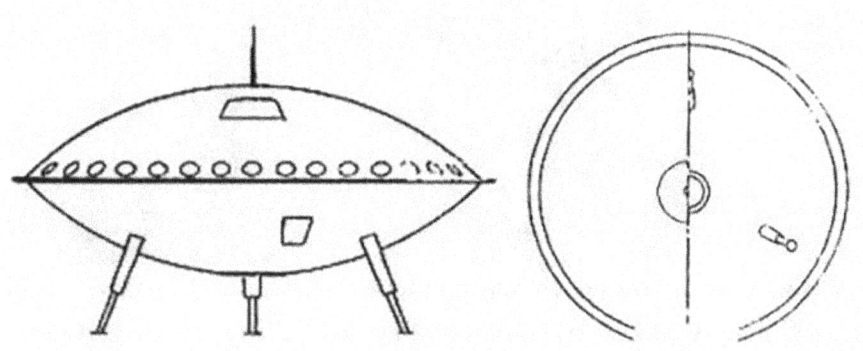

CORRELATION TO THE DULCE ABDUCTION AND MARCH 1987 EXPERIENCE

Masters says much of what he saw underground cannot be discussed for some of what happened remains too painful for him to speak about. In the *"UFO Universe"* piece, I detailed my numerous experiences which took place in an underground UFO base located under the community of Dulce, New Mexico. I saw an array of conveyor systems in this underground facility and at every checkpoint there was a computer console. Also, Donavon saw what he could only call "a computerized elevator," which correlates with the magnetic elevator I was taken on. There is also the matter of the pungent smell when he came close to the large barrels.

We both saw human entities and small grey aliens working in the same area. What the purpose is for them to be working side by side remains unknown; researchers still have found no answers to this enigma.

According to some experiencers, there could be thousands of human/alien hybrids on the planet. Many of the hybrids are remarkably human in appearance.

What is unfortunate is that Donavon's marriage broke up because of his obsession in finding out what had transpired. I, too, have loved and lost because of my obsession with what really happened to me.

For the most part, the aliens seem oblivious to our emotions. Can you imagine how horrifying it must have been for Donavon to be shackled down to this conveyor system and actually feel the tattoo being embedded into his side? The tattoo is apparently only visible under some special type of lighting the aliens have. It brings to my mind our branding and tagging of animals to track them. This is exactly what I believe happened to Donavon Masters.

Donavon has had other abductions, but this one particularly stood out in his mind because he recognized me as being on board and he felt helpless because he wanted to try and assist my escape.

Another interesting aspect to this experience for Donavon is the fact that the people he labeled his "friends" were all of a different culture. He remembered being especially close to a black man who was also experiencing the same tattoo. They both were angry because they had no control over the situation.

But while there have been certain negative aspects to this encounter, overall these experiences have had a positive impact on Donavon's life. In many ways, he feels different and special.

MORE FROM CHRISTA

On March 30/31, 1987, I had a strange abduction south of Tulsa, Oklahoma, where I was taken on board a UFO and given another physical examination. I remember looking to the left and seeing a young blond man just standing there with tears in his eyes. I telepathically heard the head alien tell the man to leave immediately. I have to wonder, could that young man have been Donavon?

Donavon sent me some of his medical records in which it is stated that there was some type of strange object found under his skin. It still haunts him to this day.

I have to wonder just how many of us have had similar experiences and have never reported them to anyone? Maybe sharing the experiences will help all of us. I know it helps me!

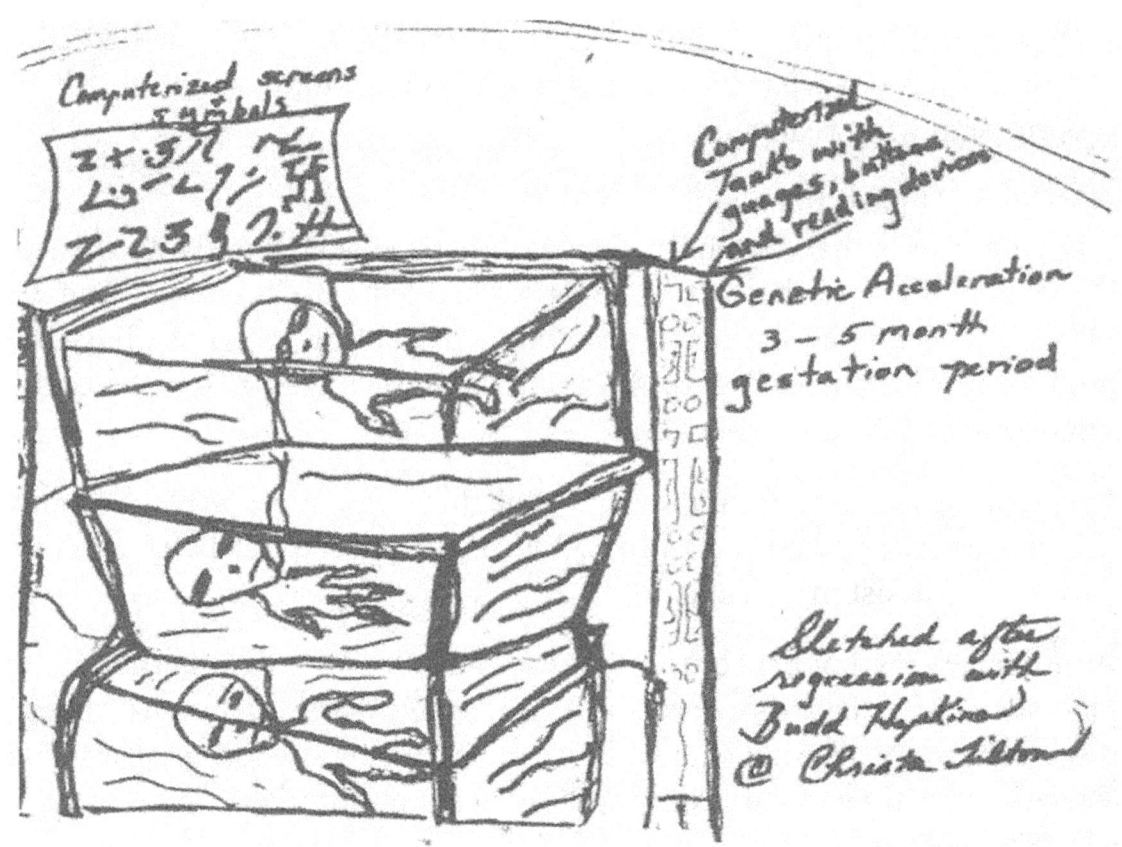

Fetuses and incubators seen on board a craft by Christa Tilton in 1988. She was told, in no uncertain terms, not to touch anything in the chamber.

THE NEVER ENDING STORY

It would be nice if Donavon's experiences ended here, but unfortunately - for him - they did not. Soon after he reported seeing objects in the sky and this strange man approached his wife asking far too personal questions, Donavon began noticing a black car driving around the trailer park he owned. This man poses as a man working in conjunction with the government and even began scaring the neighbors. No one knew who this man was or where he really came from. In a small town like Liberty, South Carolina, everyone knows what is going on with all their residents. He never approached Donavon, but would park across the road in his black car and just sit there for hours.

Scared and confused, this is when Donavon contacted me at researcher Wendelle Stevens' home. I tried to comfort him, but it is difficult when you truly feel your life is in danger. Then mysterious, unmarked, black helicopters began flying low over the trailer park. Donavon felt they were of government origin, but could not be certain. Donavon began to feel weak and his health deteriorated during the next few months. I received a letter from him the other day which bordered on the bizarre. It was as if Donavon was not writing the letter, but I knew it was his handwriting. He had never come across as being overly religious in any sense, but the letter was quite the opposite. Maybe this is Donavon's way of dealing with his experiences. I know I have a closer relationship with God because of my experiences. But again, men-in-black activity haunted him for quite some time. It is too bad that more has not been written on the subject of these strange MIB. More investigating is certainly required if we are to understand and help the victims of unwanted harassment by the strong arm of some unknown agency.

POSSIBLE GENETIC TAMPERING

When first interviewing a man about his alien examinations I always try to allow them to tell me "all" the story. Sometimes, for a man, revealing things of a sexual nature to a woman he has never met can be quite disconcerting. So I spoke to Donavon on many occasions before he ever mentioned the possibility of genetic tampering with him.

This reminds me of the case of Jocelino de Mattos from Maringa, Brazil. Jocelino was taken to an exam room inside a UFO and laid down on a table. The beings examined him, taking sperm samples with a tubular device and placing the specimen in a clear package. Later, Jocelino and his brother Roberto had sexual relations with two of the beings on board the craft.

For Donavon, I believe, something such as this may have happened to him and it is being suppressed by his subconscious. Donavon has often showed interest in trying hypnosis, but in the years gone by, I believe the thought is just too painful for him to dredge up at this point.

At some stage, I believe there was some speculation on Donavon's part that he and I could possibly be linked in such a way. I try to play this down because even though it could be humanly possible, it would be hard to prove that both Donavon and myself were on the same craft or in the same underground facility at the time this happened to him. For now, Donavon is happily living alone. His wife divorced him right after these strange events and Donavon has chosen not to marry again. He seems happy and has not had any events occur recently, although the aliens have been known to wait for years before contacting their subject again. I believe the tattoo might be the answer to many of our questions.

The puzzle of the underground facility still remains. At the time Donovan reported his experience to me, he had not read any material on the underground experiences of others. I think that many of us here on Earth are herded up like cattle and maybe given some type of invisible implant underneath our skin in the form of a number. In Donavon's case he had only one implanted, if true. But, in my case and in many other instances, we remember numerous implants placed in many areas of our bodies. What do these implants do for the aliens? What do they do for us? The study will continue and there will be many more like Donavon who have these encounters with beings from another world.

We are being manipulated by some force outside of our realm of understanding. Maybe by reporting more stories such as Donavon's we can place the pieces of the puzzle together. The best we can do for now is give support to our friends who do not understand. An update may be warranted in the future, but let us hope Donavon will be left in peace. For this is all we want here on Earth anyway, PEACE.

* * * * * * * *

Donavan's real name is Samuel Paul Holcombe. This is an update dated 2005 from his web site.

One of the more recent inexplicable events is as follows, September 28, 2005. I left my friend's house driving home at 11:00 P.M. As I was approaching a roadside park, which is 4.4 miles from my friend's house, I was thinking that I needed to stop by my post office box and pick up my mail. That was my last conscious memory, until I was standing in my bedroom with a nose bleed and my friend's truck was parked behind my house, I looked at the clock. It was 1:30 A.M. I was feeling as though I had been drugged and went straight to bed. The following morning I didn't wake up until 11:30 A.M., still feeling as though I had been drugged. That feeling lasted for about three hours after I awoke, and my legs were weak and unsteady. It is 4.4 miles from my friend's house to the aforementioned roadside park and 5.3 miles from that park to my home. A trip distance of 9.7 miles, which would have normally taken no longer than 20 minutes, but lasted for more than two and a half hours, with absolutely no recall of what happened from the roadside park to my home. Consequently, I never did stop at the post office to pick up my mail that night.

16.

LED BY THE HAND THROUGH A DEEP AND DARK LAND

A Q AND A WITH CHRISTA TILTON
By Tom Adams

UFO abductee Christa Tilton claims to have been abducted by human military personnel and taken belowground to the Dulce base. Christa was married to UFO researcher Tom Adams in 1987, and Tom conducted this interview with Christa in early 1989. Tom questions her about the effects of her experiences, her feelings toward the aliens, efforts to cope with her memories of these events and the message she would impart to other abductees. Tom and Christa divorced in 1991, and Tom passed away in 2014.

Tom interviews Christa with a tender intimacy that supports her emotionally as she recalls some traumatic and bizarre events.

INTRODUCTION BY CHRISTA: I've been investigating underground bases and Dulce, actually underground bases all over the world since 1987. I've had some good experiences and I've had some bad experiences [with aliens, etc.]

QUESTION: Have you seen any people who were being held captive underground during your abductions to Dulce and other bases?

ANSWER: First of all let me state [that] there is more evidence NOW to prove that a base DID indeed exist back in 1987 when I was abducted, and it was in the process of being dismantled. A lot of times the government will have underground bases for different purposes, and then will shut them down, board them up, concrete them in or whatever, and go on and build another base somewhere else.

What I will tell you is this. Let me stick with the question. You asked me did I see any people being held captive during that abduction to Dulce? I remember seeing some individuals as I was walking by. They looked as if they were in suspended animation. I went up to the clear casings that they were being held in. I put my hands on the casing and leaned towards them to see if I could get some kind of a response. I did not. I could not discern whether they were dead or alive at that point in time. They were just not moving, and I could not see whether or not there was any fluid.

I think that the casings were free of any fluid in this particular case. As far as my being taken to any other bases right now, I'm not going to comment on that because I'm still researching that. There has been speculation by, and information from, an Air Force officer at Kirtland Air Force Base that I, along with some other women and men, have been more than likely abducted and taken to the underground research facility near Kirtland AFB. It's in the Manzano mountain range south of Kirtland AFB where the nuclear testing was going on at that time.

Q: Did any of your alien or human contacts mention the Dulce Wars?

A: No. The alien beings that I came in contact with while underground did not speak to me. The human contacts did but no, they did not mention any kind of wars going on there. So at that particular time I was not aware of any kind of a power struggle going on. I was just taken there for a specific purpose I think, and once that was done I was rushed out of there and I don't think any kind of knowledge like that in particular would have been given to me, there wouldn't have been any reason to give it to me.

Q: What kinds of reptilians, if any, have you encountered?

A: I am almost virtually positive that... I don't believe I have come across any reptilian aliens at all. The only types that I've been associated with most of my life have been small grey aliens, the ones that I call workers. These are beings that I believe are soulless beings that are workers FOR an established alien race. They are given certain chores, certain jobs, just like we would if we worked for a large company...

There are some taller grey alien beings that I have encountered. Even though their eyes are large and dark, they don't have that "reptilian" look. I know. I know what you're talking about and no, I really haven't encountered any of those.

Q: Do you know of any other bases that researchers may be unaware of?

A: That's a great question, really, because right now I'm working with two individuals from Great Britain. They're two wonderful researchers who have been associated with Timothy Good. I don't know if you've read his material, *"Above Top Secret."* It's a wonderful book to get and read. Also *"Alien Liaison"* is another one. But yes, I am aware of many, many, many underground facilities or bases that are being used for different purposes. Most of the underground bases are being used for covert purposes or otherwise purposes involving governments' who are doing certain types of testing that they consider would be safer to do underground.

And then there are the bases, one in particular north of Tucson, Arizona, where I'm almost positive I was taken to, it goes under the cover or name of "Evergreen Aviation." They have all the planes there and everything, but what I found during my ten years of research is that this is a CIA-backed or based facility. I got very, very close to the facility, I climbed over the wired fence and sneaked in with a pilot friend of mine not long ago and got some great photographs of some black helicopters. These black helicopters were unmarked.

There were other types of aircraft there, and so we really believe that there are many, many bases in many states. I've heard of bases in almost every state here in the United States. Now the two individuals that I'm doing work for or research with in Great Britain especially are researching underground bases in America and in Great Britain. I guess they contacted me because they felt like there was a tie-in or some kind of connection and that it would be a good thing to work together and share information and see what types of facilities we can find out about.

In a lot of the facilities they are doing medical testing; some are actual laboratories like Los Alamos Laboratories. They do massive amounts of covert work for Black Projects of our own government, so we're talking about installations, underground and aboveground, that are doing things that we probably have no idea about. We hear rumors of course of different things that are going on. What I would venture to guess is that more than likely these rumors have been proven about 90% of the time to be true.

Q: My belief is that the greys operate from base animal or predatory instincts in their agendas to increase their power-base and exploit other cultures, and that they will continue to do so as a collective until they are stopped by force. Some of the greys I believe might be "tamed" by humans, so to speak, and attain a degree of emotional individuality IF they can be severed from the collective HIVE mind. What are your views on this?

A: I agree with you on most of that... Certainly the greys seem to do things like a massive collective consciousness. I've noticed that they do things together; there is almost no discussion among themselves. They seem to be working on projects or on certain things that are given to them by higher-ups, or higher alien beings and/or humans. I really couldn't tell you.

I have my doubts that humans would be able to "tame" any kind of alien intelligence here on Earth. If indeed it looks like humans are working among the greys together, that more than likely it was because of a pact or some type of a government agreement... I believe these aliens have come here for reasons, and certain individuals in the government have been given orders by their higher-ups to either give them opportunities to work alongside of these [aliens] for maybe a one-world purpose. Unless it could be shown to me to be true that the humans tamed these greys that were working alongside with me, or on me, that would be very difficult for me to believe.

Q: Have you had encounters with any Nazi-type aliens like those described by Barney Hill, Alex Christopher, Vladimir Terziski and others, alien "fascists" who date back to the secret Nazi flying disk experiments and who are allegedly working with the greys and reptilians?

A: I've heard of these Nazi aliens. Of course where I first heard about them was from TAL LeVesque back in 1987. No, I have never come in contact with what I would call Nazi-type aliens, although since most of my experiences have involved medical experimentation, genetic experimentation on me and my daughter or family, I would have to say that it reeks almost of... If you think about the medical experiments that were done on the Jews during the Holocaust, that is what I equate some of the experiments that happened to me with.

It's strange, because I'm part German, I come from a family that originally came from Germany, so I do have some German blood in me, but I'm not leaning one way or the other. And as far as being a bigot is concerned, I'm very, very open to all races, creeds, and colors of people working together to establish a wonderful world, if that would be possible. But anyway, no I have not encountered these Nazi types, and I've certainly heard a lot about them, I've heard they are very mean-spirited aliens, I don't know what their agenda is... Since I've not had contacts with these types I really have no reason to do any research on them, and also the same goes for the [tall] reptilians, although many, many friends and other researchers have contacted me telling their tales about reptilian alien races…

Q: What are your views of a possible congressionally backed take-over of the Dulce base in the future, and what would be your views on dealing with the problem supposing the greys don't surrender?

A: Through all of the research that I've done, and all of the proof that I've come up with the many times that I've been up there poking around with researchers and other individuals, we're almost positive now - I don't know if you've even heard, you may have heard the rumor, or thought it was a rumor - but I am of the belief system now that this base is or was deserted and is no longer being used by OUR government…for what reason I'm not sure.

I believe a lot of it had to do with - if there was indeed a military action there, which we have found proof of. We found some spent military cartridge shells up near where we think one of the base openings is. We found C-Ration cans, we found different types of antennas that the government would have used for communications. These are things that have been found up in these mountainous areas. If you've ever been there you'll know what I'm talking about. These things tell me and my research partner that indeed there was some type of a military response there in the past.

The areas I speak about, that my research partner who lives in the area claims were some of the openings to the base, have been concreted, cemented up. Now that's been done by somebody. So we know that some type of government official company… we believe it was a CIA-backed organization that was there… In my Dulce Papers I show an area of a ranch just north of the Archuleta mesa area, and we've been unable to track or find the individuals who have owned this property now for many years. What we've been told by the individuals who lived in or around the area, is that there is a landing strip on that particular property, there are large towers…

I did get onto the property, and close up enough to get pictures of these bullet-proof towers that were sitting on the property. There were about 20, and there are only five there now. We're wondering why they were taken out, and where were they taken? Anyway, I've got pictures of those. These are not just fire towers. Some people try to explain them away by saying "Oh, those are just so our ranchers could go up into the towers and look for fires," and things like that.

DULCE WARRIORS

The strange part about this is that you walk up the towers and there is dark black glass... you can't look in to see, and it's bullet proof. And what's strange is the opening... you are unable to get into these towers. We don't know if they were just put there for show, we don't really know exactly what they are, but we believe they were placed there for some reason. We have no understanding of that. There have been sightings of planes, small Lear jets landing in and out of that area over the years. Nobody in the town of Dulce seems to know who owns that property...

My research partner did track down someone who did own the property over 20 years ago, but after that it seemed to go into covert hands. The property also had what looked like a small wooden house. You could just walk in there, but it's been evacuated and there's nothing in there. This type of facility or front for an underground base in that area would be perfect; because this area was cordoned off by what we believe at one time was an electrified fence which they said was used to keep the cattle out.

We believe that it was used for another purpose because of the signs posted all over - NO TRESPASSING, and these were the types of signs that you would see up near Area-51, and so we have to wonder what was going on up on that property. I don't know if you've ever seen the movie "The Andromeda Strain." I saw it the other day, but I just haven't seen it in a long time. The underground facility that they went to [in the movie] was stationed on kind of a muck-up farm, where they went into the farm house and went into something like a tool shed, and then all of a sudden this elevator starts going down and down and down. And what they found once they went down was a massive underground biological testing facility.

I have to believe that these types of facilities are all over in every state. So then, back to the question...if there was a military takeover it already happened, and the base was closed...again there's no proof there. Some of the Indians who live on Jicarilla Apache land, these people are very, very closed, they don't talk to outsiders. The information that I got was only from an inside source, and I can only tell you what one Jicarilla Apache Indian told his dear friend of many years there. He said that he was going up through the mountainous areas there, up through the Archuleta mesa and back into the hills, and was walking alongside of a ledge. All of a sudden he felt some dirt falling on his head. And so of course, if you were walking around in this deserted area and you felt something fall on your head, your immediate response would be to look up. And he did, he looked up and he said what he saw horrified him. This is a man; he's a man in his 60's. This man looked up and saw...

this is what he told his friend, "I saw a grey being with large black inky eyes staring down at me over a ledge, and it looked like a large rock had been swiveled out, was sticking out of the side of the mountain."

And he did a double-take, he looked away like someone who would rub their eyes and say, "Oh, I'm just seeing things," but then he looked back up and he saw it again. Well, this time he said he took off and he ran, he was running for his life. He was very, very frightened, scared, and what's strange is that this man is friends of the men high-up in the Jicarilla Apache tribal council, but he has kept this secret from everyone except my research partner. And he told him that when he got back he was shaking, he was very, very frightened. So THIS tells me - and this just happened during the past couple years, so this tells me that there are still grey aliens inhabiting some part of that base.

Interesting question there that you had because if indeed there is still part of the base that's still inhabited by the grey beings, then certainly if there is a problem there might NEED to be a Congressional-backed military take-over of that base, or they may have just left it alone, just said "Let the people of Dulce worry about the aliens, we don't want to deal with them anymore." I don't really know what happened during the military events that they had there, I don't really know what happened, I just know that... I'm almost POSITIVE that there was some type of a confrontation!

So anyway, who knows, who can say for sure? All I know is that a lot of these individuals that come up with different stories, these are individuals who are not the type of people to just come across with a tale, in fact [many of them] are not interested in UFOs, they're not interested in any of this. In fact, when the subject is brought up, they really just don't want to talk about it to you. It's very hard to get access into that community. I have had a lot of problems getting answers, but thank God one of my research partners, his father lives there, he's lived there all his life. And this young man was brought up there (Dulce). He knows what happens there, he knows what all the rumors and tales are, and he knows what all the Indians have seen.

Q: Have you been taken to any other planets or spheres during your abductions?

A: Not that I know of. However, I [remember] that I was taken to some type of large massive ship; it had to have been a mother ship. This thing was massive; it was miles and miles and miles long. I'm not sure exactly where I was. I received some instructions while I was there. There were "light beings" there. They looked like angelic beings, only without the wings. They were wearing long robes, and I was taken into an area where they had a podium and a teacher that came out and was teaching the people who were there. These people were human. I did not see any aliens (greys) at that time, so I'm not sure exactly where I was.

Q: Did you ever get to see what was inside the "tanks"?

A: No, not during the Dulce experience. I started to walk up to the tank. It smelled very foul. It was an odor that I can only identify as being close to a sulfuric type of odor. I remember when I first went in to the medical field we were invited downtown to view an autopsy, and the formaldehyde they use there has a sickening sweet smell. It's a smell that is very difficult to try and explain to somebody who has not smelled it before, but I can say that it smelled a lot like that. The officer, the military man that was with me, guiding me, would NOT allow me up to the tank to look inside.

I can only speculate that there was something in there that may have been frightening to me, because he reacted very quickly to stop me. You asked if there were both breeding and feeding tanks. I believe so, because from what I've been told by some of the other women who saw these tanks, some of them saw body parts inside. The types of tanks that I saw were used for breeding and cultivation of small alien beings. The only thing that I can describe it as is of being [like] a fake womb. A woman carries her child in her uterus. Well, these types of breeding tanks that you're talking about were used to cultivate the fetuses that they extract from the individuals that they abduct and take there. They extract the fetus like they have done with me MANY times, and I believe they place it in this type of a tank, a glass [looking] breeding tank.

Q: What do you think most of the hybrids feel about the position they are in?

A: That's such a very good question and not many people ask that... I myself being a hybrid have felt that I do not fit in anywhere. I still feel like I don't "fit in" to this day. I know I don't, I know I'm different, and I don't try to tell everybody that either. I just have accepted it and go on with my life, but I can assure you that every hybrid I've spoken to has told me, has tried to explain to me the emptiness and the feelings that they feel. They feel almost like they don't belong here on Earth. I certainly feel [that] I don't belong here.

Q: If the outer world gets a hold of the Dulce technology and begins using it to colonize other worlds, could this alleviate the population, economic, environmental and other problems that this planet faces? In other words take away the imposed barriers that have kept us earth-bound and in essence finally let us "out of the cradle," so to speak? The greys, for one, do not wish Terrans to gain interstellar advantages and so become a threat to their own empirical agendas, and operating through various power-cults on earth they have succeeded in keeping interplanetary technology out of our hands and robbing us of our resources to finance the joint subterran and exterran projects, many of which projects and bases have been taken over entirely by their own kind and at our expense.

Once robbed of our resources the greys use their psychological slaves on Earth to set us against each other and then turn around and say: "Ha, you people are too violent to be allowed to have interstellar technology!" Although there have been technology exchanges, it would seem that they are either being used as a ruse by the greys to gain access to our society so that they can impose a global electronic dictatorship, and/or it is technology that is being provided by the Federation 'Nordics' so that they can help defend Planet Earth for the mutual benefit of themselves and their human "cousins" on Earth. What do you think about all of this?

A: I believe without a doubt that we have been working on projects to colonize the moon, underground, and also to colonize Mars... I've talked with scientists; I've talked with former NASA astronauts who believe without a doubt that this is what's going on. They don't feel like it's anything alien. Some of the astronauts say they felt like, well, this is just a technology that we've developed on our own, and that certainly population is a problem that you have to think about way in advance and that humans have come to all of these conclusions themselves. I disagree. I think that it was an alien technology that was given to us, and I think that we're running with it, and we've already started. Like with the Biosphere, a lot of people think that that is just for learning about our ecology and things like that, plants, animals and all of that. I know that was a front.

I know of a lot of things that went on underground there. That is also an underground facility, it's a massive facility and it's a wonderful facility. The technology there being tested was alien technology. All this will be used when they start to colonize the moon and Mars. These are the two "planets" right now. Actually the moon not so much being a planet but a satellite of Earth, but certainly it's a stepping-stone away from Earth to other places. And this is what's going on, I have no doubt about it. I've talked to too many scientists who've worked on covert or black projects for our government who have said that's exactly what we're doing...

I really believe that we don't have much longer here as a people to survive on Earth. The climate will be vastly changing... so we have to have the technology to go somewhere else. That's what many of the aliens did themselves [long ago]. The aliens that I've dealt with, the Ones who came from the constellation of Lyra... they actually had a massive explosion on their planet. They had to evacuate and migrated to the Pleiadean constellation where they knew other alien civilizations were already living. There are many different types of Pleiadean aliens. I cannot stress this enough to people who say, well, there's only one Pleiadean race... Some of "my" people also came into our system and settled on Mars, but something happened on that planet that forced them to go underground to live.

Q: What would you consider the greatest weakness of the greys to be?

A: I can tell you right now that the main weakness of the greys is that they have no soul, they are soulless. Do not allow them to tell you otherwise. Some of them have been known to try to impart some type of [false] religious philosophies on people that they've abducted, and the thing is you have to realize that these aliens have their own agenda, and it's not something that I feel is a positive one really. So I have found out from dealing with them most of my life, they are soulless, they have no soul, and when it comes to my religious beliefs or background - I'm not afraid to say it, I'm a Christian, I believe in God, I believe in one ultimate being... God, who created all, all alien beings of all kinds... all different constellations where people have colonized throughout the universe... beings, animals, things we probably have no idea about. Certainly I have to believe that the greys are, the only way I can describe it is that they are an empty, empty case... There's nothing there other than a superior technology type of brain apparatus up in their skull area. Otherwise they are of no use to us really, they are really of no use. They are used to impart different technologies and give us information, but as far as trusting them, I do not trust them as far as I could throw them.

Q: What do you think our greatest strength as human beings is?

A: Well, our greatest strength is our belief in God... our greatest strength is [that] ability... and our only connection with each race is our connection with that one Supreme Being, God. Now I do believe that God saw at some point in our history the need for someone to guide us into the positive way of living, I believe [that] Jesus was born as an example of the way that God would want us to live our lives... If we believe in Jesus Christ as the Son of God, the one and only God, then we have to believe that this is all true. I believe that He, Jesus, will be coming back...

I believe in angels, I collect angels [artistic representations]. My best friend in Wisconsin sends me angel cards all the time, and I send her angel this, angel that, angel jewelry, angel statues, everything, because I believe truly that angels walk among us. Believe me, I have seen them, I've dealt with them, I have spoken with them.

I have several close calls where I can only state that these angels have appeared out of just nowhere and saved my life, so I just have to believe that these are God's beings [servants]... they're wonderful.

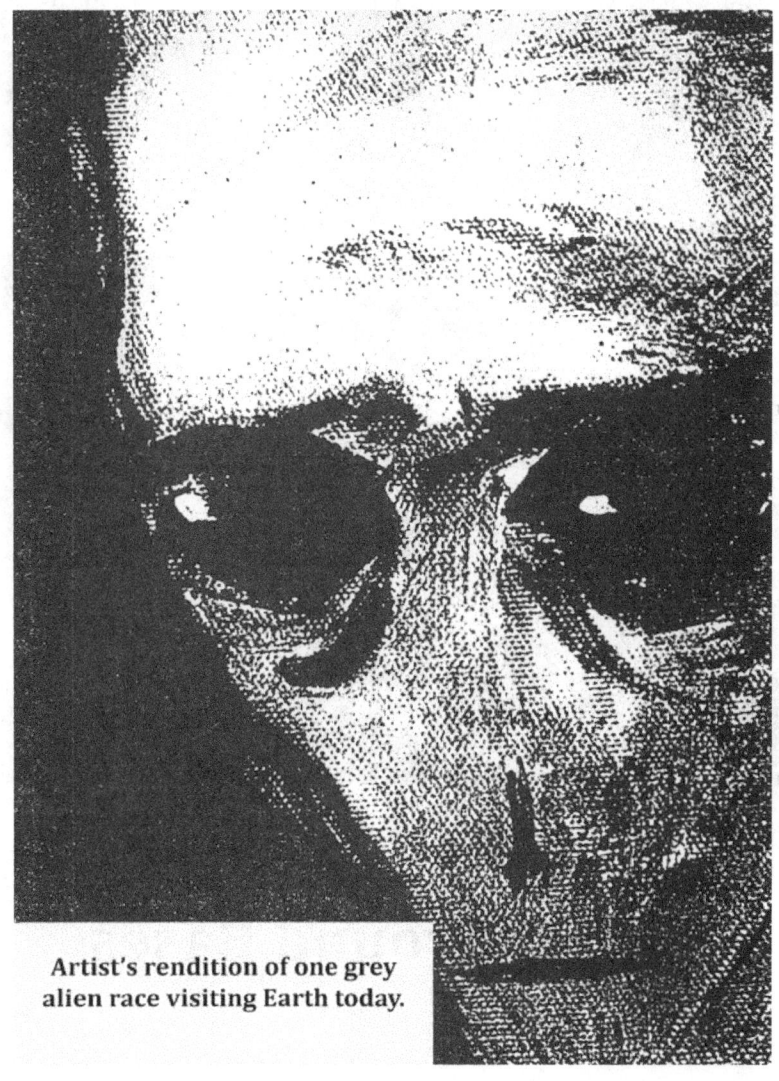

Artist's rendition of one grey alien race visiting Earth today.

SECTION THREE

Underground Bases

17.

THE DEADLY TRUTH ABOUT UNDERGROUND BASES
By Otto Binder

PUBLISHER'S NOTE: Long before the rumors of an underground joint alien/human facility said to exist in Dulce, New Mexico, there were many anecdotal accounts of aliens dwelling beneath the Earth, in the sea, and in vast natural cave systems throughout the world. The extraterrestrials are no strangers to the depths below our feet, as this chapter by researcher and author Otto Binder reveals.

****

They were just called the "little men" and were usually described as gnarled and ugly and not quite human.

Now, who do they remind you of?

Yes, the little humanoids stepping out of flying saucers, as described in numerous reports of UFO landings. All over the world, throughout history, "little men" have been seen coming up from below – and today, "little humanoids" flying around in saucers.

Any connection?

DWARFS AND SAUCER-MEN IN THE UNDERWORLD

Significant clues are piling up indicating that the legendary dwarfs and the "legendary" (according to skeptics) saucer-men may be one and the same. This would mean that the UFOnauts have long ago established themselves underground. Their brief appearances above ground through the ages, with or without saucers, might have caused the worldwide "fairy tales" about the tiny people.

Illustration of underground Cornish knockers from William Bottrell's 1873 book on the folklore of Cornwall.

But they may not be fairy tales, if we consider what the late Dr. Morris K. Jessup wrote in his book, *"The Expanding Case for the UFO"*: "There are caves in Europe which have been shaped by masonry methods. They are 10.000 to 20,000 years old. Their rooms and passages are too small for normal-sized adults of today, and children use them as playhouses."

Incidentally, it should be noted that in folklore down through the centuries various small creatures are supposed to live underground – trolls, kobolds, pixies, leprechauns, elves, goblins, gnomes. They have many names around the world.

This theme of saucer men living underground has no connection with the hollow-earth theories of various writers, or the vast catacombs wherein the "deros" lurk, according to another concept. We are speaking merely of caves and caverns and deep rocky chambers probably more extensive than has ever been imagined – which may be the "hangars" and living quarters for thousands of flying saucers and their humanoid operators.

Jessup also developed the concept that the few remaining pygmy tribes on Earth today may represent an offshoot of the original "little-men" humanoids that presumably came here eons ago. The pygmies, who exist today only in three places on Earth – Malaya, New Guinea and Africa – average about 4 ½ to five feet tall, remarkably consistent with the height of saucer humanoids as reported widely.

The biggest ethnological puzzle of all, Jessup said, is that the pygmy is not a missing link but a fully developed human being having no genetic connection with the rest of humanity. If not a product of Earthly evolution, then where did he come from?

Returning to legend again, the folklore of mining regions is always full of tales of encounters with miniature men deep in the shafts. The "metallic sprites" or kobolds (from cobalt) of Germany apparently harassed miners so much that productive mines had to be abandoned. Were they saucer humanoids who did not wish the miners to dig down into their underground domain?

In Scandinavian folklore, mines were habitually plagued by two goblins that even had names: Cutty Soams and Bluecap. Hanover had its own version of "little devils" who haunted mine shafts and whose eyes shot flames. And then we have the most basic "legend" of all – the god Pluto of the Greeks and Romans who was "king" of the underground, master of all metals and jewels, and possessing the magic power to hurl bolts of flames.

In modern UFO sightings, many humanoids are reported to point tubular devices and shoot "rays" that sometimes burn the skin of the observer...Pluto, reincarnated!

And consider this UFO sighting of June 13, 1967, at Caledonia, Canada. At approximately 2:30 a.m., Carmen Cuneo said he spied two UFOs near a mine dump. One was cigar-shaped and about 36 feet long, with four windows on a side and a boom aerial. The other was a disk 15 feet in diameter. Then Cuneo was startled to see three small men emerge with hats similar to those worn by miners. Each cap had four small amber lights at the peak. Cuneo excitedly ran to bring back another witness but by then the craft and "mini-miners" were gone.

ART AND ARTIFACTS FROM ANCIENT TIMES

More scientific evidence of cave humanoids surfaced when Chinese archeologists found a remarkable collection of stone disks in caves at the border of China and Tibet. Complete with holes and grooves, the disks resembled phonograph records, and it was found that they vibrated as if they were electrically charged. Dating back some 12,000 years, are they the "records" of an ancient humanoid hideout? For along with the disks were found the bones of undersized men with "huge craniums and underdeveloped skeletons." In other words, small humanoids.

Archeological records contain other reports of astounding discoveries that do not fit our picture of primeval times. In the Sahara, Henri Lotte, a Frenchman, stumbled upon caves whose walls were adorned with frescoes that clearly depicted what appeared to be men in space suits. A similar discovery was made in Japan, where the ancient Dogu drawings were so detailed they showed round, sealed helmets with what resembled built-in two-way walkie-talkie systems. There are cave pictures of "spacemen" – or at least ·men dressed in uniforms that look suspiciously like spacesuits – in the Val Comonique, the Swiss Alps, in Australia, and Soviet Central Asia.

And again, like the pygmies, these pictorial records are scattered all around our planet, indicating some common "model" who posed for them. What fits better than flying saucer-men who could navigate anywhere on Earth? Otherwise, how would you explain dozens of isolated tribal communities-from the Arctic to the Antarctic and all places between-at the dawn of civilization, without radio or the airplane, all depicting the same or similar "beings"? Archeology fails to provide a coherent "scientific" explanation that includes UFOs and extraterrestrial visitors.

Even more sensational – and more of a headache to anti-UFO scientific authority – was the find in 1932 of a mummy in a cave near the base of one of the Pedro Mountains in Wyoming. It wasn't the usual Egyptian mummy wrapped and laid in a golden sarcophagus...rather, this was the mummified body of a tiny "humanoid" only 14-inches tall.

But, just as headhunters shrunk heads to small proportions, it can be assumed that either by natural forces or man's technique, this humanoid was shrunk from its original living height of perhaps 4½ feet. At any rate, X-ray investigation and other tests proved it was no hoax and was indeed the petrified body of a man, approximately 65 years old, who died thousands of years ago. Whether he was "human" or not, the scientists would not conjecture. The riddle is unsolved to this day.

A WORLD UNDERGROUND

Another odd discovery, not involving humanoids at all, provides another possible answer. The Soviet newspaper *Komsomol Pravda* reported that Russian scientists had explored a coal mine above the Arctic Circle, and found the fossils of ancient animals dating back to the Paleozoic Era some 330 million years ago. They strangely described the area as a veritable "underground zoological park" where an enormous number of animals apparently had been confined in a small area. The animals were identified as natural enemies and as such never congregated within biting distance. Who, then, brought these beasts together? Is it unreasonable to think that, long ago, humanoids from the stars, living underground perhaps to avoid the fierce killer beasts above, captured some for a zoo...or for scientific study...or food?

There is other evidence that strongly reinforces the thesis of saucer humanoids living underneath our feet in hidden camps. There are many tales of weird sounds, eerie noises, and even voices and whispers in echoing caves. For instance, in Floyd Collins Crystal Gave, speleologists (cave explorers) reported hearing strange voices yelling and at times whispering, followed by footsteps. They were too experienced to be "hearing things," and said the voices simply could not have a natural origin. The leader also once heard babbling voices approaching them but they suddenly ceased and no one appeared.

In the Tampico area of Mexico stands stately Sombrero Mountain, riddled with caves near the top. From these caves come incredible sounds which, according to the local people, resemble those made by hydroelectric generating equipment. There is no hydroelectric plant within Sombrero Mountain. But take note: witnesses often have said that the UFOs they sighted made buzzing noises like electrical machinery.

Caves are also mysterious because people sometimes enter them and never come out. It is possible they might have become irretrievably lost or were killed in accidents. Isn't it also possible that the victims were abducted by the subterranean saucer-men?

Some caves, particularly in Europe, have been the source of so many disappearances that they were declared to be "cursed" and inhabited by some evil spirit or demon. A more updated version of this tale could be that saucer-men patrol these caverns arid capture or silence any human blundering into their secret domain. If the UFOnauts of today take such care to avoid humans, we can assume they have had this policy all through the ages in their underground realm.

A curious little story comes from UFO researcher Lucius Farish. He tracked down a member of the Fortean Society who had once known an old sea captain with the odd name of Harmonious. The old salt would "spin yarns," many dealing with the Old Ones who lived underground and rode around in clamshell (saucer?) craft at fantastic speeds. He claimed they came from the stars and established a vast underground network of caves, scientifically using Earth's internal heat for power. Harmonious said that portals into this hidden realm existed at Mt. Shasta in California, at a point in the South American Andes, and in Antarctica, as well as other places in between. Strangely enough, all the points he named are on the Great Earthquake Belt, or the great-circle fault that scientists now know creates earthquakes. It would be logical for huge fissures to exist along this belt, like gateways to the underground.

Harmonious told his stories solemnly, as if they were the truth. His Fortean listener could offer no proof except that for 30 years, the old sea captain – who was short and bearded like a gnome – never aged. And his story involved clam-shell "saucers" long before Kenneth Arnold and his famed Mt. Rainier sighting.

GIANTS ON AND WITHIN THE EARTH

But it is not only "little men" who lurk in the shadowy bowels of the earth. Early in 1968, a team of archeologists explored ancient tunnels and buried chambers in a remote part of Turkey. Some 900 feet below, they came upon a maze of huge passageways obviously dug by artificial means. Suddenly, they were attacked by a group of giant albino-haired men seven feet tall. One archeologist was killed, another hospitalized for months; every member of the party had serious wounds. To date, no further attempt has been made to reenter the caverns and solve the mystery.

These hairy giants sound a lot like the Yeti of abominable snowman legends or the Bigfoot/Sasquatch in the California Sierras. But note: the legends about trolls and such did not always specify that they were small men, but often huge "monster men" seven to 10 feet tall.

The legends about giant subterranean beings are as prolific as those of the little men.

Archeologists have uncovered ancient underground habitations, their proportions signifying that only enormous men could have lived there. George Hunt Williamson, famed archeologist, tells in the book, *"Road in the Sky"*, of a man named de Valda, who discovered seven skeletons of giant men and women who were between eight and nine feet tall. There is also a Mexican legend concerning a giant called Xelhua who "came out of a mountain." Williamson says that Mt. Kilimanjaro, the highest peak in Africa, has been the scene of numerous saucer sightings. According to the natives, there are "giant white men" who live in the mountain. It is a fact that eerie lights playing around the peaks have often been observed by explorers.

Proof of an ancient race of giants exists in a tribe of black people living near Kilimanjaro. Its members are up to eight feet tall! They are the well-known "Watusi." Are they the remnants of the underground giants who once wandered to the Earth's surface and stayed there?

Ferdinand Magellan and his crew claimed to have seen a race of 12 to 15-foot-tall giants while exploring the coastline of South America in the 1520s.

DULCE WARRIORS

The Bible concurs by saying: "And there were giants on the earth in those days." Anthropologists admit the discovery of genuine fossils of creatures taller than normal men. All specimens of so-called "ape-men," from *pithecanthropus* back, range above eight feet tall.

One of the most startling discoveries of recent times was made in 1945 by two pilots flying a photography mission over the terrain north of Nazca, Peru. They were astounded when their enlarged photo showed a vast network of figures previously hidden to the naked eye by the vegetation. Formed by shallow trenches, or rows of stones, the figures included triangles, squares and circles, and the enormous shapes of animals, birds, even insects!

Why was this strange pattern, extending for more than five miles, laid out to be distinctly visible only from the air? The ancient Peruvians had no aircraft that we know of. Then were these "ground beacons" set up as guides for flying saucers?

Peruvian legends persistently mention the "sky gods" who often visited Earth in "bronze eggs." Let us recall that many modern UFO reports describe egg-shaped craft of various metallic colors.

Mentioned previously were Mt. Kilimanjaro in Africa, and Mt. Shasta in California, both the sites of many UFO sightings in modern times, and also the places where strange beings were seen in the past.

Other locales around the world, particularly mountainous areas, are apparently centers of UFO activity. Included are Mt. Argentario in Italy, the Marcahuasi plateau in the Andes, and the Ozark Mountains in the U.S. Another site is Mt. Rainier in Washington State, where Arnold sighted his nine saucers and launched the modern era of saucer sightings.

The clue to the areas' UFO activity may lie in what Harmonious previously said about Mt. Shasta, that they may all be "entrances" to the saucer-men's underworld domain.

SAUCERS UNDER THE SEA

There are other possible entrances to the homes of the saucer-men – underwater, for instance. An estimated 40 percent of UFO sightings occur near rivers, lakes, bays, reservoirs and the deep sea. In a significant number of these sightings, the saucers both enter and leave the water, as the following examples illustrate:

• Dec. 13, 1959: The Swedish ship *Dorthemaersk,* nearing the coast of Venezuela, observed a strange craft shaped like a cone, and giving off fiery radiance as it plunged directly into the sea.

• Mar. 23, 1957: In Venezuela, Luis Petriera and several friends observed a glowing UFO dive into Lake Maracaibo.

The Venezuelan shores and inland waters seemed periodically to be the scenes of "sea saucers." In 1967, three different parties reported flying saucers that either plunged into the water or rose out of it. One was a spectacular sighting of the water boiling violently at first, then three saucers in single file zipping into the air and speeding away.

• Apr. 29, 1961: John P. Gallagher, a carpenter, of Newport, R.I, reported seeing a red sphere bobbing up in the bay, floating out to sea, and then suddenly flying away.

• Sept. 12, 1963: Nineteen workmen aboard Texas Tower II off Cape Cod (a radar missile-spotting station) watched for 20 minutes as a floating object swung a searchlight beam around it, gave off steamy vapors, then sank abruptly. Coast Guard cutters later found no sign of any craft or wreckage.

• October, 1967: Shag Harbor, Nova Scotia, was the scene of diving saucers several times during a single week. The most notable of the events occurred when a "flaming" object dove into the harbor waters and vanished. A search by frogmen revealed no trace of a sunken vessel.

Through the years there have been many reports of "diving saucers" that fly into or emerge from coastal waters. In December 1967, various fishermen complained of "holes" in the Gulf of Mexico "where the water boils in circles." This phenomenon coincided with a flock of sea-saucer sightings in which the craft often left the air and mysteriously disappeared into the sea.

The Gulf of Mexico has been the scene of many weird happenings. In December 1968, two men in a 21-foot boat spent a harrowing weekend on the stormy waters because their compass "went wild."

A similar incident occurred when retired Navy captain Alfred Standford, cruising off Milford, Conn., in his sloop, *Vision IV,* watched his compass make an eerie, 10-minute clockwise spin.

Many ships have reported their compasses going "haywire" over certain stretches of water, especially after UFOs were seen in the area. One theory is that the powerful electromagnetic field of the UFO is what affects the compasses, just as it knocks out car motors on land or blacks out their radios and lights.

But this leads us to the most spectacular and significant sea-saucers of all – those that are detected while submerged. These USOs – Unidentified Submarine Objects – have puzzled many a ship's crew. For example:

• July 5, 1965: Dr. Dimitri Rebikoff, a marine scientist, was conducting studies in a one-man submarine off the Florida coast when he saw a shape of unusual symmetry moving at a speed of 3½ knots. First he thought it was a strange shark, but soon realized it was some sort of machine. Dr. Rebikoff said it was the most fantastic underwater device he had ever seen.

• Jan. 12, 1965: In New Zealand, an anonymous report described a submarine "vessel" cruising at a depth of 30 feet in waters that no ordinary submarine could safely enter. This mystery USO was at least 100 feet long.

Also from New Zealand came the report of R. D. Hanning and W. J. Johnson of the *Eleoneai*. While cruising past the Rugged Islands they saw an immense structure suddenly rising to the water's surface. Both men said it looked nothing like any conventional submarines and the sighting, they added, left them badly shaken.

• In 1966, scientists aboard a research vessel loaded with electronic antisubmarine warfare gear picked up weird, intermittent signals on the sonar coming from a depth of 30,000 feet. Unable to identify the object causing them, the scientists jokingly named it the "180 rpm" animal, knowing it *wasn't* any form of marine life, but some inanimate object cruising far below.

• Aug. 29, 1964: This was truly a shocker. The *Eltanin,* an oceanographic ship equipped with a subsea camera, which could be lowered to far-reaching depths, took pictures at 13,500 feet at a location 1,000 miles west of Cape Horn, South America. They photographed a "big fish" indeed; as their developed film later showed. Hazily, but definitely visible, was an astonishing piece of machinery covered with projecting rods resembling TV antennas. The scientists aboard had to admit it could not possibly have been a marine plant at that lightless depth, nor could it have been any form of coral. When asked what it really was, one scientist couldn't answer but did say that it was man-made, and was baffled as to how anybody could have gotten it down there.

Then, during 1965-66, the famed Jacques-Yves Cousteau and his technical crew set up operations for exploring the depths of Lake Titicaca in Peru with submarines. The lake is the highest in the world at a 12,000-foot altitude.

Cousteau was ostensibly working on a Walt Disney movie, but rumors claimed that he was commissioned to find out why UFOs constantly submerged in the lake. The Peruvian Navy had officially recorded 36 UFOs that vanished in Lake Titicaca's waters in a period of only four weeks.

Cousteau found nothing at the lake's bottom-at least nothing was released to the public.

But Peru, particularly the Lake Titicaca area, is the site of many ancient legends concerning "underground giants" and their civilization. Ruins of some of their abandoned hideaways inside mountains have been discovered and authenticated by archeologists.

One final marine item may form a link in the mysterious chain of sea-saucer sightings. UFO sightings have been notoriously frequent in the West Indies, as well as Florida. Near the Bahamas shore, in August 1968, archeologist Dr. Manson Valentine announced a blockbuster of a discovery – the finding of temple ruins and marble columns under only six feet of water. In all, the relic was 100 feet long and 75 feet wide.

Cautiously, Dr. Valentine tried to attribute the visible architecture to the pre-Columbus Arawak Indians, or perhaps to the much older Mayans. But the suspicion exists that they are much older than that – perhaps dating back to Atlantis some 25,000 years ago.

Islands suddenly appear at sea regularly, as portions of the ocean floor inexplicably rise. So it is not beyond belief that some part of sunken Atlantis has recently risen into shallow waters. And Atlantis, according to legendary references, was the site of a highly-advanced civilization that possessed aircraft similar to flying saucers.

What do all the sea-saucer phenomena lead to? Simply this: most of them are seacoast and offshore sightings where underwater or tidal caves may exist – and these may give access to the underground dry-land homes of the saucer-men. Florida's extensive coastline, for instance, is known to be riddled with innumerable underwater caves. UFOs plunging into the water may simply enter these hidden apertures that could be linked to a dry underground cave system, created either by nature or men ... saucer-men, that is.

SINKHOLES ON THE RISE

And consider this. Florida is constantly beset by the sudden appearance of "sinkholes," or cave-ins, some of them disastrous. For instance, on Dec. 17, 1968, the Anclote River Bridge on Route U.S. 19, north of Tarpon Springs, suddenly collapsed due to sinkholes that abruptly opened up under it. These sinkhole pits are sometimes as big as football fields, swallowing up houses, herds of cattle, and small forests. Now, geologists know that underneath much of Florida there exists a veritable honeycomb of pits, caves, and caverns. The scientific explanation is that these were formed in ancient times when Florida was submerged and the sea-waters swirled through its basic limestone structure.

But the appearance of sinkholes is increasing, as if *more* deep caverns are being dug out. By whom? It can no longer be nature. Combine this with the enormous number of saucer sightings in Florida – both over land and off the coast – and you have a two-plus-two that adds up to a major "colony" of underground saucer-men snuggled under that state.

The sinkholes are no joke. In 1967 and 1968, no less than eight sinkholes suddenly appeared in that one area near the aforementioned Anclote River Bridge, including the following:

• A sinkhole that caused one home to collapse;

• An 18-foot wide sinkhole in the middle of Montana Avenue in New Port Richey;

• Five large sinkholes up to 30 feet wide that swallowed up trees, lawns, parts of houses, and one whole street in Tarpon Springs; and

• A sinkhole 18 feet long gobbled up part of U.S. 19 and stopped all traffic on that busy highway.

There is also another mysterious kind of geological formation – the "lava tube" – found in volcanic areas. These are amazingly straight and uniform round tunnels averaging 4,000 feet in length with smoothly polished sides. Scientists attribute them, somewhat lamely, to the seepage of water through limestone. But who ever heard of such drip-age forming symmetrical tunnels that are sometimes 40 feet wide and eight and a half miles long?

Aware that their theory is weak, the authorities stated, "Because of the persistent folklore regarding an unknown race living far, far underground, such holes or caves carry an aura of strangeness and fear... some of which (the lava tubes) are so regular that they look *man-made* ..." (author's italics).

Yes, the lava-tubes do inspire an aura of strangeness – probably because they *are* part of a much more complex and deeper system of passageways that were never made by lava or dripping water. They may be the "outlying territory" of a saucer-man network of caverns, from which they at times rise to the upper surface.

THE PECULIAR PURITY OF CAVES

Another mystery the experts cannot explain is the extreme *purity* of cave air, so pure that the National Cave Association recommends caves for hay fever sufferers, and lists 32 caves in 14 states for people to visit. These include such famous sight-seeing caverns as Mammoth Cave in Kentucky, the Cathedral Caverns of Alabama, Arkansas's Onyx Cave, Missouri's Mark Twain Cave, the Ice Caves of New Mexico, and the Forbidden Caverns of Tennessee.

Why should these and many other caves hold the purest air known, with absolutely no pollen or dust or pollutants? Why, unless an underground race of humanoids produces fresh and pure air to be pumped through their vast cave-system, some of which leaks up into the caves we know?

Are such caves related to UFO sightings? Decidedly so. A large percentage of saucer reports come from areas in the vicinity of natural caves. The following are but a few samples:

• Apr. 18, 1968: Near New Kensington, Pa., a dozen people spied a bright circular object in the sky over the Allegheny Valley. Ora Conley, Jr., and Andrew Buday, who were exploring caves in the region, also saw the UFO, which came within 50 yards of them. They described it as being as big as a room, round, with flashing lights underneath and unblinking lights at the sides, plus a glass-like dome at the top.

- July 28, 1968: A wave of UFOs was reported from the area around Huntingdon Valley, Pa., where the well-known Lincoln Caverns are located. Open to the public during the summer, these caverns contain the usual stone formations and features with colorful names – Diamond Cascade, Mystery Room, Frozen Niagara, and Giant's Castle.

With so many people visiting the caves, the UFOs seen would hardly enter them. But it's a fact that most large caverns have more than one opening to the surface. The public entrance is only the largest or most convenient. The saucers may well use another and perhaps secret entrance that bypasses the commercially exploited portion of the caverns and goes directly to the saucer-men's rocky lair.

Missouri was also the scene of a "flap" in late 1968 and early 1969, especially in the Ozark Mountains. Many UFO reports centered in the area around Hannibal, which is near the Mark Twain Cave (mentioned before).

On Feb. 11, 1969, three persons came upon a round silver ball, the size of a quarter moon, hanging in the air. It mysteriously "disappeared" after five minutes. Did it vanish underground in a diving motion too swift for the human eye to follow?

Near Springfield, Mo., are three caves open to tourists: Marvel Cave, Meramec Caverns, and Fantastic Caverns. Dozens of UFOs were reported by excited people in the vicinity in January 1969. One report from a woman and her teenage daughter told of an 18-foot round object that had landed on the highway in front of their car. Was it to let off small humanoids, which then scurried into one of the innumerable Ozark caves, many of them unexplored?

Even some of the larger, commercialized caves remain incompletely charted, according to the National Caves Association. For example, in the case of Bridal Cave, it says: "The size of the cave is undetermined, as it is explored only to the subterranean lake (Lake of the Ozarks)."

Speleologists mention "unexplored" passageways and "unknown" pits in almost all caves, large or small. Chances are that less than 10 percent of any cave system is fully known to us. Difficult passages and dangerous formations prevent even the hardiest cave explorers from going on through what may be linked caverns going on for untold miles at greater depths.

But the saucer-men could have long ago charted these lightless, mysterious mazes and converted them into comfortable and utterly safe havens, free from human interference. Otherwise, how would you explain the innumerable UFO sightings in bleak, mountainous areas which are riddled with caves?

And ponder this. On Dec. 8, 1968, the AEC conducted the Schooner Experiment and exploded in Nevada an underground nuclear bomb of 35 kilotons capacity. Five days later, the radiation level rose from 10 to 20 times – in Canada, 1,000 miles away. Since the Nuclear Test Ban prohibits aerial explosions and all A-bombs are set off underground, how did that radioactive contamination reach Canada?

There is one answer we can give the baffled scientists, which they will never accept, of course: the nuclear contamination traveled as dust through an interconnected series of caves, all the way to Canada.

We have no answers yet regarding the effect of underground nuclear explosions on subterranean saucer-men, or whether the saucer-men have protection systems against radiation. One wonders if too big a blast might not bring a swarm of angry beings boiling out of thousands of caves.

Only time will tell.

It has long been rumored that the intelligence behind UFOs have used natural caves for their secret bases.

18.

DULCE AND OTHER UNDERGROUND BASES AND TUNNELS
By William Hamilton III

PUBLISHER'S NOTE: Over the years I could always count on Bill to bring me in some very titillating material on UFO-related topics no one else seemed to be into. It was if he had a drop on the subject that few others had. He was particularly interested in the concept of aliens roaming the Earth and of the existence of underground bases of one type or another, be they occupied by ETs or some rogue military force.

Even though very active in the UFO field at one time, William F. Hamilton III managed to maintain a relatively low profile so that he could continue his work in private and without needless interruption from well-meaning but nevertheless prying eyes.

Admittedly, his name wasn't known in every household, but the fact of the matter is that 'Bill' is highly respected among his peers.

Indeed, what he had to say was as important and vital as the words of such Dulce-oriented individuals as flying ace John Lear, who has gone on record regarding the alien conspiracy.

In fact, much of what Hamilton claims is consistent with the theory that there is a massive government cover-up on UFOs and alien visitations that reaches right up to the president's private office door, and that the U.S. military has made a secret pact with a group of aliens known as the "Greys." [They] are on earth... mutilating cattle, and abducting humans for experimental purposes. Supposedly the Greys have taken over several Top-Secret underground military facilities, AND there are certain branches of the government [who] are working hand-in-hand with these entities to bring about total domination of the world, while a SECOND group of extraterrestrials is here trying to protect us.

Hamilton was a frequent contributor to *"UFO Universe"* and *"Unsolved UFO Sightings"* magazines, as well as being the author of such books as: *"Alien Magic: UFO Crashes, Abductions and Underground Bases"*, *"Cosmic Top Secret - America's Secret UFO Program"*, and *"The Pheonix Lights Mysteries."*

Of a highly controversial nature, many of Hamilton's statements may seem overly "radical" to even his closest associates, not to mention other investigators who refuse to even seriously consider the documentation he is able to present to bolster his case.

* * * * * * * *

UNDERGROUND BASES AND TUNNELS

Does a strange world exist beneath our feet? Strange legends have persisted for centuries about the mysterious cavern world and the equally strange beings who inhabit it.

Many UFOlogists have considered the possibility that UFOs may be emanating from subterranean bases and that UFO aliens have constructed these bases to carry out various missions involving Earth or humans.

Belief in a subterranean world has been handed down as myth, legend or rumor down through the generations from all over the world. Some of these stories date back to ancient times and tell tales of fantastic flora and fauna that can be found in the caverns of ancient races. Socrates spoke of huge hollows within the Earth which are inhabited by man, and vast caverns through which rivers flow.

A legendary large cavern supposedly exists below Kokoweef Peak in southwestern California. Earl Dorr, a miner and prospector, followed clues given to him by Indians. He entered Crystal Cave in the thirties and followed a passage down into Kokoweef Mountain until he attained a depth of about a mile. There, he entered a large cavern which he proceeded to explore for a distance of eight miles. At the bottom of the cavern, a river flowed, rising and falling with the lunar tides, and depositing black sands rich in placer gold along its banks. One day, crazed by fever, Dorr used dynamite to seal shut the entrance to his fabulous cavern and started a legend that still lures men to seek the fabled wealth below Kokoweef.

DULCE WARRIORS

Nowhere is the belief in a subterranean world more prevalent than with the Indians of North America. The Hopis believed they emerged from a world below the earth through a tunnel at the base of the San Francisco peaks near Flagstaff.

There are also legends about mysterious Mount Shasta in northern California. The mountain is said to have housed a race of surviving Lemurians who built a sanctuary in the depths of the Earth to escape the catastrophes which befell them. These Lumerians allied themselves with space travelers who built a saucer base inside the mountain.

Whether ancient cities exist in caverns below the earth is anyone's guess, but it's a fact that governments have built underground tunnels and facilities for a variety of reasons. The Chinese, Russians, and Vietnamese all built subterranean tunnels and bases. It shouldn't come as a surprise that America has been building its own underground world.

Mt. Shasta is one of many mountains where local legends tell of mysterious caves and strange inhabitants that live in underground cities.

An elusive report in the August 7, 1989, edition of "*U.S. News and World Report*" reveals the secret plan to carry on government in case of a disaster. The plan is called "Continuity of Government" or COG. The article stated that COG is the government's ultimate insurance policy should Armageddon ever arrive, providing the program runs smoothly. In 1982, a new secret agency, the Defense Mobilization Planning Systems Agency, was created and reports to the President. In the event of a nuclear attack, special teams equipped with war plans, military codes, and other essential data would accompany each designated presidential successor to secret command posts around the country. Besides the president, another 46 key officials named in the Joint Emergency Evacuation Plan (JEEP) would be evacuated. There are 50 of these underground command post bunkers located in 10 different regions of the country, and each is linked with others via satellite or ground-wave relays.

HOW BORING CAN YOU GET?

The U.S. Air Force sponsored research in deep underground construction as early as 1958. The RAND Corporation carried out this research and published proceedings from symposiums held on the subject of construction methods and equipment, utility installation, and the use of nuclear bursts to produce underground cavities.

A great concern to underground construction engineers was the problem of ventilation. They considered it advisable to take into account all types of ventilation contamination, and not just radioactive fallout. Underground works included ingresses, egresses, and accommodations. The first two are generally provided for by shafts or tunnels, while the third requires larger openings, such as halls, chambers, cells, vaults, or other open spaces. Many problems in design and construction are common to all three, but the problems associated with the larger openings in the rock, required for accommodation purposes, are generally more complex and difficult than those for the smaller openings of tunnels or shafts. Operation and maintenance of underground installations can also pose special problems.

Huge boring machines with large-diameter disc-grinders are used in constructing tunnels. Tunnels are needed to link one accommodation area to another, or one facility to another.

The English Chunnel project is the largest engineering project in Europe, and will link France and England through a three-tunnel railway. The eleven boring machines used in the project are so large and so long that they were assembled in underground areas 65 feet high. Six of the machines are digging the submarine tunnel between the Dover Strait and Pas de Calais and five are digging the land tunnels leading away from the channel to aboveground terminals. The front of the boring machine contains tungsten-tipped picks that workers guide with the use of laser projections on video screens.

These boring machines are like huge, steel-encased worms. Sealed in each machine are teams of 35 men who line the cavity of the tunnel with concrete and guide the muck down the track. The machines bore the hole, remove the earth, and pave the inside of the tunnel with precast concrete segments. The digging face of the machine is a 95-ton, 28-foot-6-inch diameter disc, divided into cutting blades. The borer is 300-feet long.

The September, 1983, "*Omni Magazine*" ran a picture story on the "Subterrene," a nuclear tunnel-boring machine developed at Los Alamos. The machine burrows through deep underground rock, heating it to a molten state (magma), which cools after the Subterrene moves on. The result is a tube with a smooth, glazed lining that can be used for the high-speed transport shuttles that link the sub-base complexes.

Interestingly enough, an inventor named Charles Kaempen has invented a composite pipe that has enormous tensile strength. Kaempen has developed an undersea transportation tube that uses his unique system of lock coupling and merely has to be laid on the sea floor, obviating the need for excavating and tunneling. He has made a proposal to Spain to link Spain and Morocco using his new tube technology.

Tunnel boring is undergoing a boom according to a recent article in the "*Wall Street Journal*" (Dec. 12, 1990). Susan Nelson, director of the American Underground Space Association is quoted in the article as saying, "There is simply a lot more interest in the world these days in tunneling and use of the underground in general." It says the underground is crowded with government-funded mega-projects and proposed projects. The Spanish want to put a tunnel through the Pyrenees and bore a road to Morocco on the African coast. The Norwegians want to burrow under the fiords. The Japanese are toying with tunneling through to South Korea. The Canadians are building a tunnel from Newfoundland to Prince Edwards Island. In America, there are 87 public-works projects planned in the next three years alone.

Bear in mind the fact that these are all classified as civil engineering projects. Where civil engineering goes today, military engineering has already gone yesterday. In 1959, the Rand Report carried photos of the giant Tunnel Boring Machines (TBMs). Large scale military engineering projects may have made extensive use of these machines since the fifties.

Tunneling is getting a boost because of the increasingly crowded global landscape. Planners in Northern Italy are burying stretches of a freeway in a tunnel to avoid cutting a road through historical important forest and farmlands.

Mr. Russell J. Miller of the Colorado School of Mines and director of the Center for Space Mining in Boulder, Colorado, is working on studies to determine the feasibility of putting space bases and cities underground on Mars and on the moon. Of course, someone from somewhere else may have already beaten Mr. Miller to the punch.

Informants have told us that underground facilities utilize transport tubes to shuttle workers to and from work. This is more than a subway. These tube trains use high technology. It isn't surprising, then, to learn that Frank P. Davidson of the Massachusetts Institute of Technology has a plan to unclog the airways by designing electric "wingless airplanes" that hurtle across continents and oceans in sealed tubes or tunnels that are essentially frictionless vacuum chambers. Perhaps he should meet with Dr. Kaempen and consider using his composite pipe as the tube.

Underground diggers have their own society called "Moles," who find talk of tunneling and tunnels spicier than most of us surface dwellers.

It's no secret that governments have built their own secret underground railways and tunnels. China's leaders built secret rail tunnels under Bejing that would enable them to flee in a crisis. According to a Chinese civil servant, the tunnels linked leader's homes, government buildings, the central bank and an army base. That sounds like a well-thought-out-plan. Grab your prized possessions, cash from the bank, armed guards from the base, and run like hell! The network was built up over a period of 40 years as a defense against foreign invaders. We can be sure that what China has done we have done.

Japan, dense and overcrowded, is giving serious thought to living underground. They are planning to build underground sewage plants, underground railroads, and underground cities. According to a recent issue of *"Omni,"* The Taisei

Corporation is planning to build a subterranean mall called "Alice City." There would be underground stores, offices, hotels, theaters, and sports arenas. Strolling spaces would meander through interior spaces populated with trees, birds, fish tanks, bridges, and waterfalls. The Shimizu Corporation has a blueprint for constructing an underground grid that would span 2,000 square miles underneath Tokyo. This grid would contain a number of commercial centers connected by subway trains that could shuttle workers to and from work.

ADVANTAGES TO LIVING UNDERGROUND

According to science-writer Isaac Asimov, there are advantages to living underground. For one thing, no one would worry about the weather. The temperature could be held at a fairly constant level, between 55 and 60 degrees F, and a lot of energy used for heating and cooling could be saved. Without the diurnal sun cycle, no one would know day from night. People could be working around the clock or playing around the clock, depending on their penchant. All transportation, communication, and housing could go underground, freeing the surface world from human trampling. The surface of the planet would have a few nice restaurants and recreation centers where people could observe clear blue skies, the returning planet and animal life, and have room for all to roam on a weekend hike. Earthquakes would cause only one-fifth the damage to underground structures that they cause to surface structures.

In a provocatively speculative book entitled *"Alternative 3,"* author Leslie Watkins proposes that scientist have become concerned with the state of the Earth's atmosphere, a scenario that is much easier to accept these days. Secret meetings between scientists produced three alternatives for handling the imminent danger.

"Alternative 1" was a plan to blast holes through the stratosphere to release heat and pollution.

"Alternative 2" was a plan to relocate Earth's population in massive underground caverns drawing fresh, cool air from the soil (Perhaps there is a real Alternative 2 in progress).

"Alternative 3" was to escape the Earth and go to Mars. We will consider Alternative 3 later. Whether any real such alternative plans exist is not being argued here, but the concepts are useful in examining the future directions of secret projects.

Located in Montreal, Canada, La Ville Souterraine, the underground city, has banks, hotels, universities and art displays. It is used by half a million people every day.

The Atomic Energy Commission initiated Project Plowshare in 1957 to develop peaceful uses of nuclear explosives. It has explored the use of nuclear blasts to build harbors, dams, highway cuts, and canals, and to stimulate oil and natural gas production by following up the widely used practice of detonating ordinary chemical explosions in oil-and gas-bearing strata. The first test of this technique, known as Project Gasbuggy, took place 4,240 feet below ground in a desolate area of New Mexico know as the San Juan Basin, on December 10, 1967, where a 26-kiloton nuclear "device" was exploded in a sealed well.

While Gasbuggy was only a single experiment, the A.E.C., in partnership with Austral Oil Company of Houston, subsequently began the first of what promised to be a long series of even larger nuclear explosions, on the order of two 100-kiloton shots each year, for a period of 10 years or more. The first explosion, known as Project Rulison, was a 40-kiloton shot, some 8,400 feet below ground at a site near Rifle, Colorado, on September 10th, 1969.

A method that has been suggested to build bases on the moon may already be in operation on Earth. With the use of controlled nuclear blasts it will be possible to excavate cavities beneath the lunar surface. A missile could be used to drill a hole approximately 50 feet deep, then a second blast would produce a cavity about 45 feet in diameter. An igloo would be constructed over the hole, a plastic bag dropped down the cavity and filled with air. The work area and living quarters would then be constructed.

It may prove more efficient and practical to "house" future moon colonies in artificial or natural caves beneath the lunar surface, than to attempt construction of exposed meteorite domes. Living quarters, spacious parks, lakes, and wooded areas could be constructed underground. A transportation tube would connect various colonists to other ports and distant parts of the moon.

Back on Earth, we have reports of equally suspicious parks. An ex-security officer, who once worked underground in the Groom Lake area of Nevada, said he once saw a baseball diamond and an Olympic-sized swimming pool in one of the caverns a mile below the Nevada desert.

What's going on in the deep underground tunnels below Mercury Base at the Nevada Test Site? After hearing the story of Bob Lazar on KVEG radio, a construction worker called Billy Goodman and Bob Lazar to say, "We are the construction workers...we put things together and take them apart...of the meeting of seven people, there are two who will come forward to support you." This mysterious caller further said, "There are more than just tunnels down there. There's everything you can imagine down there. I know because we put it up. We installed. We did everything."

Informants have mentioned underground tunnels and facilities in New Mexico at Dulce, Sunspot, Datil, Corona, Taos Pueblo, and Albuquerque; in Arizona in the Santa Catalina Mountains; in Colorado at Delta, Grand Mesa, and Colorado Springs; in California at Needles, Edwards AFB, Tehachapi Mountains, Ft. Irwin, Norton AFB, and Morongo Valley; in Nevada at Blue Diamond, Nellis AFB, Groom Lake, and Papoose Lake areas, Quartzite Mountain, and Tonopah.

I became interested in a possible underground installation in the Tehachapi Mountains in the summer of 1988. A young couple, Ray and Nancy, reported that they had gone to a plateau in the mountains after Ray's shift work had completed at the Northrop Plant. Ray was inspector on the B-2 project. The plateau is adjacent to the perimeter of the leased Tejon Ranch where Northrop has built a secret underground facility. It was about one o'clock in the morning when Ray and Nancy spotted a brilliant orb coming out of the ground which flashed light in their direction. They could not account for two-and-half hours of missing time. Ray thought that they had the orb under observation for about an hour, yet the next memory is of sunrise! Under hypnosis, Ray recalls being abducted and taken to an underground base populated by little grey EBEs and Air Force and security personnel. The EBEs were examining Nancy who had been restrained on a metal table. Ray's emotions swelled under hypnotic recall of the incident.

A local man claims he saw a flying saucer emerge and take-off from a silo on the property.

A disgruntled contractor reported that he worked on constructing the tunnels in the underground area and was bothered by the Air Force probes that were often seen hovering in the tunnels. He described these probes as small orbs, and said that this facility was nicknamed "The ANTHILL" because of its resemblance to underground ant colonies. The tunnels have round doorways without doors. Adjacent to the doorways are security panels with red and green lights. There are some kinds of cylinders embedded in the doorway jams that protect a field of energy of some sort.

Black helicopters have been sighted around Boynton and Secret Canyon near Sedona, Arizona. A man living in Long Canyon has sighted a lot of strange things in the canyon areas, and residents suspect a secret government installation has been established in, of all places, Secret Mountain. One of my investigators hiked to Secret Canyon late one night and was stopped by a voice on a loudspeaker and a laser-targeting light on his chest. He was told he had entered a restricted area and to turn around and leave.

We have now spotted and photographed the small orbs around the "Anthill." These orbs definitely exhibit the peculiar characteristics reported in other UFO sightings.

Since that time, we have located two other secret facilities. One is at a place in the Mojave-Desert called Llano. It is an extremely secure facility, but witnesses have seen an extremely bright light burning atop a pylon inside of a movable behemoth-sized structure. This light does not illuminate the interior of the structure! Orbs have been seen in the vicinity of this facility as well.

We can only conjecture about what secret programs are being conducted away from preying eyes. The underground can and does hold all sorts of secrets. Some of the most amazing revelations about what goes on in the underground projects comes from a mysterious informant named Thomas, and who claims there is, indeed, a deep dark secret harbored underneath the imposing mountainous elevations of Northern New Mexico.

THE DEEP DARK SIDE OF DULCE

Dulce is a sleepy little town in northern New Mexico with a population of about 900 and located above 7,000 feet on the Jicarilla Apache Indian Reservation. There is only one major motel and a few stores. It's not a resort town and it is not bustling with activity. But, according to a few outsiders, Dulce harbors a deep, dark secret. The secret is harbored deep below the tangled brush of Archuleta Mesa. The secret is said to be a joint government-alien biogenetic laboratory designed to carry out bizarre experiments on humans and animals.

New Mexico State Police Officer Gabe Valdez was drawn into the mysteries of Dulce when called to investigate a mutilated cow in a pasture 13 miles east of Dulce on the Manual Gomez ranch. Gomez had lost four cattle to mutilations between 1976 and June 1978 when a team of investigators which included Tom Adams arrived from Paris, Texas, to examine the site of the carcasses.

Curious as to how cattle were being selected by the mysterious mutilators, an interesting experiment was conducted on July 5, 1978 by Valdez, Gomez, and retired scientist Howard Burgess. They pinned up about 120 of the Gomez beef cattle and moved them through a squeeze chute under an ultraviolet light. They found a "glittery substance on the right side of the neck, the right ear, and the right leg." Samples of the affected hides were removed as well as control samples from the same animals. Schoenfeld Clinical Laboratories in Albuquerque analyzed the samples and found significant deposits of potassium and magnesium. The potassium content was 70 times above normal.

Some investigators attribute the mutilations to aliens from UFOs. UFOs have been seen frequently around Dulce. Sightings of strange lights and other aerial phenomena have been reported in many areas where the cows have been found at the time of the reported mutilation.

On April 19, 1988, I arrived in Dulce to visit with Gabe Valdez and inquire about the sightings, the mutes, and the rumors of an underground alien base. Snow was still on the ground. I checked into the Best Western Motel and called Valdez to make an appointment to see me at 9:30 PM. I found Gabe to be a very congenial host, offering to show me around the roads of Dulce that night and point out various locations where he had found mutilated cows or had seen strange aerial lights. He made the astounding statement that he was still seeing unidentified aircraft at the rate of one every two nights. We took a look at the Gomez Ranch, the road by the Navajo River, and the imposing Archuleta Mesa. Gabe had found landing tracks and crawler marks near the site of the mutes, and was convinced that scientist Paul Bennewitz of Thunder Scientific Labs in Albuquerque, was definitely on the right track in his attempts to locate the underground alien facility in the vicinity of Dulce. No one knew for sure where the facility was located or how humans or aliens gained secret entry to the facility.

I had first heard of Paul Bennewitz in 1980 when my friend Walter called me from Albuquerque and told me he had been working with Paul on electronic instruments. Walter informed me that Paul had not only photographed UFOs, but had established a communication link with their underground base at Dulce. Bennewitz had first come to prominence during the August, 1980, sightings over the Manzano Weapons Storage Area at Kirtland AFB. A Kirtland AFB incident report dated October 28, 1980 mentions that Bennewitz had taken film of the UFOs over Kirtland. Paul, who was president of the Thunder Scientific Labs which was adjacent to Kirtland gave a briefing in Albuquerque detailing how he had seen the aliens on a video screen. At the time, the aliens were transmitting signals to him from a base underneath Archuleta Mesa.

Researcher William Moore claims that the government agents became interested in Bennewitz's activities and were trying to defuse him by pumping as much disinformation through him as he could absorb. Whether Paul's communication with supposed aliens at the Dulce Base was part of this disinformation campaign is unclear. If we believe that Paul is the single source of reports on the Dulce Facility, then discounting Paul's story and discrediting him could be a tactical maneuver. The actual disinformation maneuver would result in making the public believe there was nothing to the Dulce story.

PROJECT BETA

In a report entitled *"PROJECT BETA,"* Paul states that he had spent two years tracking the alien craft; that he had constant reception of video from an alien ship and underground base view screen; that he had established constant direct communications with the aliens using a computer and a form of hexadecimal code with graphics and print-out; and claims to have used aerial and ground photography to locate the alien ship's launch ports charged beam weapons. Paul claimed that the aliens were devious, employed deception, and did not adhere to agreements. He and Walter were working on a weapon that would counter the aliens.

Have we crossed over from the land of the real world to the land of science-fiction? But then, bizarre phenomena may have its roots in a bizarre reality. As we continue our studies, the world of science-fiction will become the world of science-fact.

Paul Bennewitz had investigated the case of abductee Myrna Hansen of New Mexico, who reported having been taken to an underground facility in May 1980. Christa Tilton of Oklahoma claims she had an experience of missing time in July, 1987, when she had been abducted by two small grey aliens and transported in their craft to a hillside location where she encountered a man dressed in a red military-type jump suit. She was taken into a tunnel through computerized check-points displaying security cameras. She reports having been taken on a transit vehicle to another area where she stepped on a scale-like device facing a computer screen. After the computer issued her an identification card, she was told by her guide that they had just entered Level One of a seven-level underground facility. Christa goes on relating how she was eventually take down to Level Five, where she reports having seen alien craft and little grey alien entities in some of the areas that she passed through.

In one large room where she saw computerized gauges hooked to large tanks and large arms that extended from some tubing down into the tanks. She noticed a humming sound, smelled formaldehyde, and had the impression that a liquid was being stirred in the tanks. She was not shown the contents of these tanks. Christa has made drawings of much of what she claims to have witnessed during her abduction.

These tanks were also depicted in a set of controversial papers called the "*Dulce Papers*," which were allegedly stolen from the Dulce underground facility along with over 30 black and white photos and a video tape. The mysterious security officer who took the papers claims to have worked at Dulce until 1979 when he decided that the time had come to part company with his employers.

The rest of this chapter relates how this security officer met with a colleague of mine in order to tell us the truth about the aliens, the U.S. Government, and the

Dulce Base. His intention was to come out of hiding and present hard evidence to back his claims.

In late 1979, Thomas C. could no longer cope with the awesome reality he had to confront. As a high level security officer at the joint alien-U.S. Government underground base near Dulce he had learned of and had seen disturbing things. After much inner conflict, he decided to desert the facility and take various items with him.

Using a small camera, he took over 30 photos of areas within the multi-level complex. He collected documents and removed a security video tape from the Control Center which showed various security camera views of the hallways, labs, aliens, and U.S. Government personnel to take with him. Then, by shutting off the alarm and camera system in one of the over 100 exits to the surface, he left the facility with the photos, video, and documents. The "originals" were hidden after five sets of copies were made.

Thomas was ready to go into hiding. But, when he went to pick up his wife and young son, he found a van and government agents waiting. His wife and child had been kidnapped. He had been betrayed by K. Lomas (a fellow worker). The agents wanted what Thomas had taken from the facility in order to get his wife and son back. When it became apparent to him they would be used in biological experiments and were not going to be returned unharmed, he decided to get lost. That was over ten years ago. How did Thomas get involved in all this covert intrigue?

Thomas, now is his 50's, was in his mid-twenties when he received top secret training in photography at an underground facility in West Virginia. For seven years he worked in high security photography in the Air Force. In 1971, he left and went to work for the Rand Corp. in Santa Monica, California. In 1977 he was transferred to the Dulce facility. He bought a home in Santa Fe, New Mexico, and worked Monday through Friday. He commuted to work via a deep underground tube-shuttle system.

At this time, a fellow researcher was working security in Santa Fe, N.M. and was privately investigating UFO sightings, animal mutilations, Masonic and Wicca groups in the area. Thomas had a mutual friend who came to Santa Fe in 1979 to visit both the researcher and Thomas. This visitor later viewed the photos, the video tape, and documents taken from the Dulce Base. Drawings were made from what was seen and later circulated in the UFO research community as the *"Dulce Papers."*

DULCE WARRIORS

Thomas alleges that there were over 18,000 short "greys" at the Dulce Facility, and that he saw reptilian humanoids. A colleague had come face-to-face with a 6-foot tall Reptoid which had materialized in his house. The Reptoid showed an interest in research maps of New Mexico and Colorado which were on the wall. The maps were full of colored push-pins and markers to indicate sites of animal mutilations, caverns, locations of high UFO activity, repeated flight paths, abduction sites, ancient ruins, and suspected alien underground bases.

The multi-level facility at Dulce is reported to have a central HUB which is controlled by base security. The security level goes up as one descends to lower levels. Thomas had an ULTRA-7 clearance. He knew of seven sub-levels, but there may have been more. Most of the aliens supposedly are on levels 5, 6 and 7 with alien housing on level 5. The only sign in English was over the tube shuttle station hallway which read "to Los Alamos." Connections go from Dulce to the Page, Arizona facility, then onto an underground base below Area 51 in Nevada. Tube shuttles go to and from Dulce to facilities below Taos, N.M.; Datil, N.M.; Colorado Springs, Colorado; Creed, Colorado; Sandia' then on to Carlsbad, New Mexico.

There appears to be a vast network of tube shuttle connections under the U.S. which extends into a global system of tunnels and sub-cities.

At the Dulce Base, most signs on doors and hallways are in the alien symbol language and a universal symbol system understood by humans and aliens. Thomas stated that after the second level, everyone is weighed in the nude, and then given a uniform. Visitors are given off-white uniforms; jump suits with a zipper. The weight of the person is put on a computer I.D. card each day. Any change in weight is noted; if over three pounds, a physical exam and X-ray is required.

Scales are located in front of all sensitive areas and are built into the floor near doorways and the door control panels. An individual places his computer I.D. card into the door slot, and then enters a numerical code onto a keypad. The person's weight and code must match the card or the door will not open. Any discrepancy will summon security. No one is allowed to carry anything into sensitive areas. All supplies are put on a conveyor belt and X-rayed. The same method is used in leaving sensitive areas.

All elevators are controlled magnetically; there are no elevator cables. The magnetic system is inside the walls of the elevator shaft, there are no normal electrical controls. Everything is controlled by advanced magnetics, including lighting. There are no regular light bulbs and the tunnels are illuminated by phosphorous units with broad structure-less emission bands. Some deep tunnels use a form of phosphorous pentoxide to temporarily illuminate areas. The aliens won't go near these areas for reasons unknown.

Level 1 contains the garage for street maintenance. Level 2 contains the garage for trains, shuttles, tunnel-boring machines and disc maintenance. The studies on Level 4 include human-aura research, as well as all aspects of telepathy, hypnosis, and dreams. Thomas says that they know how to separate the bioplasmic body from the physical body to place an "alien entity" life-force-matrix within a human body after removing the "soul" life force-matrix of the human.

Level 6 is privately called "Nightmare Hall." It holds the genetic labs, where experiments are done on fish, seals, birds, and mice that are vastly altered from their original form. There are multi-armed and multi-legged humans and several cages (and vats) of humanoid bat-like creatures as tall as 7-feet. The aliens have taught the humans a lot about genetics; things both useful and dangerous.

The Grey and reptoid species are highly analytical and technologically oriented. They have had ancient conflicts with the Nordic humans from other space societies, and may be staging here for a future conflict. Intensely into computing and bio-engineering sciences, they are led to doing reckless experiments without regard for what we consider to be ethical and empathetic conduct toward other living creatures.

Principal government organizations involved in mapping human genetics, the so-called genome projects, are within the Department of Energy (which has a heavy presence on the Nevada Test Site); the National Institute of Health; the National Science Foundation; the Howard Huges Medical Institute; and, of course, the Dulce Underground Labs which are run by the DOE. Thomas had revealed that the chief of the genetic experiments for Los Alamos and Dulce is Larry Deaven.

According to Thomas, the alien androgynal breeder is capable of parthenogenesis. At Dulce, the common form or reproduction is by poly-embryony. Each embryo can, and does, divide into six to nine individual "cunne" (pronounced cooney, i.e. siblings). The needed nutriment for the developing cunne is supplied by the "formula," which usually consists of plasma, deoxyhemoglobin, albumin, lysozyme, cation, amniotic fluid and more. The term "genome" is used to describe the totality of the chromosomes unique to a particular organism (or any cell within an organism), as distinct from the genotype, which is the information contained within those chromosomes. The human genes are mapped to specific chromosomal locations. This is an ambitious project that will take years and a lot of computer power to accomplish.

Is the alien and human BIO-TECH being used to nurture and serve us, or is it being used to control and dominate us? Why have UFO abductees been used in genetic experiments? It was when Thomas encountered humans in cages on Level 7 of the Dulce facility that things finally reached a climax for him. Row after row of thousands of humans, human-mixture remains, and embryos of humanoids were kept in cold storage. He says, "I frequently encountered humans in cages, usually dazed or drugged, but sometimes they cried and begged for help. We were told they were hopelessly insane, and involved in high-risk drug tests to cure insanity. We were told to never speak to them at all. At the beginning we believed that story. Finally in 1978 a small group of workers discovered the truth. That began the Dulce wars."

Thomas also says the aliens don't want the land, the gold, the minerals, or water that we possess, nor even the human or animal life. What they do want is magnetic power that surges on and through the Earth. The aliens harvest this magic power in a way unknown to us. Thomas says the aliens recognize this power as more valuable than any other commodity on our globe.

It may be unpalatable to digest or believe Thomas' story. In fact, it seems like part of a living nightmare. There is evidence that something strange does go on at Dulce. Does Thomas have the answer? There may be a terrible truth hidden behind the continuing phenomena of UFO sightings, abductions, and animal mutilations. Our government intelligence agencies have had an ongoing watchful eye on all UFO activities for many decades now. This extraordinary phenomenon must have an extraordinary explanation. We may be only one outpost in a vast interstellar empire.

Recently, researcher John Anderson went to Dulce, N.M., to see if there was any truth to the reported UFO activity. He says as he arrived in town he saw a caravan of cars and a McDonnell-Douglas mini-lab in a van going up a rural road near the town. He followed them to a fenced-in compound where he waited to see further developments. Suddenly, six UFOs descended rapidly over the compound, hovered long enough for him to snap a picture, then shot up and out of sight. When later stopping at a store, he told the owner about the UFO photo he had taken; the store owner listened and revealed how he had been a victim rancher of cattle mutes. Their conversation was interrupted by a phone call. The store owner told John to leave at once, then after John went to his car, he saw a mysterious van drive up to the store and a man got out and went inside. John, deciding to leave Dulce, was followed by two men in a car as he left town.

Even more recently a research team has gone up to Archuleta Mesa to take soundings under the ground. Preliminary and tentative computer analysis of these soundings seem to indicate deep cavities under the mesa.

How long will the secret of Dulce, known to insiders as Section D, remain locked up inside the mute New Mexico mountains? Forever?

* * * * * * * *

COSMIC TOP SECRETS AND THE DULCE BASE

The Sept. 10, 1990 issue of *"UFO Universe"* related the following under the title-heading, "WILLIAM F. HAMILTON III – UFOLOGY'S 'MYSTERY MAN' TO REVEAL 'COSMIC TOP SECRETS'"...

Spearheading a lengthy career in UFO research which began in the days of the contactee activity at Giant Rock, up until recently when he officially retired from the field, Wm openly acknowledged the many shortcomings and pitfalls of his endeavors.

"About ten years ago, a few scientists and engineers, who worked for NASA and shared an interest in UFO abductions, came together to form a group they called Project VISIT – Vehicle Internal Systems Investigative Team. They studied about 130 cases of UFO abductions with the goal of constructing a model of UFOs, their operation, and the entities who crew UFOs.

"They found:

"– UFOs have bright interior lighting.

"– Abductees undergo a medical-type examination with apparently highly sophisticated equipment.

"– Burns are suffered by many abductees.

"– Time loss - from 20 minutes to 3 hours - is common. Project VISIT member, Dr. Richard Niemtzow, described the crew members as four feet tall, hairless, grey in color, with no nose, a small mouth and large slanted eyes. The Grey humanoid is emotionless and communicates by telepathy.

"The Greys have earned a reputation quite different than the Nordic blondes and other reported species. Most of the abductions are done by greys and more than one variation of Grey. The Greys do most of the biological intervening on abductees. Tans, Whites, and Blues (i.e. 'Greys' of other skin colors, gray-tan, gray-white, gray-blue, etc. - Branton) have also been reported by abductees. I have personally had some sort of encounter with what I call the Whites. They are small with extremely white skin and black, wrap-around eyes."

EARTH MADE SAUCERS

In April, 1984, Lt. General George Bone, Vice Commander of the U.S. Air Force Systems Command, was killed while test-flying a secret aircraft over the Groom Lake area, a top secret facility located about 100 miles north of Las Vegas, Nevada. This facility is designated 'Area 51.' The Systems Command reputedly uses this facility to test-fly spy planes, such as the SR-71 Blackbird or its successor, the Aurora. According to the February, 1988, issue of GUNG-HO magazine, which ran a feature article on Area 51, some of the craft being flown out of that test facility would make George Lucas drool!

"In the early 1980s a radio technician working at Area 51 reported seeing a saucer on the ground. It was some 20 or 30 feet in diameter, he said, and when it flew, it moved silently through the air. The technician also viewed a number of wooden shipping crates marked 'Project Redlight.' That project may have been a forerunner of Snowbird. Presently, the Air Force is trying to acquire 89.000 acres adjacent to the Groom Lake facility and to place the nearby Groom Mountains off-limits to the public.

"Before and after the TV documentary 'UFO COVER-UP LIVE,' there had been talk of an underground alien base located in the vicinity of the Groom Lake test site, known as 'Dreamland'... This adds a whole new dimension to the idea of a secret space program and hints at fantastic secret programs that take [us] more than one step beyond.

"A friend of mine once moved to Riverton, Wyoming, to escape from terrifying mysteries he encountered in New Mexico. He said the locals at Riverton asked him, 'Are you here to work on the secret space project out at the jet airport?' Saucers were seen close to the ground in Riverton. One day my friend's truck broke down and he had to hitch a ride to town. A black Lincoln pulled up and a man dressed in black gave him a lift. The dashboard looked like a computer console. The MIB knew exactly where he wanted to be left off in front of the post office, but my friend had never told him.

"ALIEN IMPLANTS – In 1980, when I lived in Glendale, Arizona, I received a call from my friend Walter Baumgartner, who published a magazine of limited circulation called *"Energy Unlimited."* Walter was a natural technologist. He said that he had started working for a physicist by the name of PAUL BENNEWITZ at Thunder Scientific Labs in Albuquerque, New Mexico. He then proceeded to tell me the fantastic story that Mr. Bennewitz had succeeded in communicating with aliens at an underground base situated near Mt. Archuleta in the town of Dulce that was close to the Colorado border and situated on the Jicarilla Apache Indian Reservation. (Note: Bennewitz actually stated that he 'interrogated' the alien-collective via a computer-radio-video link with an 'alien' computer terminal, by tapping-in to the aliens' ship-to-base communications frequency and using a type of hexedecimal mathematical code to break the alien encryption. He first discovered the signals using specialized equipment he had developed, and later concluded that these signals were also being used to influence abductees who had been given electronic mind-control implants. - Branton).

"He told me that these little grey aliens were abducting and implanting people with a device inserted at the base of the skull for the purpose of monitoring and controlling humans. He said that the 'government' knew about this and was involved with alien activities. He also stated that the aliens feared our nuclear weapons and nuclear radiation. He told me that Paul was working on a weapon that would be effective against these aliens.

INTERJECTION BY BRANTON REGARDING 'MIND CONTROL' IMPLANTS

I know of a person who went to have some implants removed by doctors. The implants were removed, via the nasal cavity, from the nerve centers of the brain – some of her nerves being damaged in the process. This nerve damage resulted in a near-death experience following which, when she had 'awakened,' she felt like a 'new person' or that some other 'identity' that had been operating in her was now gone. Some mystics may refer to alien intelligences that possess human minds as 'walk-ins'. What many refer to as 'walk-ins' are often artificial intelligence matrix implants which are attached to the nerve centers of the human brain. These serve as 'nodes' for an alien collective in a parasite-host capacity, allowing the aliens to physically utilize the human subject after an altered state of consciousness has been induced, and the human subject's individual consciousness is incapacitated. This transfer to the 'alternate consciousness' often occurs at night. Also, both malevolent and 'relatively' benevolent otherworldly cultures often induce within human subjects one or more 'alternate' personalities which are taught or programmed to work and operate in the 'other' realm.

If the individual is left-brain dominant and right-handed in their 'conscious' life, in the 'alternate' life they may be right-brain dominant and left-handed, as is the case with my own elusive alternate identity. Other than saying that humans have one brain with two hemispheres, it would be just as legitimate to say that we have two brains in one cranium. In many cases where more 'benevolent' humanoids are concerned, the individual may have 'flashes' of memories of a 'double' or 'alternate' existence where they interact with exterran, subterran or even other-dimensional humanoid societies, often in an 'intimate' capacity, and in some cases even serve as starship crew members or pilots. In the case of the benevolent 'non-interventionists,' such an alternate personality may be a means of interacting with Terrans without violating the laws of non-intervention and interfering with an earth-persons 'conscious' life, although I myself would suggest that even this would be stretching 'non-interventionism' to the limit.

However, in the case of the malevolent ones, such alternate 'identities' are programmed through intense mind-control techniques with the intent of producing unconscious mind-slaves for the alien collective. The 'secrecy' and fear of the exposure of their interventionist agendas is in this case the motive for maintaining secrecy. What is especially confusing however is when one, as in my own personal case, has been infused with alternate personalities or identities by both benevolent and malevolent otherworldly cultures. In my personal case this involved being patched-in to an alien collective-mind [Ashtar] via implants and 'used' by the dark side of that collective – or the interventionist elements within the Ashtar collective such as the 'Orionite infiltrators' that some contactees have spoken of who desire to use their positions to establish absolute control – only to later have this or another alternate personality matrix 're-programmed' by a more benevolent faction of the 'alliance.'

This more benevolent faction would either be involved with a separate Federation, or it would be a faction that is part of the 'collective' itself yet which is involved in an ongoing conflict with its 'darker' side, a faction which is opposed to the interventionist-control agendas of the 'infiltrators'. One cannot comprehend the significance of the psychic battles that can rage through a single human mind until one has been caught in the crossfire between two opposing 'alternate personalities' -- one of which is an individualist and one of which is a collectivist -- that are slugging it out for dominance of one's unconscious existence.

The best one can do in such an event would be to try and retrieve as many suppressed memories as they are able, sort the whole mess out, and assimilate and take conscious control of those thought patterns that will be most beneficial to them and eliminate the harmful thought-patterns. I will not deceive you, such a process can be very painful at times. After all, it is the root "individual consciousness" of a human being which has the final say as to just who that person is going to be, based on the universal law of free agency. For those of you who are reading this and who feel that they may have been 'programmed' with an alternate 'alien' personality which is activated during alien encounters, I will say for an absolute fact that according to universal law this collectivist alternate personality must submit to the demands of your conscious will. Anything else would be a direct violation of the non-intervention laws. Even without the assistance of alien psycho-technology, certain psychiatrists are fully aware of how easy it is to hypnotically induce an alternate personality within a human being, IF they had access to the suppressed mind-control techniques that have been used by certain intelligence agencies and occult fraternities. - Branton)

UNDERGROUND BASES

– On April 1 and 2, I spent 24 hours visiting with John Lear at his home in Las Vegas. He took out a stack of papers and had me peruse them at my leisure. His study room had walls covered with aircraft photos and certificates. There was no doubt in my mind that John loved flying. John is a soft spoken individual and frequently, while visiting him, I have watched him putter in the garden. We discussed Area 51. John had some long distance photos of the Groom Lake facility.

The one thing that stood out in one photo was the radio telescope pointing straight up in the midst of a group of buildings. The scope was probably tracking any overhead spy satellites. He showed me the reference in the February, 1988, issue of "*Gung-Ho*" magazine, that [insisted] that spacecraft were being test-flown from this facility. John heard rumors that the Greys had a base under the Groom Mountains. This is the one we believe is called Dreamland. One of my sources [a leak] says DREAM is an acronym that stands for Data Repository Establishment And Maintenance. John told me the story of Mr. K, whose son Robert was trapped inside a joint human-alien underground base in Utah. This Robert had apparently worked at Dulce Base at one time. Mr. K felt like he was being given the runaround by the military in his attempts to locate his son...

"I learned that there were a few technical people who worked at Sandia Labs in Albuquerque who were interested in alien activity. One man I talked to, C.R., knew a mysterious Colonel Ronald Blackburn, who was reputed to have said that there were 600 aliens at the Groom Lake facility in Nevada. C.R. had investigated a UFO crash near Gallup, N.M., in 1983. This one was also investigated by Tommy Roy Blann. I heard of Colonel Edwards at Albuquerque who knew the AFOSI agent Richard Doty (BOTH of whom worked with Paul Bennewitz in his investigations of the alien activity taking place at the Dulce Base. - Branton). Doty had talked to some investigators about the government cover-up. Why? I don't know.

WEIRD HAPPENINGS AT DULCE

On April 19, 1988, my wife and I arrived at Dulce, N.M. at about 4:30 p.m. Dulce was a beautiful little mountain town sitting at an elevation exceeding 7,500 feet. There was still snow on the ground by the Best Western Motel. I checked into the motel and called Gabe Valdez. He came over to see me about 9:30 p.m. We talked about UFOs and the cattle mutilations. He said that he had not seen any mutes since 1981-82. [I] had him read a letter written by Richard Doty in which Doty denies all involvement with UFO secrecy. He said Doty wasn't telling the truth. This proved true, because Doty started talking again.

"He told me that Doty wrote a report that stated that Paul Bennewitz was being investigated. Later Gabe offered us a ride around Dulce. He took us in his patrol car and showed us some of the routes. He said he saw glowing orange-lighted airships flying silently around the area frequently. He never saw these airships in daylight. We took a look at the Gomez Ranch, site of some of the mutes that took place in 1978. We asked about Bennewitz's belief that there was a secret underground alien base in the area. He said he believed about 80 percent of what Bennewitz said concerning alien activities in the area... he definitely seemed to think there was a base in the area, but his idea of where it is located was different than Paul's. He thought that the base might be south of Dulce, closer to the Gomez Ranch. He said he had not found any entries to the base. He had found landing tracks and crawler marks near the site of the mutes. He invited me to come back sometime and climb Mt. Archuleta. Someday I would come back to Dulce, but I had no idea when...

"A lot started happening in October, 1988. I started investigating the case of a couple who had gone up to a plateau on the south side of the Tehachapi Mountains (outside of Edwards AFB. - Branton) not far from my house. At two in the morning they witnessed a large flashing orb come up from the ground and rise slowly into the sky. They experienced about two hours of missing time. Under hypnosis performed by a local hypnotherapist who had taken an interest in UFO abductees, we had found that the man recalled having been taken to an underground facility. He kept mentioning 'the Colonel!'..."

(Excerpt from *"Cosmic Top Secret"* by William H. Hamilton III)

19.

MALTA - ENTRANCE TO THE CAVERN WORLD
By C. Lois Jessop

PUBLISHER'S NOTE: There are many passageways that lead downward and away from the Earth's surface. All sorts of denizens are said to live beneath our feet, be they aliens or cavern dwellers of a type undetermined. Here is a chilling, but typical, journey of detention.

Miss Lois Jessop, working for the British Embassy in Malta, wrote an account of an experience she had inside the Hypogeum. She described how, on her first visit, she convinced the guide to allow her to investigate one of the so-called "burial chambers" near the floor of the last chamber in the lower level.

In her own words, she asked "What's down there?" and pointed to a small opening off the walls. To quote from Jessop's account, the guide said: "Go there at your own risk, and you won't go far," he replied.

From that ominous beginning, Jessop continues her story.

https://borderlandsciences.org/journal/vol/17/n02/Jessop_Malta_Cavern_World.html#Crabb-Saucers-Destiny-ref

* * * * * * * * *

MALTA, ENTRANCE TO THE CAVERN WORLD

By C. Lois Jessop – Secretary, New York Saucer Information Bureau

I visited some friends on the Island of Malta in the Mediterranean in the mid-1930s. One afternoon six of us decided to hire a car and visit some of the many historical tourist attractions on the island. One of our party suggested that, since the weather was very hot, our best bet was to visit some of the caves and underground temples. At least there we could keep cool for a few hours.

Some few miles out of Valetta, the capitol of Malta, is the little town of Paula. It has only one main street, Hal Saflini, and on this is the entrance to an underground temple known as the Hypogaeum of Hal Saflini. We stopped here and sought out the guide for a tour of the cave or catacombs of the Hypogaeum.

There was a fairly large cave entrance with ancient mural decorations of whirls and wavy lines, diamond patches here and there, also oval patterns seemingly painted with red ochre. The entrance itself smelt damp and moldy, but inside the cave there was not a trace of mustiness. Joe, the guide, told us there were three floors of underground rooms and gave each of us a lighted candle.

One by one we bent down low to walk through a narrow passage which led to a step or two, and again we were able to stand up in a fair-sized room which had been built out of the Malta sandstone eons ago in the Stone-Age. Joe told of a powerful oracle (or wishing well) deep down, and how it had worked wonders in the old days for the initiated who knew the correct sound to use. I think the oracle still works today unless it was damaged. Malta was heavily bombarded during World War II.

The oracle was supposed to work only if a male voice called to it but as the guide was saying this I slipped down a small step and gave a yell that was picked up by something and magnified throughout the whole cave.

We followed the guide through some more narrow passages which led down, down, down, then straightened our backs again when we came into another room. In this large opening was a circular stone table or altar in the center of the room. Cut out of the rock walls around were layers of stone beds or resting places of some kind, with hollows scooped out for head, body, and narrowing to the feet. I guess these were places for adults about four feet tall, with smaller scooped out beds. It looked like mother, father and child either slept or were buried here, although we saw no bodies here.

Down, down, down again, stooping and crawling through a narrow passage into another large room, with slits or narrow openings in the stone wall.

"They buried their dead in here," said the guide.

Photo: Richard Ellis' "Hypogeum of Hal-Saflieni" (1924)

I peered through a slit and saw skeletons. Through another slit I peered into a cave where, the guide said, they kept their prisoners. A three foot thick stone door, about four feet high and four feet wide, guarded the entrance.

"What kind of people, and how strong were these pigmies, to be able to carve out these rooms to a definite pattern and to move doors this thick and heavy?" I thought.

"This is the end of the tour," Joe, the guide, said. "We must now turn and retrace our steps."

"What's down there?" I asked him; for on turning I noticed another opening off one of the walls.

"Go there at your own risk," he replied, "and you won't go far."

I was all for more exploring and, talking it over with my friends, three of them decided to go with me and two waited with the guide. I was wearing a long sash around my dress and since I decided to lead the group I asked the next one behind me to hold on to it. Holding our half-burnt candles the four of us ducked into this passage, which was narrower and lower than the others.

Groping and laughing our way along, I came out first, onto a ledge pathway about two feet wide, with a sheer drop about fifty feet or more on my right and a wall on my left. I took a step forward, close to the rock wall side. The person behind me, still holding on to my sash, had not yet emerged from the passage. Thinking it was quite a drop and perhaps I should go no further without the guide I held up my candle.

There across the cave, from an opening deep below me, emerged twenty persons of giant stature. In single file they walked along a narrow ledge. Their height I judged to be about twenty or twenty-five feet, since their heads came about half way up the opposite wall. They walked very slowly, taking long strides. Then they all stopped, turned and raised their heads in my direction. All simultaneously raised their arms and with their hands beckoned me. The movement was something like snatching or feeling for something, as the palms of their hands were face down. Terror rooted me to the spot.

"Go on, we're all getting stuck in the passage!" My friend jerked at my sash. "What's the matter?"

"Well, there's nothing much to see," I stammered, taking another step forward.

My candle was in my right hand. I put my left hand on the wall to steady myself and stopped again. My hand wasn't on cold rock but on something soft and wet. As it moved a strong gust of wind came from nowhere and blew out my candle! Now I really was scared in the darkness!

"Go back," I yelled to the others, "go back and guide me back by my sash. My candle has gone out and I cannot see!"

In utter panic I backed into the narrow little passageway and forced the others back, too, until we had backed into the large room where Joe and my friends were waiting. What a relief that was!

"Well, did you see anything?" asked one of them.

"No," I quickly replied, "There was a draft in there that blew my candle out."

"Let's go," said Joe, the guide.

I looked up at him. Our eyes met. I knew that at one time he had seen what I had seen. There was an expression of caution in his eyes, adding to my reluctance to tell anyone. I decided not to.

Out in the open again and in the hot Malta sunshine we thanked the guide, and as we tipped him he looked at me.

"If you really are interested in exploring further it would be wise to join a group. There is a schoolteacher who is going to take a party exploring soon," he said.

I left my address with him and asked him to have the schoolteacher get in touch with me, but I never heard any more about it, until one of my friends called me to read an item from the Valetta paper.

"I say, Lois, remember that tunnel you wanted to explore? It says here in the paper that a schoolmaster and thirty students went exploring, and apparently got as far as we did. They were roped together and the end of the rope was tied to the opening of the cave. As the last student turned the corner where your candle blew out the rope was clean cut, and none of the party was found because the walls caved in."

The shock of this information didn't change my determination not to say anything about my experience in the Hypogaeum, but several months later my sister visited Malta and insisted on making a tour of the underground temple on Hal Saflini. Reluctantly, I went along, retracing the same route; but there was a different guide this time. When we got down to the lowest level, to the room where I had taken off to explore, the tunnel entrance was boarded up!

"Wasn't it here that the schoolmaster and the thirty students got trapped?" I asked the guide.

"Perhaps," he replied, with a noncommittal shrug of the shoulders, and refused to say anything more. You cannot get a thing out of the Maltese when they don't want to talk.

"You are new here, aren't you?" I asked him. "Where's Joe, the guide who was here a couple of months ago?"

C. Lois Jessop claimed that she convinced a guide to allow her to investigate a burial chamber at the Hypogeum in Malta. There, she came across a seemingly bottomless cavern where she saw several giant humanoids on a ledge across the chasm.

"I don't know any Joe." He shook his head. "I alone have been showing people around this catacomb for years."

Who was this guide? And why did Joe disappear after we left Hal Saflini that first time? And why is it impossible to get any facts on the disappearing schoolchildren story? In the summer of 1960, Louise Becker, N.Y.S.I.B.'s treasurer, visited Malta during her European trip. She searched old newspaper files and the Museum, trying to get some facts to substantiate my story, but in vain. The Maltese are tight-lipped about the secrets of their island.

* * * * * * * * *

Your editor's third lecture, *"Flying Saucers and America's Destiny,"* contains brief references to the cavern world in the interior of the Earth; and it was after hearing this talk to her New York saucer group that Miss Jessop told Mrs. Crabb and me the Malta experience described above.

We spent two days with Lois Jessop during our eastern trip in April, 1960, and found her a charming hostess, cosmopolitan as a much-traveled Englishwoman can be, and a student of the borderland. Lois has a level-headed, level-eyed way of looking at life and people, which is very refreshing; nevertheless, I found her Malta story difficult to believe until Mrs. Crabb and I returned home and I had a chance to look up Malta at the San Diego library. Two Malta articles in the *"National Geographic"* are especially fruitful for the underground researcher: Griffith's *"Malta, Halting Place of Nations,"* May, 1920, and Walter's *"Wanderers Awheel In Malta,"* August, 1940. (p. 267, 272)

Walters and another young American friend made a leisurely bicycle tour of Malta in 1939, with plenty of time to get acquainted and to ride around with island teenagers. They visited Hal Saflini, too, and proved the startling amplifying power of the "oracle." They also picked up this sad information from their Maltese friends.

"Years ago one could walk underground from one end of Malta to the other, but all entrances were closed by the government because of a tragedy. On a sight-seeing trip, comparable to a nature study tour in our own schools, a number of elementary children and their teachers descended into the tunneled maze and did not return. For weeks mothers declared that they heard wailing and screaming from underground. But numerous excavations and searching parties brought no trace of the lost souls. After three weeks they were finally given up for dead."

Griffiths noted a hollow-sounding floor in one of the rooms of Hal Saflini, indicating yet unexplored lower levels. He also gives a few facts which back up Richard Shaver's contention that the Deros, the evil cavern dwellers, are cannibals and enjoy eating human flesh. Hal Saflini was discovered in 1902 but before the Valetta museum director could open it up for the tourists, dirt, broken pottery, and enough normal-sized human bones to account for 33,000 people had to be removed from the rooms of the Hypogaeum. Archaeologists and other innocents believe that catacombs like Hal Saflini were burial tombs; I rather think that it was a cavern restaurant for the degenerate, undersized descendants of the Atlanteans who were forced into the caves thousands of years ago.

Here is Griffith's description of the "oracle" in the cave: "At about the level of a man's mouth is a hemispherical hole in the wall about two feet in diameter. Here it was noticed only a few months ago that any word spoken into this place was magnified a hundredfold and audible throughout the entire structure. A curved projection is especially carved out of the back of the cave near this hole and acts as a sounding board, showing that the designers had a good knowledge of sound-wave motion. The impression upon the credulous can be imagined when the oracle spoke and the words came thundering forth through the dark and mysterious places with terrifying impressiveness."

GIANTS IN THE EARTH

Lois Jessop was reminded of the peculiar appearance of the twenty-foot giants she saw in Hal Saflini by a couple of 35mm slide illustrations in my No. 4 Saucer lecture, concerned with mediumship. These slides are copies of Max Heindel's drawings of the human aura, from his book, *"Cosmo-Conception,"* depicting curved lines radiating out beyond the body.

Of the huge cavern dwellers she saw she said, "Their covering seemed to be like long white hair, combed downward and shaggy looking. Their heads were oval and elongated at the chin and top; and the hair on their heads fell about the shoulders like a draped monk's cowl."

Now these underground beings, whatever their origin, have no resemblance to Shaver's Deros. At least we have the fact of their existence; and in this experience of Lois Jessop's, and in the Hal Saflini material in the *"National Geographic,"* we do have some of the best factual support of the Shaver Mystery your editor has yet seen. In fact it was this material which encouraged me to go ahead and put together talk No. 5, *"The Reality of the Underground,"* including a portion of Miss Jessop's experience and a review of Shaver's basic theories as spelled out by Ray Palmer in the early *"Mystic Magazine"* back in 1954 and 1955.

My basic premise is that there are many different races in the interior of the Earth, of all shapes, sizes and colors, and of different degrees of density, depending on what level or plane of vibration is normal to them. Along with our former director, Meade Layne, I believe that some of these underground races can shift back and forth across the border between 3-D and 4-D; so that sometimes they are visible to normal human sight and at other times they are invisible — to our great bewilderment!

Those involved with the Italian "Friendship" UFO case said that many of the extraterrestrials they encountered were giants over 8-feet-tall. As well, their secret bases were located deep underground.

WHAT SAY THE PROBERT CONTROLS

The subject of the interior of the earth and Deros came up a few times at the early Mark Probert séances in San Diego. Here is what one member of the Inner Circle, Rajah Natcha, had to say about it, 8/16/50:

"The interior of your Earth is largely hollow. If it became solid, in that moment what you call your force of gravity would be... instantly raised many hundreds of times... you would be mashed to the Earth... Nor is the Earth a great mass of fire inside. There are, under the Earth, places where one can live comfortably; and indeed where he would be relieved of many of his ills. No, he would not find total darkness, for at certain depths there is light, a diffused glow from rocks and plant life, a kind of phosphorescent light.

"Do you know where the Christian story of the Devil comes from? Many centuries ago when Atlantis went down, many of her people fled into caves. They stayed down there for many generations. Now, their skin did not turn red like your pictures of 'the Old Boy,' but rather an extreme white and tones of green. This was brought about by the lack of ultra-violet rays of the sun, and the green was due to absorption from minerals below the surface. From time to time these individuals came to the surface – some unintentionally came on a surface opening and were seen by the superstitious people of certain sections. And being so different in appearance, you can imagine the fright this created in those who saw them. Most of the hair of the body had completely disappeared; the eyes had grown smaller – due to lack of light and of vitamins from sun-grown vegetables.

"That which I was speaking of was the origin of your Dero. Some of those who went underground morally degenerated, and with moral degeneration went physical degeneration. That always follows, doesn't it? Some of them are quite like your Australian Bushmen. There are some races that are quite out of fashion and have been extinct for many thousands of years. You should try to meet some of your fond ancestors. They would look quite badly in a tuxedo or formal evening dress!"

CAVERN COMMENT BY THE YADA DI SHI'ITE

In March 1953, Meade Layne had finished reading Robert Ernest Dickhoff's little 125-page book "*Agharta*", available then from Dickhoff for $2.50, 315 E 107 St., New York 29. Dickhoff wrote knowingly of the Tashi Lama and his underground city of Agharta, of the great tunnel system drilled through the Earth by a race of pre-glacial Martians, of the evil Serpent Race who walk on two feet, erect as humans, and of Rainbow City in the Antarctic. After reading this mish-mash of occult lore, Meade went to his fount of all wisdom, the Inner Circle, for comment and received this surprising reply from the Yada.

"It is true that the Serpent People once overran this planet, and that they came from Venus. They abandoned it because conditions here were not favorable to them.

They were of great size and had scaly bodies and large frog eyes, and were very advanced mentally. Morally they were not evolved, but were extremely cruel and vicious. They are still to be found in the interior of Venus. The Venusians of the present day, however, are not descendants of this early type. Venusians visiting your Earth at present want to bring peace, and have no desire to occupy the Earth.

"Most of what Dr. Dickhoff says about the tunnel system is correct. These were constructed by Atlanteans, partly for communication, sometimes in connection with the search for metals or ores, but chiefly in order to escape extreme solar radiation and various bacteria from the surface of the globe. The tunnels themselves were not primarily designed for underground living, but in many cases they led into vast caverns, natural and artificially hollowed out, where a great number of persons spent all their lives. It is true that the tunnel opening under the pyramid of Gizeh leads into caverns under Tibet. As to size, a common diameter of these tunnels was about 150 feet.

"They were constructed by mechanical or chemical means; that is, by the application of superheat deteriorators. It was like burning their way through Earth. Yes, it resembled the heat of the atomic bomb, if such heat could be controlled and directed. It was a very dangerous process, for if the heat-blast went out of control the whole globe might suffer most serious consequences. The process was very rapid. The molecules disintegrated. The substance of the Earth is very porous and the gases were largely absorbed by it.

TIBETAN LAMA LHASSA & ROMAN CATHOLIC ROME

"In some quarters much is still known about these tunnels. The two great religious hierarchies of your plane have such knowledge, and in fact have stored great supplies of food in underground depots. They are aware of the approach of their twilight hour." (Here you have a prophecy by the Yada which had already come true for the corrupt, organized priesthood of Lhassa and Agharta. Their surface organization has been shattered by the Chinese Communists, though it is difficult to believe that the wily old Tashi Lama has been smoked out of his underground lair, Agharta. The catacombs beneath the Vatican in Rome are certainly no secret, but the Yada's hint that these connect with the cavern world may be something of a surprise. The Church has had a stranglehold on Malta for hundreds of years, with dozens of churches and cathedrals on the little twelve-mile island, and at least one male member of every family in the priesthood.)

"The one God of the world of matter is the God of Change," concluded the Yada. "All things move into and out of manifestation in the three dimensions. Where does form come from? Mind built it and will change it according to the need for change. The object lost to three dimensions still holds form on another plane. To know this and know that we know it, is to escape much sorrow when forms – of cherished things, beloved persons – vanish from the world of our sense perceptions." (March 10, 1953, Round Robin for March-April 1953.)

Agharta as envisioned by artist Carol Ann Rodriguez.

20.

ADDITIONAL BASES SCATTERED AROUND THE GLOBE
From The Files Of Researcher Albert Rosales

PUBLISHER'S NOTE: UFO archivist Albert Rosales should be crowned "King of The Humanoids," for his catalog of 50,000 plus cases has to be the largest in the world. What researcher Otto Binder started, Albert expands upon in our search for tunnels, caverns and subsurface bases, alien or "otherwise."

Rosales was born in Cuba. He immigrated to the U.S. in 1966. He had several unusual incidents as a young man while living in Cuba, and such incidents continued for him as an adult here in the U.S. Rosales became interested in unusual phenomena and UFOs at a young age, but soon directed his focus to the crux of the phenomena, the humanoids, entities, extraterrestrials, Ufonauts, etc. He began collecting data on such encounters from worldwide sources in the late 1980s. He currently has a database of over 18,000 entries, which is updated and corrected daily. He has published four books so far, and we are expecting more soon. Rosales can be contacted at:

garu-da79@comcast.net or alberthumanoid@gmail.com

Albert says he pays tribute to all the great authors and UFOlogists that came before him, Jacques Vallee, Dr. J. Allen Hynek, Carol and Jim Lorenzen, Gordon Creighton, Frank Edwards, Jerome Clark, etc. – too many to mention. "But they help guide me in my weird and wonderful quest, a lonely quest at times, perhaps not understood by most, but something I feel compelled to do and that I think is and will be important."

At last count, Rosales had compiled 18 volumes of valuable references to be found on the topic. It's hard to imagine the countless hours it must have taken to compile this mountain of information. The best way to find out more is to march in orderly fashion over to Albert's Amazon Author's page:

www.amazon.com/Albert-S-Rosales/e/B01CUB65OQ%3Fref=dbs_a_mng_rwt_scns_share

Albert Rosales is the author of the book series
"Humanoid Encounters: The Others Among Us."

Having Albert on "Exploring the Bizarre" is always a pleasure and a fascinating experience. One of the programs, which we called "Earth Vs. The Humanoids," and our introduction to Albert's appearance is below. It wasn't long into the modern "UFO era" (starting in 1947) before witnesses started seeing creatures coming out of landed UFOs. Most reports of the creatures are anthropomorphic humanoids. Sometimes these creatures would communicate with their startled audience, other times they simply would go about their tasks, run away after being spotted, or even attack those who were unlucky enough to get too close. Much like UFOs, the beings associated with UFOs come in a wild variety of shapes and sizes. This brings us to this week's guest, Albert Rosales. Rosales has spent years researching and compiling reports of strange humanoid encounters (some have been seen with UFOs, while others have not).

His dedication to his research has led to some amazing cases that go back centuries. Considering the amount of data that Rosales has collected, there is no doubt that something bizarre is, and probably always has been, taking place between humans and some other intelligence. The question remains, just who, or what, is this "other intelligence"?

You're welcome to check out this episode, but swing low to avoid interference by one of those pesky little humanoids, especially the ones with the tin helmets! https://kcorradio.com/Library/archive/exploring-the-bizarre/2020/march/albert-rosales.mp3

Now you can read a tiny extract from Albert's huge stockpile of information.

* * * * * * * * *

AN ILLUMINATED CITY WITH TALL METALLIC BUILDINGS

Location, Cerro Del Rosario La Rioja, Argentina

Date: September 23 1970 Time: 1800

A goat herder was out pasturing his animals in an isolated area when a very strong wind suddenly came up; it grew in strength to almost cyclonic proportions. The witness found shelter in a nearby cave. Thinking that it was an old abandoned mine he began exploring the cave. He found some stone steps that descended in a twisting manner. As he descended lower, he began noticing an orange light that illuminated the area. As he reached the bottom he was amazed to see a luminous underground city filled with tall metallic buildings. He saw transparent roadways and circular metallic objects that seemed to fly just above the ground. He also saw numerous very tall men and women; the men were dressed in black robes and the women in white robes. These beings completely ignored the witness. The witness walked across the roads and found another stone stairway that led back to the surface. Later, searchers failed to locate the entrance to the "city" as the cave appeared to have been totally buried in rocks. (Subterranean city in the Andes or another dimension?)

Source: Fabio Zerpa, Los Hombres De Negro Y Los Ovnis

* * * * * * * * *

DULCE WARRIORS

CONCRETE CITIES BOTHER THEM

Location, Rosario, Argentina

Date: May 11 2001 Time: 03:00 AM

M. suddenly finds herself standing in front of an alien on the ground and not inside a ship. This place is apparently located between the cities of Roldan and Funes in a field near some trees. The beings tell her that the "vibrations" emitted by the concrete of the cities is very harmful for them and that is why this location was chosen. Then she sees numerous images of cities and locations in Argentina and Brazil that appear in front of her in a sort of holographic screen.

Soon she and the being sat on the ground next to a eucalyptus tree, despite the cold night, M felt very comfortable. She was told by this being that various civilizations were visiting the Earth. She was also told that there had been a titanic explosion in an area of the Universe that created hundreds of asteroids that destroyed several planets. Many of the survivors were now migrating to different points. She was told that some of the "visitors" lived and had extensive underground installations in several locations on Earth. The alien explained that they were following a "Universal Cosmic Plan" here on Earth that the humans were not following too well. They were here on a mission and they were not going to be deterred.

Source: Horacio Roberto, Nuevos Tiempos Argentina

* * * * * * * * *

A LONG TUNNEL AND A ROCKY VALLEY

Location, Rosario, Argentina

Date: July 9 2001 Time: midnight

M, (involved in the previous encounters) woke up in the middle of the night feeling extreme thirst and very hot. She then felt very cold as she traveled up into space. A hand then reached forward and pulled her into a zigzagging tunnel filled with curves and very sinewy. She heard a constant monotonous hum during her trip through the tunnel. At the end of the tunnel there was a bright light. After the light she found herself in a rocky valley surrounded by high, corroded cliffs. She felt very cold in this totally desolate environment. Soon she found herself among many different humans from different parts of the planet. Some appeared to have just arrived, others were apparently leaving. After walking through a rocky tunnel, she found herself inside a beautiful, glowing, apparently subterranean city. The buildings were apparently constructed of some type of transparent crystal. The place appeared to be empty and she did not see any moving vehicles.

At this point she noticed that she and the other humans were wearing some type of tight-fitting silvery clothing that seemed to adjust to the contours of the body. She saw an underground river that traversed the city. Again, the now familiar humanoid figure appeared and told her to relax and that everything was going to be fine. He told her that she was a unique specimen and that's why she had been contacted. He also said that planet Earth was in danger of extinction due to the lack of care and love among humans between themselves. The humanoid said that they came from a planet that had been recently discovered by Earth scientists. And that their planet was dying, and they needed to reproduce with the help of humans (a familiar theme). At this point she noticed other humans apparently in a trance and from different parts of the world; many just stood around and stared. Soon she found herself back in her bedroom.

Source: Horacio Roberto, Nuevos Tiempos, Argentina

* * * * * * * * *

STRANGE LOOKING TROOPS ENTER MOUNTAIN BASE

Location, West of Tucson, Arizona

Date: Fall 2001 Time: 2300

The main witness had just crossed the Arizona/California border heading back home with a friend. He was low on gas and needed to refill badly. They were nowhere near a city but, in the distance, he noticed a convenience store with some pumps. When he finally got there, he noticed five or six military trucks. He was kind of surprised since he knew they were nowhere near an Army base (not a known one anyway). Not thinking much of it he walked in and handed the cashier $40 for gas. His friend had also entered the station for some food and sodas. About two minutes later, as he was pumping gas, his friend came out empty-handed. The witness could tell that something was wrong by the look on his friend's face. He assumed his friend had lost his wallet and asked him what was wrong as he neared him. But his friend waited until he was right in front of him before he said anything. His friend then asked, "Did you notice anything strange about those soldiers?" He said no and asked why. His friend said that every single one of them looked identical, same size, same color skin, and the same features. He added that their skin looked synthetic, like plastic or rubber.

Without hesitation he walked into the convenience store and realized that his friend was right. According to the witness, he saw five soldiers in the store, and they all looked "fake" or as if they were quintuplets. He did not want to be obvious and began to grab things off the shelves and noticed that the soldiers were only buying ice and water, which seemed strange since it was 54-degrees outside. As he stood in line behind them he noticed that not one of them said a word, not to the cashier, not to one another, and each of them had what looked to be some type of clear coat on their skin, almost a shiny finish, like heavy sweat, but definitely not. Once on the freeway the witnesses noticed that the Army trucks were heading straight into a mountain off in the distance less than half a mile away. He stopped his truck and watched as every single Army truck disappeared into a mountain, which he knew did not have a road or any kind of known entryway.

Source: direct from agentneedham@gmail.com

Comments: The witness seems to believe that these were "hybrids." I asked are these the so-called "super soldiers" shown to in the final episodes of the cult classic "The X-Files"?

* * * * * * * * *

THE CREATURE LOOKED LIKE IT WAS MADE OUT OF STONE

Location, "Small town" in Romania

Date: 1997 Time: Late afternoon

The main witness was eight years old and at the time he used to travel to this location for the holidays. On the date of the encounter he was accompanied by his female cousin, one year younger, named "Dorothy." Both were playing at a place where the owners of the property had a pool under construction. The owners were not home at the time. Inside the mud hole they observed what seemed to be a hole in the wall. Dorothy peeked into the strange hole, noticing that this area of the mud wall of the pool was fragile, not like the other sections around it. She touched the wall and it collapsed immediately. A 5x5 foot hole remained in the mud wall. Dorothy then went straight inside, without even thinking about her safety, and the boy then went after her. She was standing inside, frozen. The area resembled an old mine, with rotting wood keeping this "hollow Earth-like" mine from collapsing.

There was something moving which resembled a grey, stone-like biped being, carrying something heavy on its shoulder. The creature was around six feet tall, and it did look like it was made out of stone. Every part of its body was made from the same material and same color, exactly like a moving statue. However, it did not look like a human statue at all, more like a Minotaur or demon. The incident lasted only a few seconds and the creature didn't seem to notice the young witnesses. Dorothy screamed and ran out in fear, quickly followed by the main witness, who ran straight home as fast as he could. His mother only believed the part of the abandoned mine and waited for his father to get home before they went there to investigate. They discovered the hole in the wall of the pool, but no sign of anything else. They called the police, who found it very strange for a mine to be so close to the community. Around the same time, most homeowners in the area sold their houses, fearing the collapse of an underground, previously unknown mine.

Source: Your True Tales, January 2012. Comments: Rare report of underground creature?

* * * * * * * * * *

DESCENDING INTO AN UNDERGROUND ROOM

Location, Rostov-on-Don, North Caucasus, Russia

Date: Beginning of May 1997 Time: 05:00 AM

A young widow, Elena, awoke in the middle of the night and saw what appeared to be needle-like traces on her palm. Usually she goes to bed very late, but on this date she had gone to bed early, around 2100. The next morning, she again found additional needle marks. She remembered experiencing something similar about a year before. She had found needle marks and bruises; this time there were no bruises.

That night she experienced a restless sleep in which she dreamt that someone was taking the blood from her body. Who was doing it and where was it happening she couldn't tell. She only remembered seeing a thick large needle being inserted into her body and feeling much pain. She perceived all this in a dream-like state but somehow connected it to UFOs and aliens. Before his death her husband had confessed to her that he had experienced a UFO sighting and contact (no details). During a hypnotic regression she remembered some of the details of that night before the morning when she found the needle marks. That evening she again went to bed early and awakened sometime in the middle of the night to a knock at the door. She couldn't remember what happened next but when she awoke she realized that it was already 0500 A.M. An obsessive idea suddenly came to her mind that she must go to the hospital. She drank a cup of tea and took the city bus to the hospital. There were very few passengers on the bus and she noticed two strange men that had boarded the bus with her. The men "looked weird," wearing strange grey loose-fitting overalls, which covered their faces halfway; in general, the overalls resembled surgical gowns. Some of the other passengers also stared at the two strangers. The conductor of the bus then asked the two men to pay but they displayed red identity cards from the Federal Security Board.

Elena exited the bus near the hospital and as soon as she did she appeared to be in some strange fog or mist. Everything around suddenly became grey, and she felt like she was walking inside some kind of tunnel. The two strange men in surgical gowns were following behind her. She soon appeared in some type of structure which reminded her of some large room in a military field hospital. They entered the room and saw metallic beds and numerous persons with expressionless faces. A woman then approached Elena and began extracting blood from her; she felt much pain and began to scream. During hypnosis she described the woman as an ordinary human being. But during a more detailed examination of the situation Elena remembered that the woman had unearthly hands with the index finger stretching out at a right angle from the rest of the fingers, with yellow webbing between her fingers. The color of her skin was green. Her hands and appearance were identical to the visitor she had the previous night in her flat (see the previous case). Elena distinctly remembered when the woman took a box with glassy test tubes which contained human blood. Then they went out of the room into another dark room below which reminded her of a basement or bomb shelter and began descending down a ladder. It was dark and something resembling a candle had now appeared in the hand of the alien woman.

DULCE WARRIORS

The descended a very long distance, Elena following behind the alien woman in a trance-like state. At the bottom they came upon a dark underground room. Not far from the room Elena saw an elongated object positioned on the ground. The object reminded Elena of a small two-seater airplane. There Elena saw an alien man wearing a tight-fitting brown sports suit, but she couldn't see his face. The alien woman gave him the test tube filled with blood and he left. Elena then saw the object take off; it looked like it went out through an underground shaft. The rest of the encounter was erased from Elena's mind and she described the details only with the help of hypnosis. She described seeing a strange hall filled with human bones and remnants of decaying bodies and rag-like skin, torn dirty clothing. In general the room resembled a huge morgue in disarray. After taking her blood the aliens again took Elena through the fog and to the bus stop near the hospital. No one was following her this time. When she arrived home, she went to bed and fell asleep. When she awoke, she felt a strong headache. A lot of her memories were either "camouflaged" or erased.

* * * * * * * * * *

THE LADDER LED UNDERGROUND

Location, Klinskiy area, Moscow region, Russia

Date: Summer 1990 Time: late night

Four local female residents, Elena Ivanovna and her three daughters, ages 7, 10 and 13, reported a strange episode late one night. One of the daughters, Galya awoke late at night after hearing loud knocking on the door. In a state of somnambulism, she walked to the anteroom and opened the door, without even asking who it was. She was confronted by four entities, two males and two females, dressed in shiny suits seemingly separated into "black" segments. The alien men had what appeared to be small antenna-like devices over their ears. She became very frightened and rushed to her mother. After hearing her daughter screaming, Elena woke up and clasped her daughter tightly to her chest. The aliens approached them and one of the alien women then requested that they come with them. Terrified Elena screamed, refusing to go.

The alien woman then said, "If you don't come then we will take you by force." After that the witnesses blacked out. They vaguely remembered what happened next. They seemed to be moving around like robots obeying the alien commands. They found themselves in a round, not too high, semi-dark room, where they sensed a slight vibration, like a train moving. The room began rocking to the left and right, terrifying all the witnesses. Elena held tightly to her daughters, beseeching God to help them.

Next there appeared to have been a memory lapse and soon they found themselves standing in a forest meadow near some dense bushes. There was water nearby. They rushed to the water and began washing. Then a new memory lapse ensued. They then appeared at a new glade. Unlike the previous one, this one was very large. They soon noticed several groups of common-looking terrestrial people standing in the field. Elena and her daughters stood within one of the groups. The aliens then led the group via a ladder to somewhere underground and requested that the humans wash themselves. There was an underground river, which the humans used to wash. An alien wearing a shiny coverall was distributing towels or rags. The witnesses had the distinct feeling that the aliens were controlling their every move. After that they ascended back to the glade and sat there for a long time, apparently waiting for something. Elena noticed another ladder on the glade with broad steps that led underground. Her daughter Galya suddenly appeared within a group of people that were standing afar (as if teleported). A stream of water suddenly appeared out of nowhere and began flowing below the group. Elena then rushed to help her daughter. She does not remember what occurred next. All four witnesses appeared back in their rooms in the morning, awaking at 0700 A.M.

Source: Alexey K. Priyma, UFOs, Witnesses to the Unknown, Moscow 1997

* * * * * * * * *

ELECTRICAL DAYTIME

Location, El Saltillo, Adjuntas, Puerto Rico

Date: May 1990 Time: 20:00

Javier Francisco Sotomayor and several of his friends had gathered together at a local church when there was a sudden blackout in the area. All lights and electrical equipment shut off. As they walked outside, they saw a sudden brilliance covered the sky above the nearby wooded mountain. The whole area was illuminated like "daytime."

Moments later, strange "electrical" beams of light began to emerge directly from the bottom of the mountain. Astounded they watched as a huge illuminated disc-shaped object appeared over the mountain. The object seemed to be rotating and it suddenly dropped to the ground on the mountain. Seconds after the object had descended, from the same location, a spectacular array of lights was witnessed. These seemed to emerge from the ground and resembled laser beams which were pointed towards the sky. The men were puzzled as the wooded area lacked any power stations or any type of infrastructure. "It was really an incredible sight" said Javier. It seemed to the men that the Earth at that location had somehow opened up and from beneath the Earth the laser beams shot out.

To the men it was something strange but beautiful at the same time. They were convinced it was not a manmade phenomenon. After a few minutes the crevice on the ground seemed to close and the beams of light vanished. Other witnesses, like Luis Laracuente, reported that the object had been huge and disc-shaped and reddish in color.

Source: Jorge Martin Miranda, Puerto Rico Type: X

PUBLISHER'S NOTE: Is this evidence of underground UFO bases? Similar displays have been reported in other parts of the world. We immediately got in touch with our associate in the beautiful island of Puerto Rico for a personal summary of this incident. We have posted it below as the final report in this chapter.

* * * * * * * * *

THE SOUND OF UNDERGROUND MOTORS

Location: Marble Bar, Western Australia

Date: May 19 1978 Time: Daytime

There had been reports of underground motor sounds at the Michael Richardson's Hillside tin mine located 61 miles south of Marble Bar. Due to its isolated nature it was heard by few. Three Aborigines stopped by "Max's" camp and called his attention to the motor sounds he had already begun to hear emanating from the hills above his camp. A search was made of the rugged area where no vehicles could travel, but no cause for the sound was apparent and it continued even as they searched for its origin.

On the above date Max was visited by a tall "normal looking" male wearing coveralls. He was not exactly normal since his left hand looked transparent "as though it had been burned and it was new skin." This person, whose speech was normal, arrived in a Land Rover with unusually small wheels bearing a plate number that Max later checked and found to be registered to someone else. The name and place of residence the man gave also proved to be false. It was a hot day, but the stranger refused any liquid refreshment during the two hours he was there. Max asked him to aid in lifting some iron sheets and Max discovered the man had no strength at all. He began to tremble, toppled over, and Max had to help him up. About a week later Max had retired to his bed under the stars. Suddenly, the night sky brightened, and a glowing object came to him from two kilometers away. As it sped low overhead it became an enormous zeppelin-sized orange glowing craft with a revolving white light. The following morning Max found that the compass heading had been altered, his dog now possessed boundless energy, and he also had surprising energy. He could now lift 180 pounds of pipes with no effort at all.

About one week later, something in the sky projected a brilliant beam which bathed Max's entire camp in bright light for about three minutes. The period of "charged power" and "super energy" of Hillside Mine lasted over two weeks.

Source: Don Worley, "*UFO Review*" # 24 pp. 18-19

* * * * * * * * *

CREATURE UTILIZED HYPNOSIS INSIDE CAVE

Location, Near Novosibirsk, Russia

Date: 1985 Time: Afternoon

Colleagues from the Science Institute of Baku were exploring some isolated grottos at about 100 meters below the surface. One scientist, Constantine Bakulin, dropped himself down by rope. When he was prepared to be lifted up, he felt someone staring at him, and a strong heat emanating from the source. He felt afraid and attempted to pull the rope but was unable to move. He turned his head, obeying a strange inner compulsion. He then saw a bizarre creature, very tall with glowing eyes, covered with hair and with horns. The creature made motions with his hand as if telling Constantine to follow him. Bakulin took several steps into the cave but he then began to desperately pull on the rope. His comrades immediately pulled him up. Source: Igor Tsarev, Planet of Specters

* * * * * * * * *

SEARCHING FOR A FABLED UNDERGROUND CITY

Location, Patagonia, Argentina

Date: February 1991 Time: 03:40 a.m.

Looking for the fabled underground city of "Iberah," the main witness, Miguel Villegas (involved in other contacts) was camping on the shores of a local lake along with some other friends when suddenly in the early morning all the animals in the area became disturbed, including horses, deer, dogs, etc. Also, the surface of the lake became disturbed as huge waves became apparent, as if in anticipation of "something" to come. Villegas stood up and looked around and saw at about 30 meters away a very tall human-like figure about 2.50m in height, wearing a shimmering white gold coverall. The figure had long shoulder length blond hair and large slanted eyes. He smiled at Villegas, emitting an aura of love and tranquility. The entity communicated telepathically with Villegas and welcomed him to the "city." He told Villegas that one day, when the time came and he was ready, he along with others will enter the underground realm of Iberah. After that brief communication the entity vanished in plain sight.

Source: http://www.astroufo.com/entervistamv.htm

* * * * * * * * *

30 STORIES DOWN AT EDWARDS AFB

Date: April 1990, Time: Unknown

A construction contractor working at an underground installation 30 stories deep was walking down a hall with another man when some doors opened unexpectedly. They then caught sight of a figure at least 9-feet tall wearing a lab jacket and talking to two human engineers. The figure was humanoid with long arms almost down to his knees, a large head with huge black slanted eyes and greenish skin. Security personnel then ushered both witnesses out. — Source: Elaine Douglass, Right to Know Forum, Sep/Oct 92

DULCE WARRIORS

UNDERGROUND SUBWAY

Location, Dania, Florida Date: Spring 1980 Time: Night

Vicky Malagrino remembers being in a state between sleep and awake when she suddenly felt herself take off, vividly felt traveling very fast, like in an underground subway. She came to a stop in a few seconds. She found herself standing in front of a row of houses in New York. She entered one of the houses and went to the 3rd or 5th floor and entered an empty apartment. There she walked over to a window, which was cut open in a circular shape. She then remembers a UFO coming down and picking her up. Soon she remembered seeing the Earth getting smaller as she left. What she remembers well was that the initial travel feeling, or phase, had been underground. She also remembered standing on the "first floor" of the UFO, looking around. She saw three human-like persons to her left at the controls, which appeared to have large windows on top. The figures definitely looked human from the back and they were wearing formfitting uniforms. She also saw to her right a single bed and, on this bed, there was a military blanket, which has always stayed with her in that she thought that it was an important piece of information. She also saw "in her mind" the second floor and it was round, and the wall was full of computer consoles. That's the extent of the witness' memory of the event.

Source: http://www.etcontact.net/newsite

* * * * * * * * *

MISSING TIME IN THE DESERT

Location, Near Cimarron, New Mexico Date: May 6 1980 Time: 7:15 P.M.

A woman and her eight-year old son were driving along in the desert when they spotted three lighted objects on a nearby field. The center object was the biggest with lighted windows that emitted amber light. She became paralyzed and confused, and a four-hour time loss resulted. Later under hypnotic regression the woman remembered walking over to the field and hearing cattle "screaming" in apparent pain. Four figures approached and carried the witness into a nearby object. She kicked and screamed and felt extremely cold.

The beings were greenish in color and moved in a strange shuffling manner. A taller pale being with a high forehead and wearing a white outfit with cape approached the group. He appeared angry and said that she should not be here. At one point she was briefly touched by the tall humanoid and felt a burning sensation. She was shown her son and he seemed to be sleeping peacefully. She was apparently medically examined and experienced a lot of pain. She was then taken into a bright white room where she sees the beings apparently cutting up a cow into pieces apparently while the animal was still alive. Several beings wearing dark brown outfits with an orange insignia escorted her to another room where the tall white-garbed being waited. She then remembered landing in a desert area and being met there by several tall beings wearing shiny clothing that shuffled their feet when they walked. She was then apparently taken into an underground facility where the tall beings, described as hairless with large beautiful eyes and wearing long robes, examined her. At one point she briefly entered a large metallic room where she saw a huge container filled with floating animal and what appeared to be human body parts. She was eventually returned along with her son unharmed.

Source Linda Moulton Howe – *"Alien Harvest."*

* * * * * * * * *

ABDUCTEES TAKEN TO SECRET LAB - ASKED TO SIGN REGISTRY

Only under hypnosis do the Beverly, MA, resident's shrouded memories of the encounter come out.

They begin with a sudden awakening during the night and the discovery of two alien creatures standing next to the bed. The visitors are short, humanoid shapes with heads disproportionately larger than their bodies. They look out from slanted eyes that come to a point on either side of their heads, about where ears should be but are not. They have no mouths and their skin is a greenish black hue.

The next image is a dark tunnel that opens up into what appears to be a laboratory, perhaps inside a spacecraft. One wall is lined with glass-like jars on metal shelves. The shelves are anchored to the wall above a set of featureless drawers.

Says Marge Christensen, Section Director of the Essex County MUFON:

"Communication takes place, but no words are spoken. Thoughts seem to appear in the person's head through mental telepathy. The creatures usher their guests through a door into the laboratory and give instructions to sign some kind of register which already bears several other names, some in English and others in unintelligible scribbles.

"The Beverly resident is directed to a flat examining table and is asked to lie on it. The creatures busily move from station to station in the laboratory preparing for what turns out to be a thorough examination of their abducted specimen.

"After the tests are completed, the aliens exert some type of mind control to make the Beverly resident forget the visit."

"Tracking Down Alien Visitors" By Bob Scherer-Hoock - Town Transcript Topefield, MA August 16, 1982

* * * * * * * * *

DIMENSIONAL PORTALS? MOUNTAINS OPEN IN ADJUNTAS...AND FLYING SAUCERS FLY OUT

By Jorge Martin Miranda

Mr. Javier Francisco Sotomayor witnessed an unusual event that occurred in the El Saltillo sector of the Adjuntas municipality, in the south-central part of the island of Puerto Rico. The event occurred on a night in April or May 1990 (the exact date is not available). Javier was with several friends in a church in the area around 8:00 at night, and suddenly they all saw that the electrical power in the area went out. "Then," Javier told us about what happened, "a very bright light suddenly appeared and all that part of the sky and the mountain were illuminated. It became as if it was daytime, and then some rays of light started coming out from the mountain, similar to those of an electrical storm, but they came from below, from the mountain's foothill ... and then a luminous thing appeared, with the shape of a flying saucer. It was spinning, and then went down into the ground at that same spot in the mountain.

"In the same spot of the mountain where that saucer went down to," he continued explaining, "there was then a spectacle of lights that came out from the ground, similar to the beams of light from reflectors or spotlights, or as bright laser beams directed upwards, to the sky.

"In that place there is nothing electrical, no wiring or power plants, nothing. So, what was happening was something truly strange, incredible.

"I know this will sound exaggerated, but what we saw was as if the Earth at that point of the mountain had opened and all those rays of light came out of the hole that was formed. It was something so beautiful and so strange that I don't think something of human origin produced it.

"After a few minutes all that stopped. The hole in the ground seemed to close again and the rays of light disappeared," the young man finally said.

Many other people in the town of Adjuntas witnessed the formidable event, including Mr. Luis Laracuente, and claimed that the object they saw descending on the site was an extremely brightly lit flying saucer in which lilac and red lights predominated. Something very similar happened, also in the area of the municipality of Adjuntas, in the early morning hours of March 19, 1989. One of the witnesses to this other event, Mr. Luis Javier Marrero, told us what happened during an interview.

Marrero indicated that that morning he was in his van, which he had parked on a street in the San Joaquín de Adjuntas urbanization. "I was picking up some implements," he said, "and in that moment, around 4:00 in the morning more or less, I saw the sky light up, and then the electricity went out in the whole area. There was an electric blackout. I stepped out from my van to see what was happening, and saw that powerful rays of bright blue-white light that oscillated from side to side, similar to laser beams, were coming out from a site at the base of the Vegas Arriba Mountain.

He added, "What I saw was something as if a hole had appeared in the ground at the foothill of the mountain and from that hole those bright rays came out, similar to those seen in nightclubs, but immense and very bright. And they came out from below, from that hole, from the depths of the Earth.

"At that same moment I saw a flying saucer fly out from that hole. It was shaped like a disk, but wrapped in a reddish light. It flew over the mountain and then headed to the east. When that saucer came out and flew away, the light and the rays of light coming out from the mountain of Vegas Arriba went out, as if the hole there was closed, and then the bright light and the rays of light appeared again, but further to the east, at the foothill of the mountain Santas Pascuas, which was some distance away. It was as if another hole with lights had appeared there too at the foothill of the mountain of Santas Pascuas, and the saucer I had seen before descended and entered through that other hole in the ground and the hole closed. After that everything disappeared.

"Then the luminosity and the laser-like beams of light appeared again in Mountain Vegas Arriba for a moment, went out right away and it was all over. Nothing else was seen again."

Copyright - 1990 – *"Enigma Magazine."*

21.

BROWN MOUNTAIN, N.C. - SECRET MILITARY BASE UNDERGROUND?
An Exclusive Interview With Joshua P Warren

PUBLISHER'S NOTE: Josh and I have been knocking about for many years. I first met him under rather weird circumstances (what else is new?) when we attended the same movie festival outside of Syracuse, New York. We didn't know each other then, though we collided in the bar several times during the day, the hard seats of the reception hall getting to our sore butts. We were both aspiring film makers wanting to meet and mingle with others. It wasn't until six months later, when browsing the net, that I discovered that Mr. Warren had another side to his personality – he was a great ghost hunter and paranormal researcher. So we had something to talk about. He invited me onto his Saturday night talk show "Speaking of Strange," and the rest is history. As it is often pointed out, Joshua P (no period please) is by all means the world's leading authority on the mysterious Brown Mountain Lights of North Carolina, which, as it turns out, has an underground base connection, probably U.S. operated. But who knows? It would seem that interdimensional beings – "aliens" – of some sort are lurking nearby.

www.joshuapwarren.com

Joshua P. Warren was born and raised in the mountains of Asheville, North Carolina. At the age of 13, he wrote his first published book. Since then, he has published dozens more, including the regional best-seller, *"Haunted Asheville,"* Simon and Schuster's *"How to Hunt Ghosts,"* and his 2015 bestseller, *"Use the Force: A Jedi's Guide to the Law of Attraction."*

He is the president of his multimedia productions company, Shadowbox Enterprises, LLC. His articles have been published internationally, and he has been covered by such mainstream media as CNN, Fox News, *Popular Mechanics, Entertainment Weekly, Southern Living, Delta Sky, FATE, New Woman, The New*

York Times, FHM and Something About the Author; and made the cover of the science journal, *Electric Space Craft*. A winner of the University of North Carolina Thomas Wolfe Award for Fiction, he wrote columns for the Asheville Citizen-Times from 1992 to 1995. His first novel, "*The Evil in Asheville*," was released in 2000.

An internationally-recognized expert on paranormal research, Warren was hired by the famous Grove Park Inn Resort to be the first person to officially investigate the Pink Lady apparition in 1995 (the same year he founded L.E.M.U.R. paranormal investigations, of which he is president). Warren also led the expedition that captured the first known footage of the elusive Brown Mountain Lights, eventually resulting in scientific breakthroughs, via experiments Warren led in the lab, that help explain most of the lights and many mysterious, natural plasmas (such as ball lightning) that occur around the world. His work has been praised by the Rhine Research Center, The North Carolina Center for the Advancement of Teaching (or NCCAT, for which he often gives presentations) and numerous scholars such as New York Times bestselling author Dr. William R. Forstchen, Dr. William Roll, Dr. Andrew Nichols, and legendary researchers such as NASA engineer Charles A. Yost, Oak Ridge National Laboratory engineer David Hackett, and authors/researchers Loren Coleman and Patrick Huyghe.

Joshua P Warren

DULCE WARRIORS

The following is an interview I conducted with Warren on a trip he made to cement our relationship in Manhattan.

Beckley: You're the world's leading authority on the Brown Mountain Lights, which is a phenomenon that's been seen for hundreds of years in the Blue Ridge Mountains of North Carolina. I was down there myself many years ago with Jim Moseley and Allen Greenfield and quite a few other individuals. And we staked out the Brown Mountain Lights. We didn't see too much that was strange. Maybe one flash of light off in the woods which may or may not have been a Brown Mountain Light. But we did have the opportunity to meet with this gentleman, who was the local contactee, by the name of Ralph Lael, who had a little convenience store, a little shack, I guess you would call it, and a little man under the counter, which we don't know whether he was a pygmy or something from another planet.

But Ralph claimed that he was in contact on a regular basis with the beings that resided or had a base at least inside the mountain. And to convince us of the truth of his stories, he had boxes full of giant crystals, which were used as some energizing device or something by the aliens. Or perhaps by himself to entice people to buy his little booklet for a buck and a quarter and a bottle of Diet Coke. It seems almost like at every locale of this nature you always find one or two individuals who have some interesting story to tell. But how did you first find out about the Brown Mountain Lights?

Warren: Well, having lived in western North Carolina my whole life, I'd always heard legends growing up regarding the Brown Mountain Lights. In fact, there was a popular bluegrass song that was sung in the 1950s, sort of a hit in our region, called "The Ballad of the Brown Mountain Lights." My father, he used to talk about it quite a bit, because he liked the song. And so when I was around twelve or thirteen, my parents took me and my sister over to the overlook.

Beckley: Is that plaque still there?

Warren: No. Supposedly there's a plaque somewhere on the parkway that has been recently put up, but not at the overlook that I usually go to, the 181 Overlook. It's kind of odd, because I have talked to some of the people in Burk County before about putting more signs up, but they don't want to. They say that it inspires vandalism. And even at Wiseman's View, there is a plaque that has all the mountains there and points out the names of the mountains and there's nothing related to the Brown

Mountain Lights on this plaque, even. So it's almost like they, in some cases, intentionally do not talk about it. I tried to get the tourism commission to work with me one time about maybe a festival or something, a Brown Mountain Lights festival, because I heard they were doing that in Marfa, Texas, with the Marfa Lights. But they were not interested in doing that. Recently there is a private group of people that have done a festival for the past couple of years, but the world of officialdom doesn't really want to acknowledge much about the lights. Which is odd, especially when you consider that I've talked to a lot of people there, locals, who have told me about weird military activity that may or may not be related to the lights. But if not, it's certainly a bit much for coincidence.

I'll give you some examples. Of course, let me start by saying that after fifteen years of camping up there and getting permits from the forest service and bringing all kinds of scientists up there, my team and I concluded that the lights are most likely, or most of the lights that are considered Brown Mountain Lights, are likely plasmas which are being naturally produced by the mountain. Because the mountain has some special geologic and atmospheric conditions. I also know for a fact that the military has been working on using plasma for weapons for quite some time. And so it may be that the military learned a long time ago that Brown Mountain was producing plasmas and has been studying them and nature in order to determine the best way to condense it into some sort of technology. So that might be some motivation for the government.

But the types of stories I'm talking about are stories from hunters. I talked to a hunter who told me that he was way out in the middle of the woods and thought he was pretty much alone. And all of a sudden this government vehicle, some kind of all-terrain vehicle, just came blazing past him and almost ran over him. He said, "Where did this thing come from?" And he walked a little farther down the trail and the trail and the roadway ended. And he said, "Where did it go? Where did it come from?" Then, when he finally worked his way back to the gate for the road, he said the gate had recently been painted, and he noticed that it had been painted shut. He could tell that the gate had not been opened. So this vehicle appeared out of nowhere and then disappeared. He thought it must have gone inside the mountain. There must have been some hole. Because he didn't get the impression it was going to fly away or dematerialize.

I've also talked to other people. For example, there is a local cafeteria there that claims that once in a while they get these big contracts to feed hundreds of men who are related to the military. And all they do is show up with a couple of trucks of all this food, and they meet some MPs at a gate and give them the food. They never say what it's for and they never see where it goes.

Here's another good one. I was talking to a hiker who told me that one day he was out walking around and saw something shining in the nearby field, something metallic. And when he made his way over to the spot, he couldn't find out what was shining, but he noticed that at the spot where he thought something was shining, there was a little hole in the ground. He couldn't tell how deep it went, but he just thought that was odd. So later that evening, when he was about to go back home, he realized there was a lot of light in the area of the field where he had earlier seen this strange shiny spot. So he went back over there and now all of these government vehicles were in a big formation, with their headlights turned on. And they were examining something at this particular spot.

He thought, "Huh! This is weird. They must be looking at what I was looking at earlier." And he started to walk over and ask them, and then he said all of a sudden three or four people just let loose with machine guns. He said it was the most terrifying racket he had ever heard. And he turned and hauled ass. He said they weren't shooting at him. He didn't think they even knew he was there. They were shooting at something else at that same spot.

Beckley: Were they shooting at a plasma?

Warren: I don't know why they would shoot a plasma.

Beckley: Was this in the daytime?

Warren: Well, the shooting was happening at night. But a plasma that appears in the daytime can reflect sunlight. So if there was a plasma coming from the ground there, if there were one, it might also look like a shining metallic object. But how that relates to all these military people, going ape-shit and firing all their guns off like that at something at that spot, I don't know. But let's just say-use our imagination- maybe there are UFOs that are coming to Brown Mountain, because they also are utilizing these natural forces, that it plays into the dynamics of their craft.

Beckley: Ralph Lael was right.

Warren: Maybe. And so there may be an alien presence there as well. And it's possible that the military sees that as a conflict and for all I know they were shooting at aliens.

Beckley: The only thing that takes me away from the plasma theory that you speak of is that I've talked to a number of people there back in my travels and on the telephone over the years, and they describe what appears to be an intelligence behind these balls of light. And one would assume that plasma is not intelligent.

Warren: No, it shouldn't be. I have some thoughts on that as well. First off, I've seen the lights numerous times, and I've never seen personally what I would consider an intelligent interactive behavior. So I would need to see that to try to see what patterns and correlations could be gleaned from it. I've blinked lights at them and all that and I've never gotten a response. So I don't know if maybe someone is seeing the lights and reading something into that, that someone sees the lights maneuver in a certain way-because the lights do interact with each other. Which could be explained by plasmas having an electromagnetic field that naturally balances off other fields. On the other hand, just because many of these lights manifest in a form that we call plasma, that doesn't mean it accounts for all the activity. It may be when you have a place that naturally produces so much energy it also triggers other more paranormal phenomena.

I just want to make one more comment about the lights having intelligence. I have talked to people who have sworn that they have seen a light close up, and there is a little person inside of it, like a fairy or a form of some sort. Now, I've never seen anything like that. I talked to one guy who said he touched a light. He said it was about the size of a basketball or a little larger and hovering about three feet over the ground. And he walked up and touched it and it shocked him. It did not discharge him, but it definitely also contributes to the electrical part if that's indeed true.

Beckley: I know people who have claimed that they have followed the lights and whenever they get to where they think they're going to be close to them, the light will suddenly appear behind them or would move without seeming to have moved. That would appear to be some intelligence beyond...

Warren: Well, it depends, because if you are walking in an area where you have these layers that are discharging the energy creating the plasmas, it seems like it can actually transfer through the layer. So for example, you might have two lights and one of them will dim while the other one brightens and then vice-versa. We have video footage of this happening. If you're standing between each of them, you might think that one single light is actually rematerializing in a different position or something like that. But we can't be sure that they don't have intelligence, because if they have intelligence, then it would certainly be more complex than anything we know how to understand. To say that they're a plasma doesn't necessarily imply that they have no intelligence any more than saying that a human is a solid means they have no intelligence. That's just a description of our physical composition. It may be that-well, if you believe that the Earth itself is an intelligent, living thing, and I sort of do actually-

Beckley: That's the concept of the book we did, "Our Alien Planet."

Warren: And I tend to think that the Earth is a living thing. And so it may very well be some aspect of the Earth trying to communicate. Or if not communicating, at least some aspect that does bear consciousness.

Beckley: Now, why do you think that there seems to be such a negative attitude among the scientific community or an attempt to sweep all this under the carpet? Because if it were true, would this not tell us a little bit more about our planet, our environment? And intelligence and matter and physics and so on?

Warren: Well, there actually are a lot of scientists who are interested. I've gone up there, for example, with a physicist from the Oak Ridge National Laboratory. And he agrees that they're also plasmas. And our work has been applauded by the Navy Physics Laboratory. We made the cover of a science journal. However, you have a handful of people out there usually who know very little about the phenomenon and don't want to take it seriously just because that for so many years it was called ghosts. It's just an old ghost story. These were spirits of Native Americans who were battling. Or there's a story about it being a slave searching for his master because the master never came back. I think it's just the people who don't want to go out and do what we have done for themselves, to see it. They find that it's easier to simply say, oh, these guys are just ghost hunters, so why should I trust them? It's a matter of putting the blinders on. In fact, at this point in time, I don't know of anybody who can really intelligently debate the fact that these are not possibly plasmas. One guy who was a critic of ours for a long time, named Dr. Dan Kayton from Appalachian State University, was always the guy that the newspapers would go to, to have like that one fellow who's going to say that everything we say is bullshit. They call that balance supposedly.

And so for the longest time, he said, "Oh, there are no Brown Mountain Lights." There were all these condescending remarks made about me and about our organization. In fact, when I met him in person one time and asked him to debate this in a gentlemanly way, he wouldn't do it. He won't ask me any questions when I give him the opportunity, but then he'll go around and say to people that we didn't know what we're talking about. Now, even he has begun telling people that he thinks there's a good chance that these are plasmas like ball lighting as well. And almost like he has discovered this stuff. So, you know, it's a little bit frustrating that there are people who – I don't ask anybody to believe me. I say, "Here is this report of exactly what we did." Because for fifteen years we took meticulous notes. Every piece of equipment, every date we went up there, what the conditions were, what we found. All of this is free on our website, brownmountainlights.com. It's in the public domain; we've given it to the world. And I want people to go and take the same equipment that we used and go there and see for themselves and document it for themselves. You don't have to take my word for it. We've come up with four different factors that will help you predict when the lights can be seen. And once you get to the point where you can kind of predict when something is going to happen, well, that's when you're getting close to really solving the mystery.

When it comes to ghosts, if we ever get to the point where I can tell you, "All right, Tim, go to this house on this street at this time on this date and Old Man Withers will come from the closet." Then that's when you'll know that ghosts are truly real, so to speak. It's all about being able to predict when these things are going to appear.

Beckley: So are you able to predict? A ghost or any of those manifestations?

Warren: Oh, yeah. The Brown Mountain Lights – we're quite good – but it's still a very complicated system, because of Mother Nature. Science is designed to help us solve the simplest problems first. And all of the variables involved in something like this, what we think is a natural phenomenon on Brown Mountain, makes it difficult to tell with 100 percent certainty. But I think it certainly is possible that we'll reach that point.

The four factors right now are, number one, time of year. You're better off if you go looking for them in late October or early November, because it seems like at night when the mountain cools and contracts, it produces the activity. And there is a greater temperature difference between night and day in the fall than at other times of year. Also, the leaves are off the trees in the fall and you have better visibility. Number two is if the KP Index is a five or above. This is a measurement of how disturbed the Earth's magnetosphere is. And also, if you go to the website, you'll see a little indicator there with that information. Third, if it's during or just after a rainy period, because the rain water that goes through the mountain seems to build up some of these charges. And then lastly, is if there happens to be an excessive amount of carbon in the air, from camp fires or even a forest fire. The time when I saw them the most prominently was when there was a big forest fire that was a few miles down the road. The extra carbon in the air seems to act as a fuel to help create the lights. Those are the best four things for the time being.

Our work, again, is out there, it's available, and now I want other people to reproduce it so they can verify it themselves and hopefully use it to learn even more.

Beckley: Let's end this by talking about your current projects. What's next?

Warren: I probably am not ready to talk about this new movie that I'm shooting right now, but I am working on an independent production, a documentary. And I will say that it has to do with religion and some of the strange things associated with religion. In the coming year, I'm going to be taking more trips. I'm going to go to some islands that I've never been to in the Caribbean investigating pirate ghosts.

I guess just in summary, one thing that I think is really important is to take more of the stuff that we have learned in the field for so many years and apply it to laboratory experiments. That's something that has not been done much in this field. I've spent fifteen years out there collecting a lot of field data and I'm now ready to sit down and adapt that information to experiments. That's what we did with Brown Mountain. We eventually created a plasma chamber and reproduced a phenomenon like the Brown Mountain Lights on a miniature scale. And that's why we earned the cover of the science journal, because we demonstrated something in a laboratory when we knew what all the variables were.

I have a whole list of experiments that I want to do, because I see all the field data just keep piling up and piling up and finally I'm ready to start doing more with it. We have some experiments that are very simple but have just never been done. If they've been done, I think I would have heard about it by now. We have a guy who is creating a box for us that has 100 LEDs. And the LEDs range from infrared through the visible spectrum into ultraviolet. So you shouldn't be able to see the LEDs on either end, just the section in the middle. Then we're going to take 100 people, 50 who say they've seen something ghostly and 50 who say they have not and test their eyes and see specifically what frequency ranges they're seeing and try to determine if there is some consistency there in those who have or have not seen a ghost.

Beckley: You could throw in a few UFO observers too.

Warren: Yup. That's right. You could expand it to any of these strange things that people observe. So there are many experiments like that that are simple, are relatively inexpensive to produce, but it just takes time and effort and access to the right people – trustworthy people. And then you learn more about how we perceive these things. Because it may be that we are never going to be satisfied by just getting some random field that moves through at the same time someone reports something weird. Because at most you can say, wow, that was really interesting. We can't explain it, but no one knows exactly what to do from that point on. So we have to know more about how these fields are affecting people, not just by triggering hallucinations. But also trying to determine if the human is capable of documenting these things that cannot otherwise be measured with a little box that beeps and has lights on it.

I'd like to take some of these people who call themselves ghost hunters, regardless of whether you see them on TV or it's the guy down the street and ask him, what is an electromagnetic field? How does that little box that you have in your hand actually work? I think you would be surprised at how few people can tell you what an electromagnetic field is after they've been sitting there talking about getting strange electromagnetic field readings. We need to do more basic elementary stuff in terms of educating people about how to use the equipment as well as exploring how these things can be sensed by humans in addition to the equipment.

22.

RALPH LAEL AND THE LIGHTS FROM VENUS

An old-time resident of the Brown Mountain area was Ralph Lael, who was born in Alexander County on a small hillside farm in 1909. He ran for Congress in 1948 and lost by a few thousand votes. He operated the "Outer Space Rock Shop Museum" on highway 181, just outside Morganton.

Lael claimed not only to have seen the lights up close but to have communicated with them on numerous occasions as well. Deciding that the only way to uncover the source of these lights was to go into the almost impassable mountain area itself, Lael started his own investigation. One night, shortly after midnight, he got within 100 feet of a light that had risen up from a large hole in the ground.

Ralph Lael

Within 10 or 15 minutes, the first light had been joined by as many as 20 more. Shortly after, they all took off into the timber and disappeared from Lael's view. A half hour later others began popping up along the mountainside in a smaller valley below. One came so close, within 10 feet, that Lael felt he could have read a book by it.

Several expeditions, and months later, Lael discovered that by asking the lights questions, they would answer by either moving up and down for yes or back and forth for no. After this form of communicating had been established, one of the lights led Ralph to a door, which leads inside of Brown Mountain. Once inside he was led to a room about eight feet square, the walls made of crystal "as clear as glass," enabling him to see for what seemed to be miles. Suddenly a voice said: "Do not fear; there is no danger here." The voice continued by saying that Lael has been chosen to tell the people of Earth about their true history; that man was created on another planet named Pewam which our ancestors destroyed. Pewam is now the waste of the asteroids which lie between Mars and Jupiter.

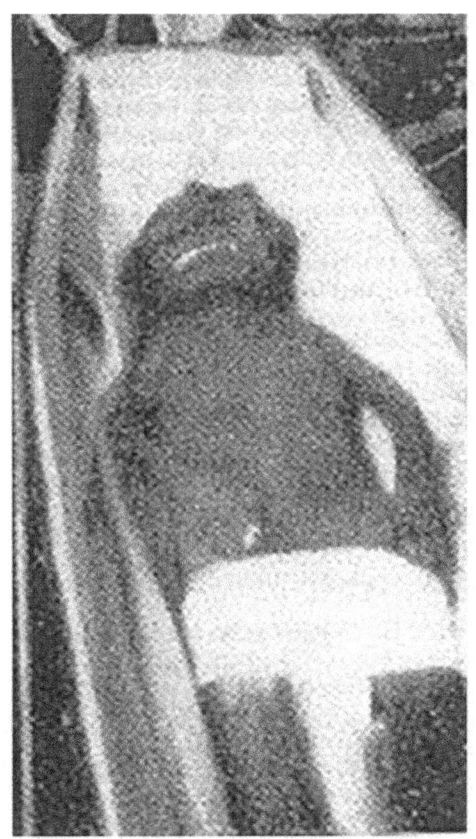

The only known photo of Ralph Lael's "Alien Mummy."

The voices explained that they are not Earthbound beings and cannot eat or drink, but live on Pethine, a "gas we absorb from the light you see around us. We perish in your atmosphere of sunlight. We live on Venus, which is a planet of pure crystal as you see surrounding you...notice that the crystal is as clear as your air. Venus is completely surrounded by water vapor about 150 miles above its surface."

In October of 1962 Lael returned to the rock, entered and was offered a ride to Venus-which he accepted. Arriving two days later on Earth's sister planet, he was introduced to men who were said to have been direct descendants of the people from the planet Pewam.

One was a rather attractive woman named Noma, who was quite beautifully dressed in a bra and panties set. While on Venus, Lael was shown what appeared to be newsreels of the destruction of Pewam as well as scenes going on back on Earth. Lael was also warned that there are certain "forces" that could decide that man should be destroyed from the Earth. A dial was turned on the wall screen and he was shown how another planet, also the same size as our world, was rendered lifeless. First he was shown the ice caps at this planet's North and South poles. "Then I saw a great cloud of vapor moving out from the sphere as the waters and oceans began to rush up the mountain sides and into the valleys. Trees were uprooted by the rushing waters, great licking flames of water shot up for miles from the surface of the planet. Much of it remained at great heights as it became vapor.

"As the picture drew near on the screen, I saw heaps of bodies of some type of animal like our buffalo being tossed around against cliffs of the mountains and higher parts of the valley. As the axis of the sphere seemed to become perpendicular, there was so much mist that I could not see the surface. As the camera or whatever was used to make the picture drew away, the view looked like the planet Venus as we approach it in reverse."

Though Lael was very secretive about this matter, for a long while he kept a "tiny creature," or "little man" that looked "highly preserved" in a glass case in the back room of his roadside Brown Mountain Rock Shop and General Store, which he operated in order to finance his extended trips back into Brown Mountain. He would "disappear" for weeks at a time presumably to visit with his alien friends in their underground bunker located on the spot.

Lael hinted that this dwarf-like being was actually from some distant world, had died in the area, and had been turned over to Lael because of his love and trust of those not of this place or time.

Although unbelievable as this story may seem, so are the Brown Mountain lights. Ralph Lael told us that "there are many things I have seen and heard that I cannot reveal here because of my obligations to the Brown Mountain Lights.

"Whether you believe or disbelieve what I have told is of no importance. You and others who have read these things should have more brotherly love for the people of Earth and those of the whole universe."

Ralph Lael documented his strange encounters in his book *"The Brown Mountain Lights."*

23.

MYSTERY OF ALIEN INFESTATIONS: ARE STRIP MINES AND NOISY UNDERGROUND CONSTRUCTION PARTS OF THE ALIEN PHENOMENA?

By Don Worley

PUBLISHER'S NOTE: Don Worley investigated, by his own estimation, over 300 UFO cases. Not so much sightings of unexplained objects in the sky, but more about what happens at ground level to those observers who have been selected for close-level, often repeated encounters. He was an active representative of both the Tucson-based Aerial Phenomena Research Organization (APRO) and Dr. J. Allen Hynek's Center for UFO Studies (CUFOS), as well as a frequent contributor to Tim Beckley's *"UFO Universe"* and *"UFO Review"* publications. Don passed away in January 2018. The following has been extracted and updated from an issue of *"UFO Review."*

* * * * * * * * * *

When Coral and Jim Lorenzen of the Tucson-based UFO group APRO sent me into the isolated strip mines area of South Central Indiana, I was little prepared for what I was to uncover. The intensity and boldness of the aliens during the 1966-67 sighting wave was unbelievable. Domed discs and oval-shaped craft were being seen by many witnesses and at close range.

For example, on the Curry and Smith farms, burnt circles 20 feet in diameter were found. So much was going on that there was really no way to keep up with it all in the limited time I could spend on the scene. As a result of all the activity, many people thought that the UFOs must be hiding in the bottom of the strip mine lakes, though no "hard" evidence to prove this theory was ever forthcoming.

One amazed farmer, George Pratt, said he often watched UFOs playing around over his farm. The round, yellow, bright light came so often from the strip mines nearby that he used the expression "It came up," like he was talking about the moon or sun.

"This thing came all summer long in the evening," Pratt said. "It didn't make any sound, but it sure tore up my radio. It would set up there for about 15 minutes, then usually move off to the south. As the days grew longer in the summer, it was a round sliver thing in the daylight. People laughed at me in town, but when they came out here on the road they would spot it on the way. About 14 others have seen it. One night three of them jets came in from Terre Haute and chased the light. I could see their wing lights and hear their motors. That thing flitted about the sky like a firefly and played a game with the jets. They never could get near it. I don't know. I still don't believe they come from space."

In those young wild days, I was startled at the scope of the infestation in the strip mines area, but now we know that it was really nothing new and probably not even comparable to events elsewhere.

Alien abduction researcher Don Worley investigated, by his own estimation, over 300 UFO cases.

There are instances where the concentration seems to be in just a small locality affecting few persons. When Bernice Neblett moved to her small island home near Vancouver, British Columbia, she discovered that she was in the midst of a teeming UFO swarm. For weeks she watched all kinds of strange flying objects around her lonely island. She learned that they were not going to hurt her. She even named one "the red flasher," and one night actually heard laughter issue from the small barrel-shaped craft.

A somewhat wider radius was involved during the latter part of 1976 and early 1977 in Michigan's Upper Peninsula. Briar Mountain (near the town of Norway) was the focal point of a 20 miles-in-diameter area that has seen intense UFO activity over a period of three decades. Most of the 50 employees of the ski lodge on Briar Mountain have seen as many as 20 or more UFOs. To them, it was a disconcerting sight to see glowing craft zipping down the slopes much like skiers would. One observer, a shocked publishing magnate, returned home with his friends and remained silent about what they had seen at the lodge.

Infestations also occur over bodies of water. Many Canadians living on the shores of Lake Ontario, between Oakville and Toronto, are convinced that a base for UFOs exists under the restless water of the lake. For years many witnesses have seen lights shooting in and out of the lake, and a number of photos have been taken. Harry Picket, an aeronautical engineer, pilot, and owner of an aircraft research firm, has watched the lights for years from his Niagara-on-the-Lake home. The orange lights are seen to hover, fly in erratic patterns, and sometimes zip straight up in the air and out of sight. What are all these lights and why are they being seen in these locations?

South America has been an incredible hotbed of UFO activity for ages. Near the little town of Demerval Lobo, in northeastern Brazil, in the spring of 1984, the antics of egg-shaped craft were so prevalent that laborers working in the fields abandoned their jobs and fled.

Everyone was certain there was a UFO base nearby. In an area formed by the Brazilian town of Odios, Mente Alogre, and Santarem, in the Amazon River basin, it was believed a base existed under the water. Fishermen pulled up their lines because of the boldness of the objects. Charles Tucker and an investigator from the USA, as well as a Brazilian Air Force investigator, went into the region in the summer of

1981. I never found out what happened to them, but I'm sure they came up empty-handed on the hidden base theory.

At other South American locations so many UFOs were seen shooting out of or entering the gulfs of San Maties and San Jorge that they became commonplace and received little attention. Several Argentine UFO groups, after accumulating years of data, became convinced that submerged alien bases surely exist in the sea off the southern coast of Patagonia.

Another phenomenon in other areas has been the perplexing underground motor sounds. The sound of underground motors can often affect many witnesses, but the case that occurred at Michael Richardson's hillside tin mine (located 61 miles south of Marble Bar in Australia), was by its isolated nature heard by few. Three Aborigines stopped by "Max's" camp and called his attention to the motor sounds he had already begun to hear emanating from the hills above his camp. A search was made of the rugged area where no vehicle could travel, but no cause for the sound was apparent and it continued even as they searched for its origin.

But it is the "other" events that took place during the motor sounds period that are really quite interesting.

On May 19, 1978, Max was visited by a tall, "normal-looking" male, wearing overalls. We cannot say exactly normal, since the visitor's left hand looked transparent, "as though it had been burned and it was new skin." This person, whose speech is normal, arrived in a Land Rover with unusually small wheels bearing a plate number that Max later checked and found to be registered to someone else. The name and place of residence the man gave also proved to be false. The man seemed obsessed with beryllium and kept questioning Max on it. This is an interesting sideline of the case, because I recall that in one high intensity cow mutilation area of Colorado, the sweet smell of beryllium often filled the air and even the wind didn't disperse the odor.

It was a hot day, but the stranger refused any liquid refreshment during the two hours he was there. Max asked him to aid in lifting some iron sheets and Max discovered the man had no strength at all. He began to tremble, then toppled over. Max had to help him up.

About a week later, Max had retired to his bed under the stars. Suddenly, the night sky brightened as a glowing object came at him from two kilometers away. As it sped low overhead it became an enormous zeppelin-sized orange glowing craft with a revolving white light. The following morning, Max found that his compass heading had been altered, his dog now possessed boundless energy, and he also had surprising energy. He could now lift 180 pound pipes with no effort at all.

About one week later, something in the sky projected a brilliant beam which bathed Max's entire camp in bright light for about three minutes. The period of "charged power" and "super-energy" at Hillside Mine lasted over two weeks. It would be foolish not to suspect that whatever was making the motor sounds in the hills above the camp also was capable of the other strange things that occurred. We are offered additional clues about concentrations when we note other broader scale infestations and the mind staggering phenomena that can become associated with them. Landings, contact with UFO occupants, surgical cow mutilations, and encounters with ape-like entitles often begin to occur. Campers around Big Bear Lake on the eastern edge of the San Gabriel Mountains in California had seen some 30 UFOs over the course of three weeks.

In 1980, two Chilean men, architect Oscar Zamorro, and a friend, came across a landed UFO while on a hike in the Andes Mountains. The two men reported that they saw a six-foot-tall "Bigfoot-like creature" enter the craft, which then rose up into the air like a helicopter and shoot away at incredible speed.

They also encountered great ape-like figures. It was also discovered that you could pick up strange mechanical sounds upon planting a microphone on the forest floor. Within one hundred miles of Calvert, Texas, there were missile silos, radar units, as well as Air Force and Army bases. However, all the multiple phenomena that engulfed this region in 1973 did not seem to have anything to do with these establishments, since alien concentrations also occur in areas not having defense establishments. There were many UFO reports, plus landings, alien contact, mutilations, and, again, strange underground sounds.

The Yakima Indian Reservation, located in South Central Washington State, is a region of hundreds of square miles of rugged forest land. During periods of high UFO activity, forest lookouts in fire control towers watched glowing objects maneuvering over distant ridges and moving about down into the canyons. Most of the other usual phenomena we have come to expect were present. When aerial activity was the heaviest, Chief Fire Control Officer Bill Vogel reported a sound similar to turbines or large truck motors which could be heard running underground. It sounded like a truck laboring to get up a hill and never getting there, it was reported.

Meanwhile, just south of the reservation and north of the Columbia River, another investigator (who formerly worked twenty years as a Los Angeles law enforcement official) reported yet another unbelievable situation. The area had been the scene of much UFO activity for some ten years. One ranch family believed the UFOs must be engaged in some kind of mining operation. The source of the machinery sound seemed deep underground. Ape-like entities (Big Foot critters) had shown up so much that the ranch horses and dogs no longer went into a panic when they appeared.

This family also claimed they had seen weird animals, such as pure white and black cougar-like cats with long front legs, short back legs, and a ringed tall. They also reported a pink flamingo-like bird, huge beaver-tailed porcupines, strange insects (such as pure white "black widow" spiders), and enormous moths. The family thought some of the creatures they had seen could be tropical in nature. I came away convinced of the reality of their claims.

The great profusion of assorted UFOs and other eerie happenings in the forested northwestern region of New Jersey in the 1975-76 time period was also most amazing. This sparsely settled region of hills, lakes, swamps, and forests in the counties of Morris, Warren, Hunterdon, and Sussex, was the site of another one of those macabre infestation scenes. Great sky flashes, brilliant ruby-red UFOs, and an estimate that there could have been as many as 600 sightings of ape-entities gives you some idea of the "problem" that afflicted the inhabitants.

The hairy ones seemed to do a lot of howling and crying all over the place and left many tracks. We are primarily concerned here with the truck sounds reported by so many citizens for several years. Near White Meadow Lake, N.J., witnesses reported sounds resembling underground construction work or subterranean machinery. The sound of a truck climbing a hill was frequently described. The sounds would often last much of the night. One housewife thought they came from the direction of high voltage lines in the distant woods. Another witness, who had heard the sounds off and on for several years, pinpointed their location as that of a water storage tank behind his home. He also heard the sound of a baby crying, which came from the same direction.

Otherworldly creatures are depicted on the movie poster for Seth Breedlove's "Invasion on Chestnut Ridge." *Small Town Monsters* - www.smalltownmonsters.com

This identical baby crying sound has been known to come from the throat of the ape entitles. Another couple in the same area discovered a row of tiny unusual footprints in their yard. Dr. Harley Rutledge, a respected physicist, conducted a valuable five-year study of an intense area in southeastern Missouri. He did not solve the burning mystery of an alien presence in such abundance. A number of investigators have espoused the "magnetic fault line" theory. Like many theories, I'm afraid it has too few facts to support it and would still leave much unexplained.

What are we to think about these disturbing underground sounds? Due to descriptions that often tally, I do assume that the witnesses are accurate and the sounds are coming from beneath the ground. I believe they are not being fooled by a massive stereophonic sound penetrating everywhere and only appearing to come from the Earth. Don't think for a moment that I am in any fashion being swayed toward a foolish "they-originate-from-under-the-Earth theory." One fact is proven beyond all doubt by the alien infestation modus operandi. That fact is, there must exist a space-time dimensional entrance (and exit) from our plane to some other realm. The "nuts-and-bolts boys" will have to bow out on this one. No explanation they could ever give would ever provide them with a leg to stand on.

In any event, it's pretty certain that the government will never reveal the truth about these awesome matters. They know that on the day that Earth's masses awaken to the realization of the fantastic stellar ultra-technology we called UFOs, social disintegration could become a very real possibility.

What are the aliens doing in these infested areas? Make no mistake, the UFO intelligence is up to something. At present, its motives and ultimate purpose lie beyond our limited awareness and comprehension. Comparatively, we are like blind slugs. The aliens' covert influence upon all things human may be much more than we suspect.

24.

OPERATION TANGO – UNDERGROUND BASE IN KOREA
By Paul Dale Roberts

PUBLISHER'S NOTE: Paul Dale Roberts is a Fortean investigator who delves into ALL things paranormal – from Mothman, to the Chupacabra, UFOs, Crop Circles, Ghosts, Poltergeists, Demons and more.

Roberts is the HPI(Hegelianism Paranormal Intelligence – International) Owner. www.facebook.com/groups/HPIinternational

Significant investigations by HPI are the Skinwalker Ranch in Utah, looking for Natalee Holloway's ghost in Aruba, UFOs and Bigfoot at Mount Shasta, UFOs and USOs at Monterey Bay, Area 51, Guatemala City – Guatemala.

Roberts now writes for online magazines such as *"Chatterbrew Magazine"*: chatterbrew.com; *"Lorena's Angels"*: www.lorenasangels.com; *"Ceri Clark's All Destiny Magazine."*

Roberts was recently picked up by *"Paranormal Magazine UK"* and works for the online national news site *"Before It's News."*

* * * * * * * * *

In 1981, I was sent out to the 501st Military Intelligence Battalion at Yongson Barracks, Seoul Korea. I was an Intelligence Analyst -97 Bravo. My job was to work at PIC-K (Photo Interpretation Center - Korea). I was Army Intelligence, but we had a joint effort in working with Navy Intelligence, Air Force Intelligence, Marine Reconnaissance and elite teams like US Army's Special Forces; Air Force Special Operations; Navy Seals; Army Rangers; Army Delta Force; Army Night Stalkers. I had a Top Secret S.B.I. (Special Background Investigation) clearance. My job was also to work with Image Interpreters in identifying threats in North Korea and Red China. I heard many reports of UFO sightings in South Korea. A more recent sighting took place when North Korean leader Kim Jong-un and US President Donald Trump met in the demilitarized zone.

Reports came in that the object that was seen by many people was described as a bright white disc. The Korean and American government tried to dismiss the report by saying it was a flock of birds. South Korea scrambled fighter jets and helicopters in response to a flock of birds flying near the border with North Korea. For a good while after the UFO departed, there were black unmarked helicopters sighted. These black helicopters were most likely the US Army's Night Stalkers.

If the sighting was a mere flock of birds, why were jets scrambled to intercept this flock of birds and why did unmarked black helicopters circle the area where the UFO was seen? While I was with the 501st Military Intelligence Battalion, I was sent on a special assignment to a listening post inside of a mountain in an unknown location. This listening post was named Operation Tango. We were taken there by a bus with blacked out windows. Deep inside this mountain was an assortment of computers and listening devices. The place reminded me of a James Bond movie. Many of the intelligence troops inside this mountain were picking up on the radio frequencies of Red China and North Korea. What was very interesting at this site is the fact I had the opportunity to talk with an intelligence operative who told me that there was a tunnel that ran from Yongson Barracks to the demilitarized zone, but there was a breakaway point from that tunnel that led inside a mountain.

Inside that mountain were top level intelligence officers working with Republic of Korea Army Special Forces "Black Berets" (R.O.K Special Forces) and members of Delta Force and the Navy Seals. The operative said that, at times, these officers and elite troops were visited by extraterrestrial beings that had a special treaty with our government and the South Korean government. The extraterrestrial beings looked like a "praying mantis" type of aliens. The aliens were helping South Korea and the American government in keeping peace with North Korea. There was some sort of trade going on between the American government, the South Korean government and the extraterrestrials. At the underground base in South Korea, the American and South Korean governments were monitoring "angel stops." Angel stops are when extraterrestrials abduct humans for various experimentations.

While at the PIC-K (Photo Interpretation Center - Korea), I saw top secret photos of UFOs seen by our reconnaissance aircraft and satellites and that story can be found here: www.unexplained-mysteries.com/column.php?id=113987

DULCE WARRIORS

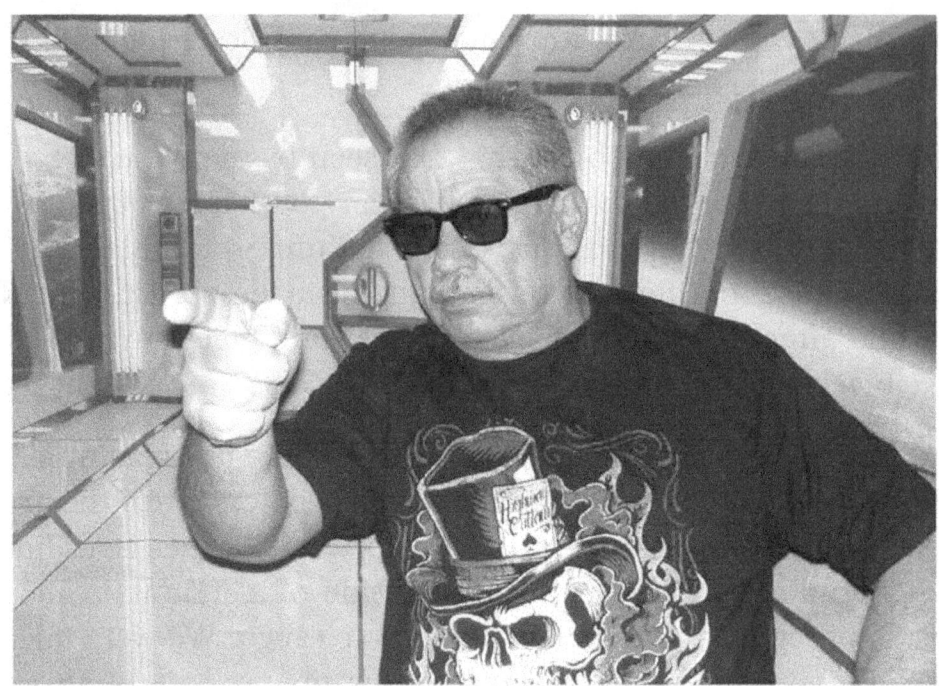

Paul Dale Roberts (Above) says that the U.S. and South Korean military maintain a secret "listening post" inside a mountain, and are occasionally visited by "praying mantis" types of aliens. These extraterrestrials allegedly are helping South Korea and the American government maintain peace with North Korea.

Besides UFOs being seen in South Korea, USOs (Unidentified Submerged Objects) are seen coming out of the ocean near South Korea and zipping into the sky, becoming UFOs. Could the possible underground base also extend out into the ocean? Before I was stationed at South Korea, I spent a few days in Tokyo, Japan, and heard many stories of USOs ripping out of the ocean near Japan. Near the south of Tokyo is the Devil's Sea, also known as the Dragon's Triangle, the Formosa Triangle and the Pacific Bermuda Triangle.

A woman named Sakura claimed that in 1978 she was abducted by greys and taken to an underground base in the ocean. She believes she was taken to the Devil's Sea. She says the underground base had a huge display of various forms of animal life in glass containers. Sakura says there were also glass containers of various types of humans on display. The animals and humans looked like they were still living, but just were not moving. Sakura's alien captors gave her a pregnancy test and after the procedure, she woke up in her bed. Sakura is positive this was not a dream.

25.

ADAM GORIGHTLY - THE SPOOKS AND KOOKS OF DULCE

The early 1980s were certainly wild and wooly times in the weird world of UFOs. Even though this was pre-internet, increasingly bizarre stories about UFOs and their alleged alien occupants were circulating around the world at an alarming rate among UFO researchers. Stories of crashed flying saucers...captured ETs... and secret treaties with alien races were being told and retold by various "UFOlogists." These stories appeared to be coming from different sources with no apparent connections, but they also had some interesting similarities. However, after years of stagnation, the hunger for any new information was so great that these new "UFO revelations" were embraced as fact and new faces were emerging everyday to add their bit to the growing quagmire.

It's easy now to look back and cluck our tongues at the naivety of the UFO community and their widespread acceptance of some of the wilder stories that were circulating at the time. Hindsight is 20/20. However, after all these years, many of the so-called "new" revelations are still being touted out today as fact. A good story, no matter how unlikely, especially if it fits someone's preconceived belief, is very difficult to give up.

One only has to take a look at what is going on in the world right now and the information that is being perpetuated as fact by certain groups. Many are all too willing to believe something if it fits within their narrow worldview, even if there's no good evidence supporting it. So with that in mind, in the decades to come, "facts" today could well become the "what in the world were they thinking?" of tomorrow.

Referring to himself as a "crackpot historian," Adam Gorightly decided to take on the decades of muck and mire surrounding the modern mythologies of crashed UFOs, secret alien treaties, and the alleged underground alien base near Dulce, New Mexico. What started out as an article titled "My Breakfast with Tal," eventually evolved into the book "*Saucers, Spooks and Kooks: UFO Disinformation in the Age of Aquarius.*"

ALL ROADS LEAD TO PAUL BENNEWITZ

Pity poor Paul Bennewitz, the man who was convinced that he had discovered evidence of alien activity near his home in Albuquerque, New Mexico. If Bennewitz had not contacted Kirtland Air Force Base concerning his evidence of UFO photos and suspicious radio transmissions, the subjects covered in Gorightly's book (and this one for that matter), may have never been conceived and disseminated to the UFO community.

The whole belief that there is a secret underground base at Dulce, New Mexico certainly seems to have originated with the Paul Bennewitz affair. No evidence has been found of any mention of an underground facility at Dulce prior to Bennewitz – not counting the cattle mutilations that were occurring in the area as reported by Gabe Valdez.

Bennewitz came to believe in the reality of a secret Dulce base thanks in part to Myrna Hansen who claimed, under hypnotic regression, that she and her son had been abducted by aliens and transported to a secret underground facility. Bennewitz somehow deduced that this underground base was located near Dulce. According to Gorightly, "All of these elements of Hansen's story ultimately became incorporated into UFO lore as we now know it. The term alien 'greys,' as far as I have been able to glean, was another trope that came straight out of the Bennewitz Affair."

The belief of the Dulce base became enforced with Bennewitz when the "alien" radio transmissions he was receiving out and out told him that they were located at a secret underground base near Dulce. With the help of his "friend," AFOSI Special Agent Rick Doty, Bennewitz flew to Dulce on several occasions, looking for evidence of the base, and even supposedly coming across what to him looked to be a UFO crash site.

The Dulce base was just one part of the whole Bennewitz affair, which seemed to be an effort by the military and intelligence community to spread a myth of evil aliens, abductions and human experimentation to the larger UFOlogical community. There have been several explanations on why this myth, especially in association with secret bases across the country, was being perpetuated. The most likely was that it was an effort to uncover foreign spies who were using an interest in UFOs in order to gain information about secret military technology.

Whatever the reason, the myth turned out to be wildly successful. The fact that we are still discussing certain aspects of it, alien abductions, crashed UFOs, government agencies secretly dealing with UFOs and alien species, is indicative of its success.

The Dulce base idea took on a life its own as a number of different people jumped onto the band wagon with their own version of the story. In his book, Gorightly says that on December 2, 1981, Paul Bennewitz sent a letter to U.S. Senator for New Mexico Pete Domenici stating that "sometime late '79 or first of '80 an argument insued (sic) over weapons and the military abandoned (Dulce base); the final circumstance of the men unknown…"

In a September 11, 1984 interview, Bennewitz told UFO researcher Jim McCampbell that: "In 1979 something happened and the base was closed. There was an argument over weapons and our people were chased out, more than 100 people involved…"

Although Bennewitz didn't implicitly state that there was an actual battle between humans and aliens at Dulce, his comments about some type of conflict, or of the humans abandoning the base, appeared to have been enough to plant the seed that later blossomed into what was later known as "The Dulce War," popularized by people such as Branton and Jason Bishop III.

Variations of this story have also cropped up concerning a similar battle/confrontation occurring at Area 51. In fact, the entire Dulce mythos seems to be a beta test of what would later happen at Area 51. The similarities of "alien and UFO" stories surrounding both Dulce and Area 51 don't seem to be coincidental. It leads to some speculation that Dulce could have been an early attempt to draw attention away from Area 51. If that was the case, it was not very successful.

Another part that Gorightly brings up in *"Saucers, Spooks and Kooks"* is there seems to be a lot of common themes that run between events surrounding Paul Bennewitz and stories such as Roswell, Dulce, Area 51, Project SERPO and the MJ-12 Papers.

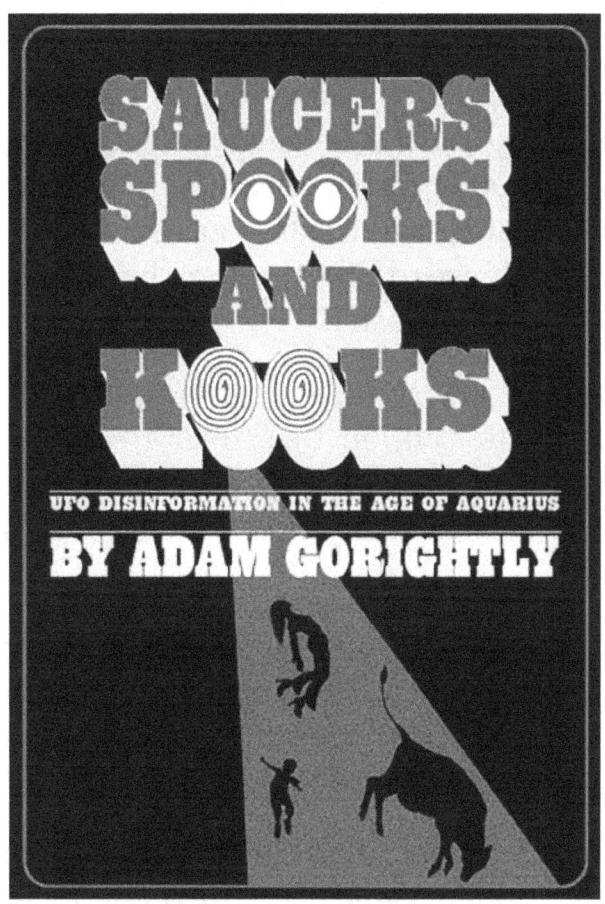

"You see the same recurring cast of characters who promoted these stories that are featured in my book, among them John Lear, Tal Levesque, Richard Doty, Bill Moore and a handful of others that formed this nexus of 'influencers.' Bill Moore would later disavow many of these claims, and ostensibly remove himself from this nexus of characters, who he said were pushing false stories that had ultimately driven Paul Bennewitz bonkers."

Also added to this interesting mix of eccentric characters is John Lear.

"John Lear, who admittedly had ties to the intelligence community, was an avid MJ-12 papers promoter," Gorightly said. "At the same time, during the mid-1980s, he was leaking information to the media about a secret stealth aircraft testing program at Area 51. The specter of stealth technology was forever lurking on the edges of these tall tales related to Dulce Base, Kirtland and Area 51, part of what appeared to be an effort to shape the overall narrative and muddy the waters about what was actually going on at these military testing sites."

DULCE WARRIORS

DISINFORMATION RATHER THAN DISCLOSURE

Of course, what makes the myth so compelling is the idea that it incorporates a mixture of truth and fiction to make it believable. The UFO phenomena is certainly real...recent revelations of Navy involvement with UFO activity involving fighter jets show that we are not just dealing with swamp gas or weather balloons. That leaves us to endlessly speculate with everything that was being released to Bennewitz and others on what was true and what wasn't.

It certainly wouldn't be a huge surprise that some sort of underground facility didn't exist around Dulce. After all, on December 10, 1967, a 29-kiloton hydrogen bomb was exploded south-west of Dulce with the intention of fracturing rock to free up natural gas and create a huge cavity that would act as a reservoir to store the released gas.

Unfortunately, the gas drawn from the well was too radioactive to ever be used and the ground was so contaminated that most of it had to be hauled away. As well, radioactivity in vegetation downwind from the blast site was increased by 10 times over natural levels and still remains high to this day.

Those that live in the area of the Jicarilla Apache Reservation wonder if the government had built an underground base in order to monitor the subsequent radioactivity (among other secret military activities) after the blast. That could also explain the cattle mutilations...research on how radiation affects plant, wildlife and domestic animals in the long term. There is also the matter of the alleged crashed UFO spotted by Bennewitz in the area of the Archuleta Mesa. It has been suggested that rather than a grounded extraterrestrial spaceship, Bennewitz actually spotted the remains of a test stealth aircraft. Rick Doty later admitted to encouraging the belief of the Dulce base by having the Air Force dump old equipment around Archuleta Mesa—vents connected to nothing, antennas sticking out of the ground, soldiers appearing to guard a complex built into the mountain. This seems to be a lot of effort all in order to fool one guy looking for UFOs and an underground base.

Could it be that the area around Dulce did have something mysterious going on? Due to its location, it may have been part of the top secret stealth aircraft development and testing program that was going on at the time. It certainly was conveniently located, with Kirtland Air Force Base to the south and Area 51 to the west.

New Mexico State Police Officer Gabe Valdez, who had spent years investigating local cattle mutilations, was convinced that the sky above Dulce was being used to test black budget aircraft. Valdez even said that he had accidentally taken photos of these aircraft that were invisible to the naked eye.

Valdez's son, Greg Valdez, in his book *"Dulce Base: the Truth and Evidence from the Case Files of Gabe Valdez,"* writes: "They were testing advanced aircraft from a nearby off-site air base. The aircraft was invisible and silent and used optic camouflage."

Many of the key players in the "Dulce Wars" mythos have faded away into obscurity. Nevertheless, the stories that they helped disseminate remain with us today, continually being resurrected by those who believe that they are uncovering something exciting and new. Adam Gorightly puts it best as he advises new UFO researchers who attempt to navigate those stormy seas.

"I'd suggest looking back in the annals of ufology and examining its past. Do that before jumping aboard any particular UFO shark, because there seems to be nothing new under the sun when it comes to a lot of these recurring themes that continually crop up in UFO lore."

Adam Gorightly was always a favorite guest on "Exploring the Bizarre" with Timothy Green Beckley and Tim R. Swartz.

If You Enjoyed This Book...Check Out Some of Our Other Books, All Available on Amazon.com

If You Enjoyed This Book...Check Out Some of Our Other Books, All Available on Amazon.com

If You Enjoyed This Book...Check Out Some of Our Other Books, All Available on Amazon.com

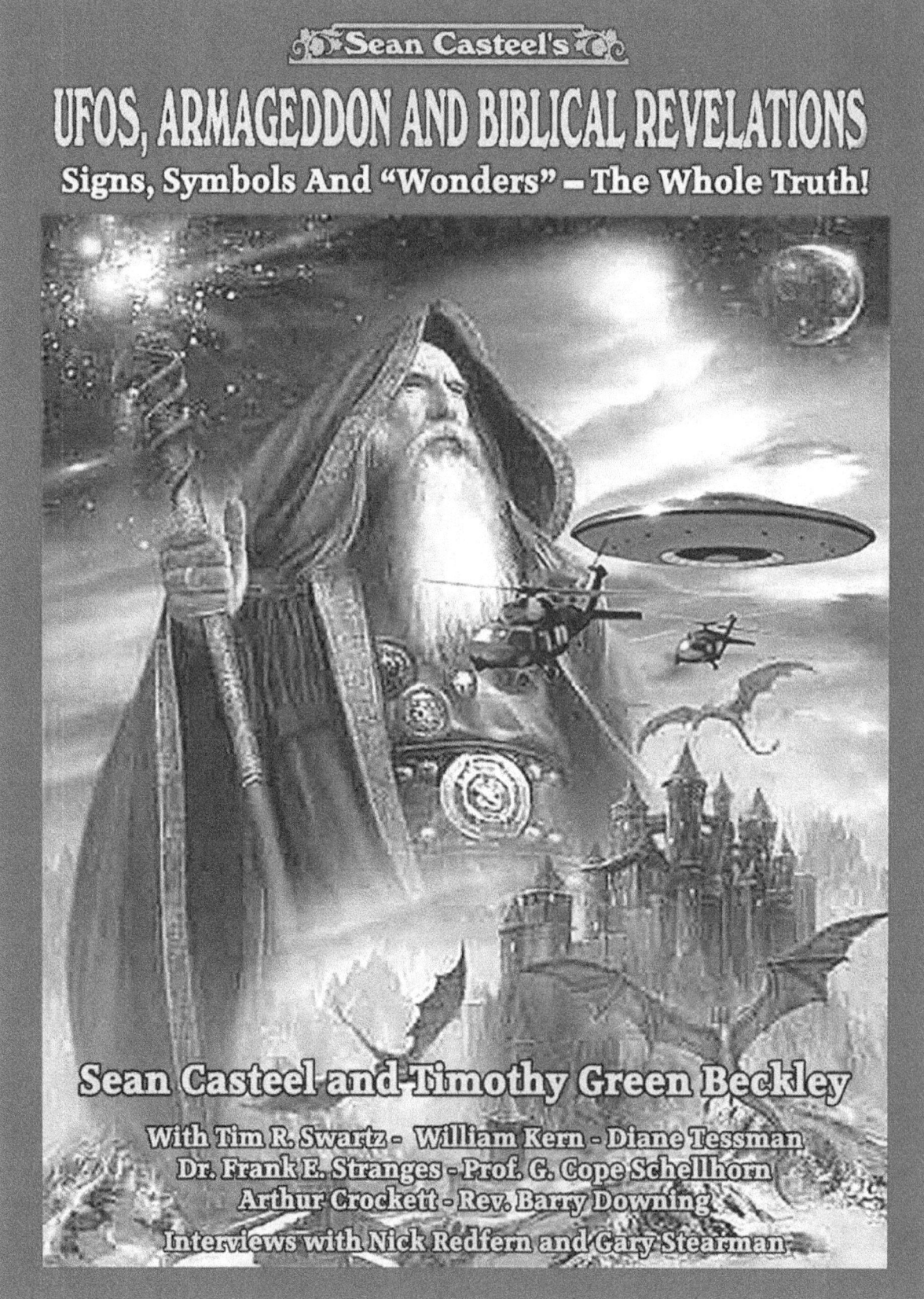

If You Enjoyed This Book...Check Out Some of Our Other Books, All Available on Amazon.com

TIM R. SWARTZ'S BIG BOOK OF...
INCREDIBLE ALIEN ENCOUNTERS

A Global Guide To Space Aliens, Interdimensional Beings And Ultra-Terrestrials

By Tim R. Swartz, Timothy Green Beckley, Sean Casteel

CONTRIBUTORS:

Brian Allan, Hakan Blomqvist, Barry Chamish, Scott Corrales, Maria D' Andrea, Preston Dennett, Ben and Paul Eno, Olavo T. Fontes, T. Allen Greenfield, Adam Gorightly, Rick Hilberg, Cynthia Hind, Hercules Invictus, William Kern, Erica Lukes, Philip Mantle, Aleksandar Petakov, Brent Raynes, Paul Dale Roberts, Malcolm Robinson, Carol Ann Rodriguez, Susan Demeter-St. Clair, Brad and Sherry Steiger, Diane Tessman, Nigel Watson, Charles J. Wilhelm, Linda Zimmermann

Visit Our Website at: www.conspiracyjournal.com

www.ingramcontent.com/pod-product-compliance
Lightning Source LLC
Chambersburg PA
CBHW081914170426
43200CB00014B/2725